Praise for Detecting The Scam: Nelson Mandela's Gift

So how does one draw a connection between the statesmanship of Nelson Mandela, the sleaziness of Bernie Madoff and Ken Lay and the surreal world of Hans Christian Andersen? Well, Michael Friedlander does it brilliantly, logically explaining in an immensely readable, personable and witty way how Mandela's political principles can be employed as a didactic device to detect financial scams and cry out, like that fantastic child, "But the emperor isn't wearing anything at all!"

Steve Linde, Managing Editor, The Jerusalem Post

DETECTING THE SCAM:

NELSON MANDELA'S GIFT

Library of Congress Cataloging in Publication Data
Friedlander, Michael
Detecting the Scam: Nelson Mandela's Gift

ISBN: 145153664X
UPC/EAN-13 #9781451536645
LCCN: 2010905740

To order additional copies, please contact us.
www.detectingthescam.com
orders@detectingthescam.com

To Nelson Mandela:

> *For the qualities that have made you the most inspirational man of our time...*

To my two boys:

> *For the joy you have brought to our lives...*

To my wife:

> *For having that sense of humor I said you would need when we got married...*

To my folks:

> *For clinging to the irrational delusion that your sons are devilishly handsome and quite smart...*

"The world is a dangerous place, not because of those who do evil, but because of those who look on and do nothing."

Albert Einstein

"The reality of the other person lies not in what he reveals to you, but in what he cannot reveal to you. Therefore, if you would understand him, listen not to what he says, but rather to what he does not say."

Kahlil Kibran

"Who are you going to believe, me or your own eyes?"

Groucho Marx

TABLE OF CONTENTS

Preface .... *i*

PART ONE: THE START OF THE JOURNEY

CHAPTER ONE: The need to ask 1

CHAPTER TWO: The Duck School 15

CHAPTER THREE: Enron's prize 27

PART TWO: NELSON MANDELA

CHAPTER FOUR: An overview of the man 39

CHAPTER FIVE: Early life to Robben Island 47

CHAPTER SIX: Robben Island to release 83

CHAPTER SEVEN: Release and the aftermath.................... 127

PART THREE: ENRON, AHMED CHALABI,
                   AND BERNARD MADOFF

CHAPTER EIGHT: Canaries in the Enron coal mine 167

CHAPTER NINE: How they solved their problems 197

CHAPTER TEN: Canaries in the Chalabi coal mine 209

CHAPTER ELEVEN: Bernard Madoff 229

CHAPTER TWELVE: The Emperor's new clothes.................. 241

Selected bibliography 257

Index 263

PREFACE

BLAME BILL CLINTON

"The man who can smile when things
go wrong has thought of someone
else he can blame it on."

Robert Albert Bloch

H igh-profile scams have always fascinated me. Perhaps it was the perverse pleasure in seeing some
of our finest and brightest scammed. In each case,
though, something was wrong. Were the scammers really
that brilliant or was there another more troubling explanation?

Nelson Mandela has also always fascinated me. Perhaps it
was because I grew up in apartheid South Africa and I knew
about the ruthlessness of those he faced. *I was there.* I can
still marvel at his courage, extraordinary moral authority,
and his remarkable negotiating skills.

Looking back at the recent high-profile scams and those who were closest to the scammers, I couldn't find a *hint* of anyone with the courage needed to confront the scammers. Nor could I find a *trace* of anyone with the negotiating skills needed to expose the looming scams. Nor could I find anyone who even *pretended* to have any moral authority. That was when I saw the connection between the two objects of my fascination—scams and Nelson Mandela. And thus was born this book...

So, why was I smiling? Things were not going well with my book. This was not nearly as easy as I had hoped, and I knew I had to blame someone. It was obviously not my fault. It never is. Ask my wife. No, this was Bill Clinton's fault. Although we had never met, he had teased and tormented me into writing it. And, to add insult to my profound injury, he had yet to apologize. I was conflicted. Should I forgive him? I couldn't decide. Perhaps I should explain...

It had happened in the wee small hours one morning years ago as I was channel-surfing mindlessly. All was quiet and still in the kingdom. I can remember thinking about those financial talking heads that blanketed every television news channel. These were the same experts who had expressed such shock at the implosion of Enron, the company they had most admired and supported. I can remember them blaming it all on a diabolical and undetectable scam.

I smiled at the irony: if only they had done their jobs, they would have warned us. Indeed, some *had* warned us, but most hadn't. Instead, many would claim they were the victims of the very scams they should have detected. I remember this left me scratching my head, but, back to Bill Clinton.

Midnight had long come and gone. My channel-surfing was relentless. I knew I had to keep moving to escape those talking heads. On one channel, I can remember seeing some bozo wearing a cowboy hat talking excitedly about bull riding. I squeezed my remote. Another bozo replaced him. This one was wearing a baseball cap as he rode a strange contraption he claimed could clear the forest behind my ranch. Sadly, this just wasn't his day. I didn't have a ranch, let alone a forest behind it, so I again squeezed my remote. A hatless Mr. Clinton appeared. He was pitching his new book to an openly spellbound audience. I couldn't resist. I stopped to listen and watch—and you may wonder why...

Thanks to the Bush family, I'd come to admire anyone who could string together a few coherent sentences in the English language—preferably without a teleprompter. Whatever his other frailties, President Clinton had this increasingly rare gift.

Something caught my attention. I turned up the volume. When you turn fifty, he was saying, take a deep breath and look back. Think about some of the more important life lessons you've learned. Just imagine, he wondered, if, as a young adult, you could have drawn on your parents' and grandparents' life lessons. *What greater gift could they have given you?* Of course, he was right, but he was not done. Think back on those years, he continued, and write down those lessons. Offer them to your kids. And, who knows, maybe they might even read them. This intrigued me and my favorite Oscar Wilde quote immediately came to mind:

> *"When I was a boy of fourteen, my father was so ignorant I could hardly stand to have the old man around. But when I got to be twenty-one, I was astonished at how much the old man had learned in seven years."*

Well, I had already turned fifty. Maybe I could show them how much I'd learned...

As I thought about the lessons I might pass on to my kids, I again thought about the recent high-profile scams. I wondered about the remarkable lack of curiosity of some of our very finest and brightest and their lack of any moral authority. I thought about the questions they hadn't asked.

This made me think back to Nelson Mandela. In 1918, he was born in a village in the Transkei in South Africa. His parents were illiterate. They lived in a mud hut with no electricity, plumbing, paved roads, or other modern amenities. Their son grew up with remarkable values and a driving sense of curiosity so lacking in some of our finest and brightest. As he later became a lawyer, he also became a leader with unequalled moral authority and unparalleled negotiating skills.

I couldn't help but wonder how his qualities, skills, and moral authority might have saved us from the recent high-profile scams.

It was then that my earlier smile turned into a broad grin. I remembered thinking about how our self-delusion had aided the scammers. I remembered how I had stumbled upon an unlikely connection between Enron and Nelson Mandela. Much to my delight, I had discovered that Enron had actually awarded him its highest prize for the very qualities *it did not have.* My next discovery only added to my delight. Only a few months earlier, Harvard University had honored him for the very qualities *it had failed to teach* some of Enron's top executives. I was on a roll. I then discovered that President George W. Bush had awarded him the Presidential Medal of Freedom for his statesmanship— *at the very time the president was widely ridiculed for his own diplomatic efforts prior to the Iraq war.* And, finally, not even Mr. Clinton was spared. When he awarded Mr. Mandela the congressional gold medal, he recognized Mr. Mandela's enormous moral authority. *This was at a time Mr. Clinton was embroiled in the Monica Lewinsky scandal.*

I couldn't possibly have made any of this up. Self-delusion was clearly alive and well and living in the United States and, if the scammers were smiling, you had to forgive them.

So, I made my decision—albeit with a twist. If Bill Clinton wanted life lessons, they wouldn't be mine. Instead, I would first draw on Nelson Mandela's life lessons. I would see how he developed and used those formidable skills. Then I would briefly explore three recent high-profile scams to test those lessons and to answer a few troubling questions.

I would tie this all together by exploring Hans Christian Andersen's classic children's tale *"The Emperor's New Clothes"* and by showing the connection between the tale and the Enron, Ahmed Chalabi, and Bernard Madoff adventures.

Finally, I would do this knowing that not all scams were detectable, but also knowing that we would at least have a better shot at detecting and avoiding them if we made good use of Nelson Mandela's gift.

And thus was born this book. Blame Bill Clinton, who will never know about the anxiety and self-doubt he would cause me that night...

Part One:

THE JOURNEY

One day Alice was lost. She came to a fork in the road and saw a Cheshire cat in a tree.

"Which road do I take?" she asked.

"Where do you want to go?" was his response.

"I don't know" Alice answered.

"Then," said the cat, *"it doesn't matter."*

CHAPTER ONE

THE NEED TO ASK

"Before beginning a Hunt, it is wise to ask
someone what you are looking for
before you begin looking for it."

Winnie the Pooh

"He who asks is a fool for five
minutes. He who does not ask
remains a fool forever."

Ancient Chinese Scribe

I am a practicing coward. No way would I begin our journey by confronting Winnie the Pooh or some mysterious unnamed ancient Chinese scribe. No way. Not me. Instead, I would take the easy path: I would follow their advice and begin by asking what we were looking for and why. I would ask what skills we would need to detect the modern scams and who could teach us those skills.

After identifying Nelson Mandela as our teacher, I would ask how he came to master his skills and how he applied them. And then I would test what we had learned against the Enron, Ahmed Chalabi, and Bernard Madoff adventures. My hope was that perhaps the gift of his skills and moral compass would improve our chances of detecting and avoiding the scam. This was the destination for our journey.

A STARTING POINT: WHAT IS A SCAM?

A scam is a swindle. It is built on a lie or on a fabric of lies designed to persuade us to do something or not do something. *It is therefore all about the scammers' power to persuade us—and our power to resist their persuasion.*

What do all scammers have in common? Many are quite charming and likable, because they know we like to do business with people we like. Many exude enormous hubris, because they know how impressed we are by people of apparent stature. So they work on being likable and presenting themselves as people with stature.

As for their lies, the better scammers do not bother with small lies. After all, what's the point in getting caught in a small lie? No, their lies are generally whoppers.

Finally, what do all scams have in common? They are all *calls to action.* Unless the scammers can persuade us to do what they want, their scams will wither and die. It is all about whether or not we can resist their powers of persuasion. If we can, we survive. If we cannot, we have a problem.

THE CHANGING SCAM

For years, when we thought about scams, we might have thought about Robert Redford and Paul Newman swindling the swindlers in *The Sting.* These were romantic and heroic rogues, but that was Hollywood. In reality, the old-time scammers were neither romantic nor heroic. Instead, they were smooth-talking con men on the fringes of society. Their con was direct and personal, often delivered with daz-

zling and bewildering charm. Their goal was always to become their marks' friend. They knew how difficult it was for
a friend to say "no" to a friend, even a new friend. So, they
would become very good at making new friends.

The scammers in the modern high-profile scams are noticeably different. They are not on the fringes of society.
They are often the very pillars of society. While Carlo Ponzi
might have once been a dishwasher, his modern counterparts are respectable and well educated.

In another sense, too, they are different. Unlike the old
timers, the modern scammers use layers of respectable surrogates to do their bidding. These surrogates help create a
foggy mist. They sometimes help structure and sometimes
even sell the scams. In doing so, they offer respectability,
credibility, and something far more important. They also offer the *plausible deniability* that was never available to the
old-timers. If anything went wrong, the scammers could
now redirect blame to the surrogates. And they would. Not
that the surrogates were worried. They were all paid handsomely for this particular service.

In looking at the new scams, therefore, we had to accept
a chilling new reality and the problem it posed: There are
now so many respectable professionals in the picture that
it is becoming increasingly difficult to distinguish between
the good guys and the bad guys. The fog and mist are every-
where.

THE LINK BETWEEN NEGOTIATING SKILLS AND SCAMS

Because the art of negotiation is the art of persuasion,
scams are effectively negotiating duels between the scammers and us. Fortunately for us, we have a significant advantage in that duel. While scammers have to persuade us
to act on their lies, *we don't have to.* When we ask questions,
all we need is *the whiff* of a possible lie to trigger even more
questions. And if the answers to those questions appear a
tad sketchy, we could always walk away. *But we have to ask
those questions...*

In our negotiating duel with scammers, there are at least two obstacles we face.

The first is staring at us in the mirror. Too often, we see only what we want to see and hear only what we want to hear. Too often, we want to believe so badly that we suspend our common sense and sense of disbelief. Too often, our insecurity stands in the way of us from asking the questions we must ask. Never has the need to ask been greater. Always, the scammers' unspoken question is Groucho's:

> *"Who are you going to believe? Me, or your own eyes?"*

Too rarely do we trust ourselves to ask the questions we must ask. Too rarely do we trust ourselves to follow our common sense in assessing the answers we receive.

The second obstacle we face is the new breed of scammer. Many are artists. Some are pure magicians. Some weave their lies into the truth so skillfully that their lies and the truth can become almost indistinguishable. And with their respectable surrogates effectively daring us to challenge their respectability to find the lies, we often doubt ourselves.

The only small comfort in any of this is that, no matter how daunting the obstacles we face, the scammers themselves face at least three clear and present real dangers.

THE FIRST DANGER SCAMMERS FACE:
A SKILLED NEGOTIATOR

The last thing any scammer wants or needs is to face a skilled negotiator, but, when he does, the scammer counters the danger ingeniously: *He creates a remarkable illusion— one that would make David Copperfield proud.*

He creates the illusion that, even as he is trying to persuade us to do what he wants, we are not really negotiating with him. *And why is this so important?* If we feel we are not in a negotiation, we are less likely to bring our most important negotiating skills to the table. We will not feel the need to ask the questions the scammers fear most.

Remarkably, in creating their illusion, scammers would receive unexpected help from an unlikely source: the best business and law schools in the kingdom. To the scammers' pure delight, many of these schools teach that negotiation occurs primarily in the context of *conflict resolution*. Take, for example, the Harvard Business Essentials Series, which draws on the expertise of the Harvard Business School, one of the most prestigious and respected schools in the kingdom. The first sentence of the introduction to the school's book entitled *Negotiation* reads:

> *"Negotiation is the means by which people deal with their differences."*

For the best scammers in the kingdom, this represented the key to the candy store. It was a dream come true. Now the path to creating their illusion was clear: *they would simply avoid any signs of differences or conflict.* For the alumni of some of our best schools, therefore, with no clear conflict visible, they apparently believed they were not in a negotiation. With the illusion established, it would be clear sailing for the scammers. And if they were smiling, you would have to forgive them.

THE SECOND DANGER: TIME

Scammers understand that the more time they give us to reflect on what they are selling, the more time we will have to ask questions. And, again, questions are the last thing the scammers want or need.

Again, over the years, the best scammers in the kingdom have come up with an ingenious solution to counter this danger: *They always demand that we act quickly and urgently.*

They tell us that, if we don't act quickly, we will lose a remarkable opportunity. And, worse, the opportunity will likely be offered to someone else.

Ironically, this should also give us the first significant clue to a brewing scam: Whenever anyone asks you to decide quickly and urgently—without giving you the time you need to consider what he is selling you—beware! *The faster he needs you to decide, the more time you should take...*

THE THIRD DANGER: OUR SENSE OF ETHICS

Our sense of ethics is the third danger all scammers face. This has the potential to stand in the way of every scam. *What is it about ethics that scammers fear?*

The late Justice Potter Stewart once wrote that to act ethically is to know the difference between what you have the right to do, and what is the right thing to do.

The very best scammers always tweak this: They will argue that if we have the right to do something, it is thereby the right thing to do—and we should do it. Sounds close, but no cigar, folks.

Many of the recent highest profile business and political scams have involved this very question. In each case, there were some who understood the distinction. When the scammers came across them, they would attack them personally and often viciously. And this would be yet another significant clue to the presence of a brewing scam: *when you ask a question and are then attacked personally, you know you have hit a nerve.*

To appreciate just how good the best scammers in the kingdom are—and to show how difficult are the ethical questions for even our very finest and brightest—we will need a brief reality check and a slight detour.

SCAMMING THE BEST OF THE BEST

The Enron scam offers a remarkable example of how the best scammers in the kingdom plied their craft. Those scammers would have to out-negotiate one of the most distinguished boards of directors in the kingdom. They would

either have to persuade them that they were not in a negotiation or that, if they had the right to do something, it was
the right thing to do no matter how potentially disastrous
the longer-term consequences of their decision.

We might begin by noting the absence of any significant
discussions at the Enron board meetings as to whether
what they were being asked to do was the right thing to do.
Instead, their only focus seemed to be on whether or not
they had the *narrow legal right* to do what they were asked
to do. Equally remarkably, when the board was given very
little time to make some quite important decisions, this apparently raised no red flags with anyone on the board. They
displayed a stunning lack of curiosity.

Judging by board members' lack of probing questions,
the Enron scammers succeeded in creating their illusion
with the board that no negotiations were taking place. Apparently the individual directors never suspected that they
were in a negotiation because none brought his or her negotiating skills to the table.

To fully appreciate the magnitude of just what the Enron
scammers accomplished, one must appreciate a little about
Enron and just how distinguished its board of directors was.

In the years preceding its implosion, Enron was the sev-
enth largest company in the kingdom. Wall Street regarded
its board as the crème de la crème of corporate boards—
and for good reason. Each director was distinguished and
experienced. Each was also well compensated. There were
no inexperienced rookies on this board.

Amongst its directors were seasoned chairmen and
presidents of other highly respected companies. Certainly,
if anyone could understand the nuances underlying the fi-
duciary duties and responsibilities of directors, these particular individual directors could.

The board also included a sprinkling of superstars from
academia and government. One director was a former dean
of the Graduate School of Business at Stanford University
and professor of accounting (emeritus). Another was a
president emeritus of the University of Texas. Again, cer-

tainly, if anyone could recognize—if only on a purely intellectual and academic level—that something presented to
them might appear a little odd or ethically questionable,
these two could.

Yet another director was a former United Kingdom secretary of state for energy. Certainly, if anyone was distinctly
well qualified to understand the volatility of the energy
markets and the problems associated with trying to deter-
mine, for example, the present and future value of a twenty-
year energy contract, he would understand.

Two other directors were a former deputy secretary of
the U.S. Treasury and a former chairman of the U.S. Commodity Futures Trading Commission. As with the others,
these two directors were certainly similarly well equipped
to sniff the occasional odd odor in the air.

And then there was the chairman of the board. He was
the darling of Wall Street, a pillar of society, and a friend of
presidents. He was also a celebrated innovator in the energy industry. His name was Ken Lay.

Another board member and the company's chief executive officer was Jeff Skilling. Wall Street regarded him as a
brilliant wunderkind. Before joining Enron, he was a super-
star with McKinsey and Company, one of the blue-chip con-
sulting firms in the kingdom. Prior to that, he was a Baker
Scholar—an honor awarded to the top 5 percent of the Harvard Business School graduating class.

The business media recognized both Ken Lay and Jeff
Skilling as executives and managers *extraordinaire*. Ironically, this was an endorsement that would later return to haunt
them in their criminal trials as they presented a defense that
I've characterized as the "idiot defense." They each asked a
jury to believe that they didn't have a clue what was happening under their very noses in their business under their
watch. Presumably without the hint of a smile, they argued
that they were the true victims of the scam. Again, this was a
nice try, but no cigar. Sadly for them and their families, their
jury was unconvinced. Sanity prevailed.

As any diligent board of directors and its management team would do, Enron also retained the finest and brightest legal and accounting talent that money could buy to advise it and protect it. And Enron had lots of money available for this form of hired help.

Sadly, despite the remarkable backgrounds and experience of Enron's board and management, and the remarkably talented and experienced, highest-priced professional help available, the scammers apparently hoodwinked them all.

That the board did not ask the hard questions was almost unbelievable. In fact, its failure to ask raised a far more troubling question *about whether or not it was even scammed.* This gave rise to a test I've called "The Subway Test."

THE SUBWAY TEST

Can you be scammed if you know about the lie, but nevertheless still do the deal? Here's the Subway Test:

> *Someone approaches you in a subway and offers you a Rolex. It looks like a Rolex, but it certainly doesn't feel like one. It is as light as a feather—quite unlike the heavy Rolexes that are sold in the stores for thousands of dollars. Your new friend tells you the price is $50. Although neither of you mouth the words, you both know it's fake. If you buy it, are you the victim of a scam?*

The answer is no, you were not scammed. You simply bought a fake Rolex, knowing it was a fake. Another more troubling question that arises, however, is this:

> *Assume you later give the fake Rolex to a friend you know is penniless. Assume, too, that you also know that he is going to use it to impress a potential business partner who thinks he has lots of money. Assume you are having dinner with him and his potential business partner. What do you do as he starts to tell his potential partner how he paid*

thousands for the watch? What if he says you were
there when he bought the watch?

When does your silence result in you joining the scammer class?

In researching the Enron scam, it was hard to avoid the conclusion that Enron's board either knew or should have known about the lies it bought and later sold. Certainly, its failure to ask even the most basic questions reflected an embarrassing lack of curiosity. Certainly, its willingness to accept advice that made no sense was strange.

The Enron scammers also always gave the board not just the cover it needed from the company's highly paid and respected professional advisors; they also gave it another level of cover: the board's two wunderkinds, Ken Lay and Jeff Skilling, were prepared to make the very decisions they were asking their fellow board members to make. It apparently never occurred to the board that the wunderkinds were also two of the best scammers in the kingdom.

NO LIE TOO OUTRAGEOUS

If you could believe the wunderkinds, nobody at Enron saw the bankruptcy coming, but not everyone at the company bought this. Only a few months before the bankruptcy, Ken Lay addressed a mass meeting of his employees. He offered this confident reassurance about the health of his company:

> *"I want to assure you I have never felt better*
> *about the prospects of the company...Our per-*
> *formance has never been stronger. Our busi-*
> *ness model has never been more robust; our*
> *growth has never been more certain."*

In Hans Christian Andersen's classic child's tale "The Emperor's New Clothes," it took a small child in the crowd to point out that the emperor was wearing no clothes. Well, at Enron's mass meeting, there was one employee who played

the role of that small child. That employee submitted a written question to Mr. Lay—which, to everyone's probable astonishment, Mr. Lay actually read to the meeting:

> *"I would like to know if you are on crack. If so,*
> *that would explain a lot. If not, you may want*
> *to start because it's going to be a long time*
> *before we trust you again."*

We now also know that at the very time Mr. Lay was re-
assuring everyone about the health of his company, he and
some of his senior management team were rushing to sell
their stock before the Enron ship hit the rocks. Also, at that
very time, and as Enron was clearly strapped for cash, Mr.
Lay "borrowed" over $60 million from the company, which
he repaid with effectively worthless Enron stock. He was effectively dumping his stock.

There were some respected analysts that realized that all
was not well at Enron. When they asked questions, Enron's
finest and brightest shouted them down in vicious personal
attacks. Not many other analysts picked up either on the un-
answered questions or on the over-reaction to these questions. Some in the financial media did raise some red flags,
but few really wanted to see those flags. This seemed to
confirm the suspicion that many just looked the other way.
And, to make matters worse was a new realization: We were
now living in a cheating culture that actually encouraged
and rewarded looking away.

OUR CHEATING CULTURE

Why is it that we have no tolerance for lying and cheating
in the world of family, sex, and traditional crime, yet, in the
world of career advancement, we view lying and cheating
quite differently?

Is there a connection between the collapse of our largest and most prestigious companies and banks, on the one
hand, and the epidemic of cheating in our high schools, colleges, and corporations? Could we really expect students
who cheated in high school to stop cheating when they

entered college? Could we really expect those who cheated in college to stop cheating when they entered graduate
school? And could we reasonably expect those who cheated
in graduate school to stop cheating when they enter the
business world?

When Enron collapsed, even President Bush acknowledged the problem might lie in our best schools:

> *"Our schools of business must be principled
> teachers of right and wrong, and not surren-
> der to moral confusion and relativism."*

Two weeks later, he spoke directly to Wall Street's leaders, saying,

> *"We need men and women of character, who
> know the difference between ambition and
> destructive greed, between justified risk
> and irresponsibility, between enterprise and
> fraud."*

The problem was staring the president in the face. It was
in his audience of Wall Street leaders.

Meanwhile, in the midst of this epidemic of corporate
cheating, the silence of our colleges was deafening. In a
rare breath of fresh air, at least one college president, Texas
A&M's Robert Gates—later to become secretary of defense,
replacing Donald Rumsfeld—acknowledged the responsibility of the nation's universities in a post-Enron era:

> *"All of these liars and cheats and thieves are
> graduates of our universities. The university
> community cannot avert its eyes and pro-
> claim that this is not our problem, that there
> is nothing we can do, or that these behaviors
> are an aberration from the norm."*

Perhaps Nelson Mandela provides part of the answer in
the starkest terms. In describing his warders' brutal behavior on Robben Island, he wrote that bad behavior that is rewarded is repeated. Isn't this exactly what we face? If we
reward those who cheat and act irresponsibly, why would
they change their ways?

OUR CHALLENGE

We therefore now face a remarkable challenge in detecting the scam. Because of our cheating culture and the fact that some of our finest and brightest have no moral compass, the scammers have no trouble in attracting some quite respectable surrogates to help them sell their lies.

Somehow, we would have to find a way to see through their lies and summon the courage to draw upon our common sense and experience to ask the right questions. Never was the need to ask more important.

Somehow we would have to hone our negotiating skills. We have to develop a greater ethical sensitivity. We would have to do the right thing to do, rather than doing simply what we have the right to do.

CHAPTER TWO

THE DUCK SCHOOL
AND THE SCAM

"He may look like an idiot and talk like an idiot,
but don't let that fool you. He really is an idiot."

Groucho Marx

"If you call a tail a leg, how many legs has a dog?
Five? No, calling a tail a leg don't make it a leg."

Abraham Lincoln

The Duck School is the school of common sense. It is
my invention, but not really. It is the oldest and largest school in the world. *It is the scammers' kryptonite.*
Even though its education is priceless, there are no tu-
ition fees. Its teachings are passed down from generation
to generation by parents, friends, strangers, and even comedians—from mud huts to modern suburbia. Its teachings
could not be easier to understand—or more difficult to fol-

low. To follow its teachings, we also all have a few personal flaws we must first overcome.

In every high- or low-profile scam, the chances are either that someone didn't apply its teachings or that someone did and then refused to stare reality in the eye.

ITS TEACHINGS

WE HAVE TO TRUST OURSELVES...

If something looks like a duck, walks like a duck, and quacks like a duck, we have to trust ourselves that we might just be looking at a duck.

FORGET THE MESSENGER...

If someone tells us the duck is a swan, it won't matter how rich, well educated, or respected that someone might be. Until we are offered a reasonable explanation as to why it is a swan, the duck will remain a duck.

DEMAND THAT EXPLANATION...

If someone tells us the duck is a swan, we are entitled to that explanation. Indeed, we should demand it.

REPETITION CHANGES NOTHING...

If someone repeats a dozen times that the duck is a swan, it won't turn the duck into a swan.

BEWARE THE NEED FOR SPEED...

If we are asked to act quickly to identify the duck as a swan, we have to ask why there is a sudden need for speed.

SMELL THE SMELL...

*If something doesn't smell quite right about
that duck or the person selling it, we should
breathe deeply and smell the smell.*

IF IT'S TOO GOOD TO BE TRUE...

*If something seems too good to be true, it
just might not be true.*

BACK TO TRUST...

*Finally, we have to trust ourselves to recog-
nize anything that might be unusual about
either the duck or the messenger—and we
should ask about it.*

OVERCOMING OUR FLAWS

Think of any bad decision we've ever made. Think of the lies
we've embraced. Think of any successful scam. In each case,
you will find one or more of the following flaws we all have
that contributed directly to why we made that bad decision or
embraced the scammers' lies.

WHAT WE SEE...

*Too often, we often tend to see only what we
want to see—and we sometimes won't even
look for what we don't want to see.*

WHAT WE DON'T SEE OR HEAR...

*We often can't see what isn't there—and
can't hear what isn't said. Often we don't
want to.*

WHAT WE FOCUS ON...

*We often tend to focus only on ourselves—
and refuse to focus on anyone or anything
else.*

OUR ASSUMPTIONS...

We often tend to view the world solely through the lens of our own assumptions—and we often simply can't free ourselves of those assumptions. And often we just don't want to.

THOSE SIMPLE EXPLANATIONS...

We often embrace the simple explanations too easily—provided, of course, they support what we want to believe.

OUR DEFERENCE TO HUBRIS AND OFFICE...

We sometimes allow the hubris and the office held by others to cloud our judgment—as if they know better than us whether the duck is a swan. They don't.

OUR OPTIMISM AND TRUST...

Our natural optimism and desire to trust those we like often turns into blind optimism and blind trust. We want to believe so badly.

OUR MYOPIA...

We often can't see the long-term consequences of our actions—and, again, we often refuse to look.

OUR FEAR OF DOING THE RIGHT THING...

We are often afraid to do the right thing because we put self-interest ahead of everything else.

So, armed with the principles and insights of the Duck School, how could we better detect and avoid the scam—the object of our affection? We could start by identifying different types of lies.

SOME DIFFERENT TYPES OF LIES

The best scammers in the kingdom challenge us to find their lies. There are at least three broad different kinds of lies of which we need to be aware.

The brazen lie

The brazen lie is an *in-your-face challenge* told with such conviction and certainty that *you are almost dared not to believe it.* For the scammer, it is presented simply as a self-evident truth.

In the brazen lie, for example, the scammers will tell you with infectious excitement that the duck is a swan. Then, with lightning speed, they will move on to their next talking point. They know the brazen lie is often difficult to check—even with time needed to check it out. Without the time, forget it...

Thus was born the scammers' ever-present unquench-able need for speed. If you want to check out that duck again, guess what? It is too late. *It is gone...*

Some believe that Ahmed Chalabi, the leader of the largest Iraqi exile group before the war, was the master of the brazen lie. He made no secret of the fact that he wanted the United States to invade Iraq and occupy Baghdad. According to reports, amongst many other items of evidence he planted, he claimed that weapons of mass destruction lay hidden in the basement of a specific hospital in Baghdad outside the view of American satellites. He claimed they were either about to be used or given to the terrorists. There was thus no way for the Bush administration to check this without entering Baghdad, which is what they anyway wanted to do. When no weapons were found at that location—or anywhere else—it was too late. We were already in Baghdad.

As for Mr. Chalabi, he had accomplished what he wanted. When later asked about this, he reportedly smiled...

The shaded lie

The shaded lies are subtle shadings of the truth. Here, the scammers will tweak the truth. Consider a financial disclosure statement in which the numbers are accurate, but that contain disclosures that shade the truthful numbers. To detect the shaded lie often requires the help of professionals, which is why the best scammers often will offer us help through their respectable surrogates.

The Enron scam is replete with examples of shaded lies that were so difficult to understand that even the most experienced analysts couldn't understand them.

The lies of omission

Of all of the lies, however, the lies of omission are the most difficult to detect. Here, quite simply, the scammer is deliberately *not* telling us something—knowing that this will mislead us. To detect lies of omission requires unusual listening and reading skills. It requires you to listen for *what is not said* and to read *what is not there*. Philosopher Kahlil Gibran captured this reality about the importance of listening—

> *"The reality of the other person lies not in what he reveals to you, but in what he cannot reveal to you. Therefore, if you would understand him, listen not to what he says, but rather to what he does not say."*

THAT SENSE OF SMELL—AND SIGHT

Almost every scam has its own distinctive "smell." Sometimes, its fragrance smells too good to be true. Sometimes, the smell is just a tad "off." To identify that smell is not as unscientific as it might sound. For years, professional interrogators have managed to detect *physical signs* of lying and discomfort. In fact, they are trained to look for "tells"—the involuntary signs that liars emit when lying. Professional interrogators do this as part of a fixed routine. Gifted nego-tiators do this instinctively.

As a young lawyer, I can remember working with a senior partner who was known for his remarkable negotiating skills. Before he and his clients would begin a negotiation, I can remember how they would make a point of socializing with the other side. As they would talk about everything but business, I would watch and listen without having any idea what they were really doing—or why they bothered.

Years later, a continuing education seminar provided the answer. A professional interrogator and psychology profes-sor was explaining how you could tell when a witness was not telling the truth. I was fascinated to hear that the first step in catching a liar in a lie is to identify a baseline for body language and other physical characteristics while he or she was under no pressure. For example, if a potential liar didn't scratch his nose or blink while discussing golf or gambling, a sudden scratching or blinking attack when busi-ness was discussed might constitute one or more "tells." And when those tells began to show up in clusters, it was time to start paying serious attention. It was then that the penny dropped. I was embarrassed finally to learn why the senior partner and his clients were so intent on schmoozing with the other side before the serious negotiations began. They were simply identifying a baseline they would use later to great effect. I was just too naive at the time to understand this.

ENRON AND THE DUCK SCHOOL

An interesting example of how the principles of the Duck School applied to the Enron scam was offered when an Enron employee described the company's approach to accounting rules. It also shines a light on the role of sur-rogates.

She described Enron's need to describe a dog as a duck on the company's financial statements. She explained how the accounting rules described a duck as something that had yellow feet, white covering, and an orange beak. After Enron had dressed the dog so that it had those features, it would have to persuade the company accountants to certify that what they were looking at was really a duck. After pointing out the dog's white covering, yellow feet and orange beak, they asked the accountants to certify it as a duck. The accountants responded by saying that, according to the rules, it was indeed a duck.

Were the accountants scammed? *No, they were not.* They simply made a choice between integrity and fees. They also chose to disregard the problem this caused when outsiders relied on their opinion. By doing so, did they become part of the scam and did they thereby join the scammer class? You decide...

The lengths to which some Enron analysts and bankers went to ignore the Duck School was also remarkable. Invoking the "trust-me" doctrine, Enron asked them to admire and endorse the company as a healthy swan when, in fact, it was an ailing duck on life support. Nobody noticed the tubes and nobody asked why such a successful and profitable company had no money...

After interviewing Wall Street analysts, Dan Ackman, writing for *Forbes,* concluded that they had "little or no understanding of how Enron reported such huge numbers." Instead of asking the hard questions, they chose to trust the company and accept the numbers they were given—numbers that were created with pixie dust. By April 2001, there were some who questioned the lack of clarity of Enron's disclosures, but others continued to recommend Enron's stock.

Some did detect an odor wafting around Enron's revenues, however. Between 1999 and 2000, Enron doubled its reported sales. Before it declared bankruptcy, Enron was about to double its revenues again. This would have made it the second largest company in the world in terms of sales revenues. *How was this possible?* How could a relatively obscure energy company become so large and so successful

so quickly—particularly when there was such mystery surrounding how it made money?

Enron's senior management responded with great assurance and certainty that their company was a healthy
and beautiful duck. Dan Ackman tried to explain the problem with the company's numbers using the analogy of an
Olympic track coach. He likened Enron to an unknown run-
ner who had apparently just broken the world record for
the mile by forty-five seconds. Any track coach, Ackman
explained, would know this was impossible. Remarkably,
hardly any of the analysts and bankers looking at Enron's
startling success reached this same conclusion. Nothing
about the incongruities in the company's performance
piqued their curiosity.

Happily, there were a few analysts who did understand.
One was Jim Chanos, the president of Kynikos Associates, a
short-selling hedge fund. In his testimony before Congress,
Mr. Chanos confirmed that many analysts who supported
Enron did not have a clue about the company:

> "In January 2001, we began contacting a
> number of analysts at various Wall Street
> firms with whom we did business and in-
> vited them to our offices to discuss Enron.
> Over the next few months a number of them
> accepted our invitation and met with us to
> discuss Enron and its valuation.
>
> We were struck by how many of them con-
> ceded that there was no way to analyze En-
> ron, but that investing in Enron was instead
> a 'trust me' story. One analyst, while admit-
> ting that Enron was a 'black box' regarding
> profits, said that, as long as Enron delivered,
> who was he to argue!
>
> It was clear to us that most of these analysts
> were hopelessly conflicted over the invest-
> ment banking and advisory fees that Enron
> was paying to their firms. We took their 'buy'
> recommendations, both current and future,
> with a very large grain of salt!"

Mr. Chanos has been described as a "financial sleuth." The more he looked into Enron, the less sense it made to him. He described his reaction to Enron's apparently successful broadband adventure:

> *"We knew telecom cold. And here's Enron bleating about this great opportunity."*

He could not understand how Enron's broadband division could be doing so well when the rest of the industry was flailing.

> *"[W]e were puzzled by Enron's and its supporters boasts in late 2000 regarding the company's initiatives in the telecommunications field, particularly in the trading of broadband capacity. Enron waxed eloquent about a huge, untapped market in such capacity and told analysts that the present value of Enron's opportunity in that market could be $20 to $30 per share of Enron stock.*
>
> *These statements were troubling to us because our portfolio already contained a number of short ideas in the telecommunications and broadband area based on the snowballing glut of capacity that was developing in that industry. By late 2000, the stocks of companies in this industry had fallen precipitously, yet Enron and its executives seemed oblivious to this!"*

He also noticed something that was there for anyone to see. While Enron's revenues were growing steadily, *the company appeared to have no cash.* And how could a business operate without cash? In fact, Enron had negative cash flow in the first nine months of 2000. Its debt was also rising. Considering it was apparently so profitable, this made little sense. *Something was wrong.* As he searched for answers, he was concerned about Enron's financial disclosures:

> *"We were also troubled by Enron's cryptic disclosure regarding various 'related party transactions' described in its 1999 Form 10-K as well as the quarterly Form 10-Qs it*

*filed with the SEC in 2000 for its March, June,
and September quarters. We read the foot-
notes in Enron's financial statements about
these transactions over and over again but
could not decipher what impact they had on
Enron's overall financial condition."*

All that was clear was that, if anyone had the courage to apply the principles of the Duck School to Enron, they would have seen what Mr. Chanos and others saw. This also served to highlight the startling refusal of our finest and brightest to ask questions.

We somehow had to acknowledge and understand that reality is the way things are—not the way we wish they would be. We had to ignore the messenger and focus on the message. And if it seemed too good to be true...

It is now time to introduce Nelson Mandela into the tale. And Enron would offer a quite unexpected segue that I couldn't have made up.

CHAPTER THREE

THE ENRON PRIZE:
YOU COULDN'T MAKE THIS UP

"Nelson Mandela epitomizes the ideals upon
which the Enron Prize for Distinguished
Public Service was established."

Enron Chairman Ken Lay

On October 26, 1999, Ken Lay and his Enron board wrapped themselves in Nelson Mandela's enormous stature. That evening at Rice University, they awarded him the Enron Prize for Distinguished Public Service. Previous recipients were Colin Powell and Mikhail Gorbachev.

He was a perfect choice: an icon and Nobel Laureate, honored throughout the world for his unsurpassed moral authority. He had peacefully liberated his country. For twenty-seven years, he had languished as the apartheid government's prisoner. Despite the harsh and brutal conditions at

the desolate Robben Island prison, he had somehow overcome hopelessness. He had begun his negotiations with his
captors from his prison cell and ultimately persuaded them
to abandon apartheid.

That year, Enron was not alone in honoring Nelson Mandela. A few months earlier, Harvard University, the alma
mater of Enron's Jeff Skilling, had conferred upon him an
honorary degree. In his introductory remarks at the award
ceremony, Harvard's president, Neil L. Rudenstine, offered a
brief snapshot of Nelson Mandela's early life:

> *"Nelson Mandela's remarkable life has*
> *shaped, in absolutely decisive ways, the*
> *course of his country's history since the early*
> *decades of our century.*
>
> *Born eighty years ago into a royal lineage*
> *in South Africa's Eastern Cape, he went as*
> *a boy to live in the household of the regent*
> *of his own Thembu people. He has often said*
> *how much he learned about leadership from*
> *those early years...President Mandela is a*
> *democrat who has learned from a king.*
>
> *He also took from his background a deep*
> *sense of his own dignity, and the dignity of*
> *all men and women."*

The citation on Harvard's honorary law degree laid out
the bigger picture:

> CONSCIENCE OF A PEOPLE, SOUL OF
> A NATION, HE HAS BROUGHT FORTH
> FREEDOM FROM THE CRUCIBLE OF
> OPPRESSION AND INSPIRED, BY HIS
> COURAGEOUS EXAMPLE, THE BET-
> TER ANGELS OF OUR NATURE

In honoring Nelson Mandela, Enron's message was clear:
it could share the same stage with him. For Ken Lay and Jeff
Skilling, this made total sense. Enron was known as a bea-
con of excellence and even morality in an increasingly ruthless business world. The company and its managers were
widely regarded as the very epitome of excellence. A *For-*

tune survey had named Enron *"Most Innovative Company in America"* for an unprecedented fifth year in a row. The same magazine ranked Enron *"No. 1 in Quality of Management"* and *"No. 2 in Employee Talent"* of all American companies. Enron was also named one of the *"Best Places to Work in America."* In 1999, *Business Week* named Ken Lay one of the top twenty-five managers in the world.

Enron seemed a remarkable company led by a remarkable team. Ken Lay had created a sixty-five-page Code of Ethics that resembled a constitution. It even included "Principles of Human Rights." In his foreword, he wrote—presumably with a straight face:

> *"[W]e are responsible for conducting the business affairs of the companies in accordance with all applicable laws and in a moral and honest manner...We want to be proud of Enron and to know that it enjoys a reputation for fairness and honesty and that it is respected...Enron's reputation finally depends on its people, on you and me. Let's keep that reputation high."*

In Enron's 1999 Annual Report, he stressed the company's high values—again presumably with a straight face:

RESPECT:

> *"We treat others as we would like to be treated ourselves. We do not tolerate abusive or disrespectful treatment. Ruthlessness, callousness and arrogance don't belong here."*

INTEGRITY:

> *"We work with customers and prospects openly, honestly and sincerely. When we say we will do something, we will do it."*

COMMUNICATION:

> *"We have an obligation to communicate. Here, we take the time to talk with one another...and to listen. We believe that infor-*

mation is meant to move and that informa-
tion moves people."

EXCELLENCE:
"We are satisfied with nothing less than the
very best in everything we do. We will con-
tinue to raise the bar for everyone."

Looking back, this was breathtaking in its self-delusion.

That evening at Rice University, the Enron family was giddy with euphoria. The thought of honoring the man who "epitomized" their ideals must have been intoxicating. What apparently occurred to none was that the company was honoring him for the very qualities *it did not have*—and that might have saved it.

Before Nelson Mandela addressed the gathering of dignitaries, Enron executives, and Rice University faculty and students, former Secretary of State James A. Baker III and Prince Bandar Bin Sultan of Saudi Arabia introduced him. The introduction was effusive.

As Nelson Mandela concluded his address, he turned to the students and offered them this advice: *"Trust yourselves,"* he implored, *"and do the right thing."* He warned them that this might not always be easy—and that it might sometimes take great courage and sacrifice. *He knew. He had been there.* He received a rapturous standing ovation. As the applause thundered through the auditorium, and unknown to many of those gathered, the seeds for Enron's looming implosion had already been planted. The scam was already percolating. *Two years later, the company imploded.*

While Ken Lay's written guiding principles and Enron's values might have mirrored Nelson Mandela's—at least in Ken Lay's mind, it is interesting how the two men walked the walk with respect to the one principle Mr. Mandela demanded and insisted upon of his followers, namely, that the interests of those they represented should always outweigh their personal interests. Ken Lay adopted this same guiding principle in Enron's Code of Ethics.

Now the question was how the two men walked-the-walk on at least this one issue...

HOW KEN LAY WALKED THE WALK

In 1999, Enron and Ken Lay shared a common problem: Both needed cash desperately. Enron's compensation committee had already given him a $7.5 million line of credit. From time to time, he drew down on the line and repaid it in cash in a timely manner. The company was not affected by this. It was cash out and cash in.

In May 1999, at his specific request, this arrangement changed. Now, instead of having to repay his loans with cash, he was permitted to repay his loans with company stock. *Presumably, nobody on Enron's board understood the significance of this change.* While, previously, it was cash out and cash in, now it was cash out and effectively worthless Enron stock in. if word leaked out that Ken Lay was effectively selling off his stock to pay off his debt, or if the company was effectively trying to liquidate stock to meet its financial obligations, the effect in the market would have been profound.

Apparently neither Mr. Lay nor his fellow board members, nor his closest advisors, nor the company's accountants realized that the cash-poor company could not use Ken Lay's stock to meet its payroll.

In another sense too, his new deal effectively gave him the key to the candy store for, while he could only withdraw $7.5 million at a time, *there was no restriction on the number of times he could withdraw it.* And Ken Lay had a *lot* of company stock. He was therefore faced with a crisp issue: To address his personal financial crisis, would he deplete the company's available and desperately needed cash reserves and replace it with effectively worthless Enron stock?

The facts are a devastating indictment of Ken Lay. He started drawing down his entire $7.5 million line of credit *once a month*, and then *every two weeks*, and then *several days in a row.* On each occasion, he repaid the line with company stock. In June 2001 alone—just months before the bankruptcy—he drew down *$24 million* from the line. Over the entire year prior to the company's collapse, he drew down *$77 million* from the line, which he repaid with stock.

So much for how Ken Law walked-the-walk. *All that is clear is that he didn't...*

HOW NELSON MANDELA WALKED THE WALK

By early January 1985, Nelson Mandela was in his twenty-first year of imprisonment. South Africa was in crisis. The Soweto school uprising of 1976 had bred a radical group of young black activists who were making the country ungovernable. As South Africa looked into an abyss, the government escalated its violence against blacks and other anti-apartheid groups. This, in turn, created a mood of increasing defiance in streets throughout the country. The protests and violence escalated.

At the same time, the international campaign to release Nelson Mandela had gathered momentum. He had become the greatest political problem the government faced. Releasing him became a necessity, but, by releasing him, they could not afford to show weakness and lose face.

President P. W. Botha came up with a tactical gambit that he thought was brilliant. He would offer to release Nelson Mandela and some of his fellow prisoners on condition he renounced violence. He believed that this was an offer he couldn't refuse—

> *"because, if Mandela refused, the whole world would understand why the South African government would not release him."*

His minister of justice, Mr. Kobie Coetsee, had read the reports about Nelson Mandela. He warned President Botha that Mr. Mandela would not accept the offer.

President Botha, however, remained convinced in the brilliance of his strategy. He ignored the warning. On January 31, 1985, in a debate in Parliament, the president publicly offered Mr. Mandela his freedom. It was subject to the condition that he "unconditionally rejected violence as a political instrument." He extended this offer to all political prisoners—thereby hoping to put even more pressure on him. He then added:

> "It is therefore not the South Africa government which now stands in the way of Nelson Mandela's freedom. It is he himself."

President Botha could never have anticipated the reply would be smuggled out of Robben Island so quickly. Less than two weeks later, on February 10, 1985, Nelson Mandela's daughter delivered her father's reply at a huge rally at the Soweto soccer stadium in Soweto, a black township outside Johannesburg. The reply was as eloquent as it was unambiguous. Would Mr. Mandela put his own interests of being released from prison ahead of the interests of those he represented?

He began his reply by addressing directly President Botha's demand that he renounce violence:

> "Let Botha...renounce violence. Let him say that he will dismantle apartheid. Let him unban the people's organization, the African National Congress. Let him free all who have been imprisoned, banished or exiled for their opposition to apartheid. Let him guarantee free political activity so that people may decide who will govern them."

> "I cherish my own freedom dearly, but I care even more for your freedom. Too many have died since I went to prison. Too many have suffered for the love of freedom. I owe it to their widows, to their orphans, to their mothers and to their fathers who have grieved

and wept for them. Not only I have suffered
during these long, lonely, wasted years. I am
not less life-loving than you are."

He explained his conclusion:

"But I cannot sell my birthright, nor am I
prepared to sell the birthright of the people
to be free. I am in prison as the representa-
tive of the people and of your organization,
the African National Congress, which was
banned.

What freedom am I being offered while the
organization of the people remains banned?
What freedom am I being offered when I
may be arrested on a pass offence? What
freedom am I being offered to live my life as
a family with my dear wife who remains in
banishment in Brandfort? What freedom am
I being offered when I must ask for permis-
sion to live in an urban area? What freedom
am I being offered when I need a stamp in my
pass to seek work? What freedom am I being
offered when my very South African citizen-
ship is not respected?"

His statement ended dramatically:

"Only free men can negotiate. Prisoners can-
not enter into contracts... I cannot and will
not give any undertaking at a time when I
and you, the people, are not free. Your free-
dom and mine cannot be separated. I will
return."

Even though he had been in prison for 21 years—and
even though his closest friends in prison would also have
been released had he accepted the president's offer—he
preferred to remain in jail rather than accept the president's condition. Every one of his friends accepted his decision and supported it.

By doing so, he had clearly put the interests of those he
represented ahead of his own and thereby reinforced his al-

ready overwhelming moral authority. By doing so, he even won the grudging respect of his enemies.

One can only wonder how differently Ken Lay and his management team may have addressed Enron's problems had they studied the man they had honored that evening at Rice University. Perhaps they would have done nothing differently because they were always more concerned about their personal interests than the interests of those they represented.

Perhaps the group that might have benefited the most from studying Nelson Mandela were the professionals—the lawyers, accountants and investment advisors. Perhaps one of them—or one of their younger associates—might have asked the difficult questions and might have questioned the ethical propriety of what they were being asked to do. Perhaps they would have been inspired by Nelson Mandela's experience and might have acted differently...

Part Two:

NELSON MANDELA

"CONSCIENCE OF A PEOPLE, SOUL
OF A NATION, HE HAS BROUGHT
FORTH FREEDOM FROM THE
CRUCIBLE OF OPPRESSION AND
INSPIRED, BY HIS COURAGEOUS
EXAMPLE, THE BETTER ANGELS
OF OUR NATURE."

CHAPTER FOUR

AN OVERVIEW OF THE
MAN AND HIS GIFT

During my lifetime I have dedicated
myself to this struggle of the African people, I have fought against
white domination, and I have fought
against black domination. I have
cherished the ideal of a democratic
and free society in which all persons live together in harmony and
with equal opportunities. It is an
ideal which I hope to live for and to
achieve. But if it needs be it is an
ideal for which I am prepared to die.

Nelson Mandela,
Rivonia Trial

In his historic negotiations with the apartheid government that began while he was still their prisoner, Nelson
Mandela accomplished the seemingly impossible. He
persuaded the regime to give up apartheid. To appreciate
the magnitude of this is to understand the cultural climate
of the time.

Apartheid literally means "apartness" or "separateness." For three hundred years, most Afrikaners simply believed that the white race was superior to all others. The racial supremacy that apartheid sought to legislate represented their white South African values of three hundred years. They saw any threat of the removal of apartheid as a threat to their fundamental personal and cultural identity. As Nelson Mandela and his colleagues began their negotiations for the peaceful removal of apartheid, they understood what they faced.

In 1948, the National Party, led by Dr. D. F. Malan, won the all-white election. They ran on the apartheid platform relying on white fear and anxiety—and there was plenty of that to spare. As the new prime minister acknowledged victory, he addressed the "colored question" and reflected the attitude of a majority of Afrikaners:

> *"The colored question is rapidly increasing in seriousness and urgency. I consider apartheid—that's the separation policy—to be South Africa's last chance to remain a white man's country...It lays a tremendous responsibility upon those who govern the country. A responsibility which the white man feels is his duty to help these underdeveloped people who are not capable of governing themselves. It would fall to pieces if we were not there to look after them."*

In fairness, not all Afrikaners embraced apartheid's goals. The outgoing prime minister, General Smuts—himself an Afrikaner—saw apartheid as "a crazy concept, born of prejudice and fear." He was correct.

How best to describe the injustice and horror of apartheid? After apartheid ended, South Africa's Truth and Reconciliation Commission issued a report. The introduction to Volume 7 would help shine a light on the evil that was apartheid:

"This volume is a tribute to the victims of Apartheid and a living monument to those who sacrificed so much in order that we could all enjoy the fruits of democracy. It contains the stories of those who came forward to speak of their suffering...

These summaries cannot do justice to the magnitude of the violations experienced by victims. They do not always convey a sense of the lasting impact of the violations, nor do they describe the wider picture of abuse, discrimination and human rights violations that Apartheid wreaked primarily upon the black citizens of the country.

It has been very difficult to describe acts of torture in these summaries. In most cases, acts of torture have been abbreviated to state that a person was tortured without necessarily specifying each method such as electric shocks, suspension from a tree, the 'helicopter' method, attempted suffocation by the 'tubing' method, submersion in water and so on.

Although rape and other forms of sexual torture were undoubtedly part of the repertoire of torturers, details are generally not included.

Where details are specified in the summaries, these should serve to remind readers of the full horror and scope of the use of torture in South Africa during the mandate period."

WHAT HE FACED

The government created an internal security force that the KGB would have envied. They gave it enormous power. Generally, its enemy was anyone involved in the anti-apartheid movement. Specifically, its enemy was the African National Congress and its most eloquent spokesman, Nelson Mandela. *He was the face of the enemy.*

After Mr. Mandela was arrested and convicted, the government was convinced his stature would fade over time. It was also convinced that he was more dangerous dead than alive. It did not need a martyr on its hands to rally the angry young blacks. Its main concern became to keep him alive.

In her book, *The Anatomy of a Miracle: The End of Apartheid and the Birth of South Africa,* Patti Waldmeir described how, within the walls of the Robben Island prison, Nelson Mandela was scheming to outsmart and seduce the government into dismantling apartheid. Amazingly, he succeeded.

He knew he would have to begin by persuading the government to negotiate with him and with the African National Congress. While he was convinced he could handle the negotiators, he also knew his greatest obstacle would be to get them to the negotiating table. Only then could the seduction begin.

An obstacle to those negotiations was not just the three-hundred-year old Afrikaner culture. It was also the United States and the United Kingdom, who saw the apartheid regime as an important ally in the fight against communism. *Each wanted to keep the status quo in South Africa.* Each was prepared to look the other way as the apartheid government trampled lives and rights.

In 1984, for example, Prime Minister Thatcher referred to the African National Congress as "a typical terrorist organization." She said that anyone who thought the ANC could ever form a government was "living in cloud-cuckoo land." That same year, Dr. Niël Barnard, the head of the National Intelligence Service, South Africa's equivalent of the KGB, recalled believing that some settlement between the government and the ANC was a necessity. He later described Nelson Mandela in this way:

> *"[H]e has this strange charisma, being a man who people want to listen to...so there was, in our minds, looking from an intelligence perspective, never the slightest doubt. This is the man—if you cannot find settlement with him, any settlement will be out."*

At the time, the government did not share his impression.

The negotiations about the negotiations began slowly. By 1990, President de Klerk recognized that the country was on the verge of exploding. A new generation of young blacks was making the country ungovernable. The president had only two choices. He could either bring in his military to provide yet another temporary reprieve, or he could choose another path. He could attempt to negotiate a peaceful settlement with a legitimate and respected black leader, while maintaining as much power as he could.

Both the president and Nelson Mandela recognized South Africa was looking into an abyss. Both knew that any solution would have to address the rage of the neo-Nazi groups of the Afrikaner right wing, on the one hand, and the rage of those younger victims of apartheid who were demanding vengeance and retribution, on the other.

The president reluctantly came to accept that only Nelson Mandela had the stature to control the anger in the streets. What perplexed him was that the longer he remained in jail, the more his stature grew. With the demand for his release growing around the world, and with the anger on the streets becoming uncontainable, it became clear the government could wait no longer. The president needed him.

Although Nelson Mandela had already been in jail for the past twenty-seven years, in a strange irony, the president effectively became Mr. Mandela's prisoner. When the president would later release him from jail, South Africa and the world would hold their collective breath.

For President de Klerk, this was a calculated decision—and a risk. He reasoned that the newly released seventy-one-year-old would be unable to cope with the strains of life and leadership outside prison. He was certain that disillusionment and disenchantment would follow the euphoria of his release. It was inconceivable to the president and his Cabinet that Mr. Mandela could meet his followers' impossible expectations. They were totally convinced that his charisma and standing would quickly wane. They were therefore in no rush to begin negotiations. To the contrary, they were waiting for the euphoria that greeted his release to die down. They wanted to give him the time to fall on his face. They wanted to show that the former prisoner was not a savior, but was instead a fallible man who had lost touch with the new world he had just entered.

As the negotiations eventually began, two questions persisted:

- How would a man, who had been imprisoned for twenty-seven years be able to withstand the negotiating pressure the government could exert?

- How would a man with such humble roots be able to match wits—let alone outwit—the government's sophisticated team and the military might that was available to it?

The answers to these questions lay in the man himself—and in the negotiating skills he had acquired throughout his life. Looking back, even his adversaries grudgingly acknowledged that Nelson Mandela was a *leader and negotiator extraordinaire.*

The South African apartheid-era foreign minister, Pik Botha, for example, provides an insight into how Nelson Mandela approached his epic negotiations with the South African government:

> *"When we started negotiations, Nelson Mandela, in his very first opening statement, for at least 20 minutes or more, said he made a study of the Afrikaner history, merely telling us, 'Look, I know you and I respect what you've gone through.'*
>
> *He didn't come up with a statement of bitterness, retribution. No. A man, after 27 years of being robbed of his freedom, and to then come forward and start negotiations on that basis—remarkable. There's no way you can argue against that."*

The issue wasn't whether or not he felt bitterness. He did. He also simply appreciated that the expression of bitterness would not help him reach his goal of eliminating apartheid.

HIS GIFT

His life had prepared him well for those negotiations. It had resulted in him developing extraordinary negotiating, decision-making, and leadership skills.

He understood that knowledge was power. Throughout his life, and in many different contexts and circumstances, he discovered what I have called "Ten Powers of Negotiation." These 10 beacons of knowledge made him a *negotiator extraordinaire* and a leader of unsurpassed moral authority. They would also be his gift to us for our journey:

- The power of the *process*
- The power of *preparation*
- The power of *positioning*
- The power of *common sense and logic*
- The power of *dignity, congeniality, and humor*
- The power of *truth and fairness*
- The power of *observation—listening and seeing*
- The power of *morality, courage, and attitude*
- The power of *patience*
- The power to *walk away*

DISCOVERING HOW HE DEVELOPED THOSE SKILLS

Many of his skills were learned and developed early in his life—long before his imprisonment. Other skills were developed and refined during his long days at Robben Island. During that time, he nurtured and honed his skills until they became a scalpel that he would wield with the precision of a surgeon.

His early life had a profound and lasting effect on him. It shaped both his future and that of his country. It provided him with lessons in leadership and negotiation that would form the foundation of the Ten Powers. And those Ten Powers could have helped us better detect and avoid the scam.

To appreciate fully his quite remarkable skills and qualities is to understand the context in which he developed them and the circumstances in which he applied them. What we now know with absolute certainty is that, if he could apply those skills and qualities in the face of an overwhelmingly powerful adversary, we could apply them in our everyday lives—if we could summon the moral backbone to do so.

CHAPTER FIVE

NELSON MANDELA'S LESSONS: EARLY LIFE TO ROBBEN ISLAND

"He has often said how much he
learned about leadership, from
those early years...President
Mandela is a democrat who
has learned from a king."

Neil L. Rudenstine
Harvard University President

O n July 18, 1918, he was born in Mvezo, a rural village
in the district of Umtata in Transkei, South Africa.
The Bolshevik Revolution was a year old. World War
I was coming to an end.

His parents must either have had a premonition or a fine-
ly tuned sense of humor. They gave their son the Xhosa birth
name of "Rolihlahla," which literally means "pulling the
branch off a tree"—or, in informal Xhosa terms, "trouble-

maker." Later, this would not even mildly amuse the South African apartheid government.

On his first day of school, his teacher gave him the name "Nelson" and, from that day on, he would be known as Nelson Rolihlahla Mandela. André Brink, the noted anti-apartheid writer, has suggested that his teacher might have "had delusions of imperial splendor." We'll never know.

His father, Hendry Mandela, was illiterate and polygamous. He was tall and dignified, with no sense of inferiority toward whites—a trait he passed to his son. He was also stubborn—another trait that he passed on. He was a respected man in the community and acted as counselor to two consecutive Thembu kings. One appointed him as chief of his village.

When Xhosa Chief Jongilizwe died, a dispute arose as to which of his three sons should be his successor. He sought out Nelson's father, who recommended that Jongintaba be appointed Regent. This advice was accepted—which would later prove a fateful decision for the young Nelson.

Soon after Nelson Mandela's birth, his father was involved in a dispute that resulted in him losing his chieftainship. As chief, his father was responsible not only to the Thembu king, but also to the local white magistrate. When one of his father's subjects lodged a complaint with the magistrate about an ox that had strayed, his father was ordered to appear before the magistrate. He refused. He believed that, in tribal matters, he was guided only by Thembu custom and not by the laws of the king of England. The magistrate was unimpressed and stripped him of his chieftainship for insubordination. He lost everything. Later, Nelson Mandela noted the qualities in his father that he recognized in himself: "a proud rebelliousness, a stubborn sense of fairness."

In later years, as his negotiating style developed, the rebellious spirit and sense of fairness he inherited from his father would lead him to challenge the status quo and to ask the difficult questions. His sense of fairness permeated everything he did and contributed significantly to the moral authority he exuded.

ONE EARLY LESSON: AVOIDING HUMILIATION

One of his first lessons he learned as a young boy was also one of his most profound. In his autobiography, he wrote how he learned that "to humiliate any other person is to make him suffer an unnecessary cruel fate."

He wrote how he never intentionally set out to humiliate anyone. This was a recurring theme throughout his life, whether dealing with those with opposing views, cross-examining government witnesses, dealing with his wardens at Robben Island, or negotiating with the leaders of the apartheid government.

This also had an effect on his negotiating style because he understood that a negotiation was about persuasion. He understood how difficult it would be to persuade someone who felt humiliated. He understood that humiliating anyone was always counter-productive.

> *More than seventy years later, Enron's CEO, Jeff Skilling, would ridicule this rejection of humiliation as being too "touchy-feely" for his taste. Enron was known for its culture of humiliating its employees and business adversaries.*
>
> *Again, more than seventy years later, we would see pictures of Iraqi prisoners of war being subjected to unspeakable humiliation, presumably in the hope that they would divulge important information—even though this was contrary to the view of experts who believed that the opposite was true. The experience of the experts was that humiliation almost always has the opposite effect on prisoners, making them less inclined to cooperate.*
>
> *What both experiences illustrated was that humiliation has at least two other unintended consequences: not only does it undermine the morale of everyone connected with that humiliation, it also undermines any possibility of being able to assert any moral authority.*
>
> *This makes one wonder about those negotiators who persist in believing in the benefit of negotiating by intimidation and humiliation.*

In his autobiography, Nelson Mandela wrote about how he has always believed that nurture, rather than nature, determines a person's values. He believed in the importance of parents and family in a child's development and personality. He recalled a Xhosa fable his mother told him when he was very young. It was about a traveler who was approached by an old woman with terrible cataracts on her eyes. When she asked for help, the traveler refused. She then approached another passerby, who did help. Miraculously, the scales fell from her eyes and she became young and beautiful. She and the passerby fell in love, married, and lived happily ever after.

He describes how the story and its message had a profound impact on him. He saw the tale as one in which virtue and generosity will always be rewarded in unanticipated ways.

Looking back at his life, virtue and generosity were always at the core of his belief system. And he did not just pay lip service to this. He lived his life this way—and this contributed to his ever-present moral authority. His lawyer and lifetime friend, George Bizos, made this comment:

"He believes that everybody is a good guy. Only when people show that they are not on the level with him, he becomes very angry and can become quite scathing."

Mr. Mandela has written how he believes that there is mercy and generosity in everyone and that no person is born hating another. He suggests that people must learn how to hate and that, if you can learn to hate, you can also learn to love.

When Nelson Mandela was nine, his father died unexpectedly from a lung disease. After a mourning period, his mother told him he would be leaving for Mqhekezweni, the home of Regent Jongintaba. It was his father who had recommended Jongintaba to become the next regent. This is why the regent now offered to be Nelson's guardian and to treat him as if he were one of his children. When Mrs. Mandela accepted the offer, she knew this would result in her son receiving a better education than she could otherwise provide. She saw how living in Mqhekezweni would be exciting for him. It was the provisional capital of Thembuland, and the power and influence of the regent pervaded every aspect of life there.

The young Nelson's education began immediately. One of his first impressions was profound. He remembered how the youngest Xhosa children acquired knowledge through listening and observing.

Almost as soon as he settled into his new home, he started attending tribal meetings. Once again, the importance of listening was emphasized—but now in the context of leadership. The regent would call tribal meetings to discuss national matters, such as a looming drought, the culling of cattle, or new laws decreed by the white government. All Thembus could attend those meetings—and many did. How the regent presided over these meetings would make a lasting impression on the young Nelson. He remembered how the regent conducted and approached those meetings. He remembered how the regent—

- considered everyone's opinion valuable;
- encouraged everyone to express his opinion;
- would not interrupt speakers;
- would not end meetings until everyone was heard;
- would respect differing opinions;
- would listen without comment to criticism—even when it was personal;
- would always retain his dignity;
- would only provide his own opinion at the very end of the meeting—thereby not coloring the debate;

- would offer his opinion finally to reflect a consensus he was attempting to forge.

The regent wanted to give those who attended the opportunity to be heard. This would give him the opportunity to hear all shades of opinion. And he didn't want those opinions to be influenced by the perception of what others thought he wanted to hear. This approach would therefore give him the benefit of considering many different views before reaching a decision—and in deciding how to bring together a consensus.

This made a great impression on the young Nelson. If no consensus were possible, the regent would often call another meeting. Generally, no agreement was forced upon those who disagreed. The tribal meetings were a collaborative process between people with common interests and goals.

The minority's rights were protected. The regent understood how a minority could become an effective obstacle to any planned action if they were not treated with respect and if they were not treated as full participants in deliberations. Nobody was ever punished for disagreeing with the regent. It would not have occurred to the regent, for example, that advisors would be fired for airing an opposing view. Certainly, if this were what advisors feared, they would never offer the regent opposing views.

Mandela remembered how the regent would deal with personal criticism. The regent would simply listen without defending himself. And he would show no emotion. For the young Nelson, this was an important lesson in leadership and in democracy.

Later, from jail, Nelson Mandela would reflect on the importance of a leader being able to keep together all sections of his people—"the traditionalists and the reformers, conservatives and liberals." He reflected on this:

> *"As a leader, I have always followed the principles I first saw demonstrated at the Great Place. I have always endeavored to listen to what each and every person in a discussion had to say before venturing my opin-*

ion. Oftentimes, my own opinion will simply represent a consensus of what I heard in the discussion. I always remember the regent's axiom: a leader, he said, is like a shepherd. He stays behind the flock, letting the most nimble go out ahead, whereupon the others follow, not realizing that all along they are being directed from behind."

He later added a refinement:

"It is better to lead from behind and to put others in front, especially when you celebrate victory when nice things occur. You take the front line when there is danger. Then people will appreciate your leadership."

From the earliest age, therefore, young Nelson received an education that was priceless:

- He learned the importance *of never humiliating anyone.*

- He learned the value of *virtue and generosity.*

- He learned the *power of observation* and the need to listen.

- He learned the *power of congeniality* and how to deal with people who were not congenial.

- He learned the *importance of collaboration*—and how this might need time. He understood the need for patience.

- He learned the *importance of dignity.*

- He understood the importance of *respecting the minority.*

- As important, he learned the *essence of leadership.*

These early lessons would form the basis for the Ten Powers of Negotiation. In particular, they taught him about the Power of the Process, which demonstrated to him how negotiation is an ongoing fluid process. It also shone a bright light on the Powers of Observation, Patience, Dignity and Congeniality.

At the age of twenty-one, he enrolled for a bachelor of arts degree at the University of Fort Hare. For young blacks in Africa, he recalled, this was regarded as "Oxford and Cambridge, Harvard and Yale, all rolled into one."

In his second year at Fort Hare, he was faced with the dilemma his father had faced years earlier—having to choose between his personal interests and the interests of those he represented. In that year, he was nominated for the Student Representative Council, the highest student organization at the university. Of those nominated, the student body would elect six members to the SRC at elections to be held in the final term.

Shortly before the election, the whole student body met to discuss certain grievances against the school's administration. A majority voted to boycott the SRC elections unless their grievances with the school administration were addressed. The elections were held as scheduled, but less than 20 percent of the Fort Hare students voted. Six representatives were elected to the SRC, one of whom was the young Nelson.

The six elected representatives met and tendered their resignations to the principal, Dr. Kerr. They explained that they had all supported the boycott and did not enjoy the support of the majority of the students. Dr. Kerr accepted the resignations and set a trap. He announced that new elections would be held the next day in the dining hall at suppertime. The entire student body would be present—which would remove any argument that the newly elected SRC would not have the support of the student body. The students recognized the trap. When the election was held, approximately the same number of students voted. They elected the same six students to the SRC.

When the members of the new SRC met, only the young Nelson took the position that nothing had changed. He felt that the SRC still could not claim the support of the majority of the student body—despite the presence of the entire

student body at the election. This time, he could not persuade the other five SRC members to join him in resigning.
He was the only member to resign. Like his father, he had a
stubborn sense of fairness and a rebellious streak. He had a
sense of what was the right thing to do.

When he tendered his resignation, Dr. Kerr asked him to
reconsider. He also warned him that, if he did not change his
mind, he would be expelled. This is how the young Nelson
recognized his predicament: On the one hand, he had taken
a stand based on what he regarded as his moral obligation
to the other students. On the other hand, the issue could
sabotage his academic career.

So, what did he do? He told Dr. Kerr the next morning that
he could not in good conscience serve on the SRC. Again, Dr.
Kerr gave him time to reconsider, saying that he had until
the end of the summer. What rankled him was the injustice
of the situation. He felt he had every right to resign from the
SCR if he wanted to. Like his father, he would not defer to
authority. He would not agree to serve on the SRC and, like
his father, he was to suffer the consequences. He would not
be able to return to Fort Hare.

If his greatest strength over his career was the enormous
moral authority he possessed, this Fort Hare experience il-
lustrated how he earned that authority. He always led by
example—and he demanded no less from others

ARRIVING IN JOHANNESBURG

In the early 1940s, when the young Nelson arrived in Johannesburg, World War II was raging. The atmosphere in
the city was electric. The Afrikaner culture had long identified with the professed racial superiority of Germanic peoples, their anti-Semitism, and their use of state socialism to
benefit the "master race."

It was no surprise, therefore, that many Afrikaner leaders had wanted South Africa to enter the war on Nazi Germany's side. South Africa, meanwhile, had entered the war

on the side of the British. Many of the Afrikaner leaders who were to become the architects of apartheid were interned as Nazi sympathizers.

Soon after arriving in Johannesburg in those turbulent times, young Nelson told a cousin that he wanted to become a lawyer. His cousin offered to introduce him to someone who might help. He introduced him to Walter Sisulu, who was to become his closest friend. Sixty-two years later, in 2003, when Mr. Sisulu died, Nelson Mandela summed up their relationship:

> *"We shared the joy of living, and the pain. Together we shared ideas, forged common commitments. We walked side by side through the valley of death, nursing each other's bruises, holding each other up when our steps faltered. Together we savored the taste of freedom."*

As he left Mr. Sisulu's office after their first meeting, he was surprised to learn that Mr. Sisulu had never completed high school. Mandela had learned at Fort Hare that a college degree made one a leader. Now he saw that many of the outstanding leaders had never been to a university. He was now moving in circles who regarded common sense and practical experience as more important than high academic qualifications.

At the end of 1942, he passed his final examination for his bachelor of arts degree. This was a milestone. In 1943, he enrolled for a bachelor of laws degree at the University of the Witwatersrand.

Who could doubt that we now live in a society that seems to value high academic qualifications over common sense and practical experience? In the context of all of the recent high-profile scams, the professional surrogates that surrounded the scammers were the best-educated professionals in the kingdom. Because we place such a high value on high academic qualifications, we allowed them to persuade us to ignore our common sense and practical experience.

Nelson Mandela identified three attributes that would be indispensable in his struggle against the apartheid regime:

- the importance of carefully defining and articulating goals;

- the need for a focused, solution-oriented approach in reaching those goals and handling the inevitable setbacks;

- the importance of meticulous preparation and planning.

These were the attributes that would come to define his fight against apartheid. He would hone these skills during his long and difficult stay at Robben Island and would apply them in his upcoming negotiations with the government.

In identifying these three attributes, he focused on the Power of the Process and the Power of Preparation.

The Power of the Process requires an understanding of the importance of clearly defining one's goals in a negotiation and not mistaking goals for the strategies in reaching those goals. It also emphasizes the importance of focusing on solving problems and not on assigning blame when breakdowns occurred.

Finally, as later chapters will demonstrate, meticulous preparation would have made it much more difficult for the scammers in every major high-profile scam.

THE IMPORTANCE OF DEFINING GOALS

A goal is a destination. Everything in a negotiation is how you reach that destination. While he always knew there would be questions about how he would reach his destination, there was never a question about Nelson Mandela's goal. In fact, one of his great strengths was his pragmatic approach to reaching his goals. He never confused identifying his goals, however, with how he would get there.

He understood, for example, that every negotiation was a series of negotiations, with the first being about defining the goals for the negotiation itself. Unless and until there was agreement as to where you and the other side wanted to go, *the negotiation would go nowhere.*

To reach this agreement about your joint destination, however, it was critical to understand everything you could about the other side. In Mr. Mandela's case, he studied the Afrikaner culture and became fluent in Afrikaans. This gave him an unusual ability to understand those with whom he was negotiating.

> *The Middle East peace negotiations are a classic example of the importance of reaching agreement on the fundamental goals of any negotiation before any progress is possible.*
>
> *Can there be any surprise that little or no progress has been made when one side refuses to recognize the other's right to exist?*
>
> *Similarly, in Nelson Mandela's case, because his goal in his negotiations with the apartheid government was the elimination of apartheid and because the government's goal was the retention of apartheid, initial progress was impossible.*

THE IMPORTANCE OF A SOLUTION-ORIENTED APPROACH

Throughout his life, he consistently demonstrated his solution-oriented approach to problems. He never dwelt on whose fault the problem was. When faced with a problem, he always sought a practical, constructive, and common-sense solution that also demonstrated an understanding of the concept of "positioning."

There was one early example of this. When he joined the ANC, there was the perception about its leadership that was widely shared by its younger members. They believed that

the ANC leaders were an African elite who were more interested in protecting their own interests than in promoting
the interests of those they represented. The younger members discussed how they could solve this problem. They
agreed that their goal was to change the ANC from within—
and not to break away from it. To reach this goal they decided to form a Youth League—as part of the ANC. This was
designed specifically to light a fire under the ANC's leaders.

They therefore deliberately positioned the Youth League's
policy as falling within ANC's policy, thereby giving the ANC
hierarchy no choice but to accept the Youth League.

> *This demonstrated the ability to position yourself in a man-
> ner that is attractive to those with whom you are negotiating.
> This would also highlight one of the most important skills
> of the best negotiators, namely, to see the world through the
> eyes of those with whom they are negotiating. This requires
> meticulous preparation into the background, policies, and
> goals of the other side.*
>
> *Just as the scammer will offer you what he thinks you want
> most, you must look at the scammer and his motives. You
> must ask, for example, why he chose you for this enormous
> opportunity or why he wants you to decide so quickly.*

THE IMPORTANCE OF METICULOUS PREPARATION

There were two events in 1946 that had an important
impact on Nelson Mandela and shaped his later strategies.
Both events highlighted the need to prepare effectively and
meticulously for any task at hand.

The first event was the African miners' strike. There
were over four hundred thousand African mineworkers
who were paid very little and who were provided with neither housing nor paid vacation. The African Mine Workers
Union demanded higher wages, housing, and paid vacation
for their members. The Chamber of Mines ignored their demands and seventy thousand miners went on strike.

The strike, however, was poorly organized. The government retaliated brutally and twelve miners died. The strike's leaders were arrested and the union was crushed. The lessons of poor preparation were evident.

Shortly thereafter, the government decided to curtail the free movement of Indians and restrict where they could live and work. The Indian community was outraged. It launched a mass campaign of passive resistance and, unlike the miners' strike, its organization and dedication were remarkable.

The lesson was duly noted. Meticulous preparation became an indispensable part of Nelson Mandela's negotiating arsenal. It would become the cornerstone of his approach to negotiation and one of the most important powers.

> *Later chapters will demonstrate the importance of preparation in the context of three high-profile scams. They will show how, if only we had learned more about those with whom we were dealing, we would not have given the scammers the respect and deference we gave them. These chapters will also raise issues relating to what we do with what we have found in our preparation. For example, the Power of Morality, Courage and Attitude would require us to have the courage to use our moral compass to exercise yet another power, the Power to Walk Away.*

IMPLEMENTING APARTHEID

Two years later, in 1948, Dr. Malan's National Party won the all-white election on the platform of apartheid. All of South Africa watched as the government set about implementing its policy of apartheid.

Monty Python would have been proud of them. Indeed, only the zaniest comedy writers could have made up how they approached their task of creating a body of laws that would separate the races. But these folks were not comedians. They were deadly serious. And what they were doing was an affront to all right-minded South Africans with any sense of fairness and what was right.

This is how the government went about its task:

Classifying the races

It began with an "us vs. them" approach. While there were many different racial groups in South Africa, for the government there were only two groups: us and them. The "us" group consisted of everyone it deemed "white." The other group consisted of everyone else—the "nonwhites." The nonwhite group was then divided into the black/African people, the Indians, and the Coloreds, who were of mixed race. Remembering that the object of apartheid was to separate the whites and nonwhites, a starting point had to be to decide who was "white" and who was not. And this was not as easy as the government leaders might first have thought.

They responded with some Pythonesque techniques, such as measuring the curliness of hair or the thickness of lips for determining whether or not someone was "white." They might, for example, put a pencil through the hair. If it stuck in the hair, the person would be classified as "nonwhite."

Separate areas, amenities, and facilities

Only when the government's world was neatly divided by race could it separate the races by permitting whites and nonwhites to live and work only in prescribed racial areas. It then gave each member of the nonwhite group a passbook to permit him or her to be in a prescribed area. Needless to say, the failure to carry that passbook would result in arrest and detention. The same result would occur if he or she were caught in an area not designated as permissible in that passbook. This system of passbooks did not apply to the white group.

What was the point of this physical separation? One point was to protect the well-paying, high-end jobs for whites by preventing those jobs from becoming available to the nonwhites. Another was to allow the forced eviction of tens of thousands of nonwhite people from homes their families had lived in for generations. One example was the case of District 6, a multiracial community on the edge of Cape Town city center. Under the new laws, forty thousand people were evicted and their community was bulldozed.

To keep interracial contact to the minimum and to separate the different races further, new legislation was passed. This required all races to have separate amenities such as toilets, parks, buses, and beaches. This was not separate-but-equal legislation. It was the opposite. It also created complicated issues for them.

Take, for example, the unexpected problem presented by "white beaches." On the one hand, it made total sense to the government that the best beaches be reserved for whites. On the other hand, it apparently forgot that many white families took their children to the beach with their black nannies. The new law did not permit the black nannies on those beaches. What were the white moms to do? Well, they demanded and received special dispensation for their nannies. The government quickly permitted black nannies on the "whites-only" beaches to look after white children, provided, however, that the nannies did not enter the water. This made as much sense as allowing blacks to clean Dutch Reform church buildings, but not allowing them to pray in those buildings.

Public transportation was also segregated—sometimes with tragic results. There were reports of people lying injured waiting for the racially correct ambulance to arrive. If a "whites-only" ambulance responded to a traffic accident and found seriously injured nonwhite victims, it was not permitted to help. Instead, it would have to leave those injured nonwhite passengers for a "nonwhite" ambulance. This was more than just another humiliation.

Cupid and the world of literature presented two other practical, semi-humorous problems the regime faced.

The problems posed by Cupid

The apartheid leaders understood the enormous problem Cupid posed. They understood that the whole fabric of their apartheid system could be ripped apart if white people fell in love or lust with anyone of a different color. The government's solution was obvious: It passed another law: the Immorality Act.

This piece of legislation made it a criminal offense for any sexual act to take place between a white and a nonwhite person. Again, sadly for the government, this was also not as easy as it sounded. It therefore came up with whatever tools it thought the police would need to enforce this law. For example, the government empowered the police to raid the homes of any suspects and seize their bedclothes as evidence. Obviously, this assumed that people in lust were wearing bedclothes when they were doing whatever it was they were not permitted to do. The police could also arrest persons found together in parked cars if they suspected the occupants either of having had sex or, God forbid, conspiring to do so. Again, the Monty Python writers had to be scribbling furiously for their next project.

The problems posed by literature

The world of ideas and literature posed an even more formidable problem and challenge for the government. It would have to deal with the very real danger presented by the written word—and, of course, any subversive ideas those words might generate.

Again, the solution was obvious to the government: It passed another law that created a Censorship Board to give its stamp of approval on what citizens could read and watch in apartheid South Africa.

There was one teeny-weeny and quite foreseeable problem: the sheer quantity of reading and video material. Undaunted, the board members set about their task with vigor and gusto. They would not be delayed by the time it would take actually to read and view the massive amount of material that had been generated since the invention of the printing presses hundreds of years earlier. No, they would not have to read everything before passing judgment on the material.

One example that absolutely delighted the enlightened few was when the Censorship Board banned the classic tale of a dark horse. It was the title that made the banning inevitable: It was *Black Beauty*. And, no, I am not making this up...

The problem of education

Another problem the government faced was not at all amusing. Ironically, how it addressed this problem ultimately led directly to the downfall of apartheid. It led to the Soweto children's uprising almost twenty years later.

The architects of apartheid understood the problem of education and schooling was pivotal to the success of the implementation of their policy. Here, the government's approach was chilling and resembled Stephen King more than Monty Python.

The government proceeded to segregate the school system. Different curriculum subjects were taught to different racial groups. When the intellectual architect of apartheid, Dr. Verwoerd, introduced the education bill, he used language that was reminiscent of the Nazi propaganda he once promoted:

> *"I will reform black education so that Natives will be taught from childhood to realize that equality with Europeans is not for them."*

This was as chilling as his rationale:

> *"What is the use of teaching a Bantu child mathematics when he cannot use it in practice?"*

Later, as prime minister, he recognized that expanding industries in white areas needed an expanding black labor force. He had the challenge of rationalizing the presence of black labor in his white society. He accepted the challenge: He described blacks as being like *"donkeys, oxen, and tractors"* that could someday be replaced by other machinery. Now, the next question was, how would the government enforce all of this?

The Suppression of Communism Act

The cornerstone of the government's security legislation was the Suppression of Communism Act. This declared the Communist Party and its ideology illegal. Presumably, someone in the government would have to delve into the writings and philosophy of Marx, Hegel, and Engels to define exactly what was "Communist ideology."

This conjured up the delicious thought of a group of apartheid government bureaucrats sitting around a smoke-filled table pondering the nuances of Marx's *Communist Manifesto* and *Das Kapital*. Instead, they sidestepped the problem. Undaunted by any intellectual niceties, they came up with a disingenuous solution. They simply defined Communist ideology as any scheme that aimed "at bringing about any political, industrial, social, or economic change within the Union by the promotion of disturbance or disorder" or that encouraged "feelings of hostility between the European and the non-European races of the Union the consequences of which are calculated to "further" disorder.

This was later referred to as "statutory communism," since it bore no relation or resemblance to the actual doctrines of Communism. It also raised another question: What if the government policy itself invoked "feelings of hostility" between the races. Could the government itself be guilty of infringing its own law?

The government then proceeded to use this act to silence and detain any anti-apartheid activist. It allowed the minister of justice to list members of anti-apartheid organizations and to ban them, usually for five-year periods, from attending public meetings, or from being in any specified area of South Africa.

BANNINGS AND ARRESTS

In September 1952, under the Suppression of Communism Act, fifty-two liberation leaders from around the country were banned from attending meetings for six months.
Nelson Mandela was amongst those leaders banned. He described the effect of the banning:
The bans extended to meetings of all kinds, not just political ones. Those banned could not talk to more than one
person at a time. They could not attend a family birthday or
funeral. Mr. Mandela described the experience as inducing
"a kind of psychological claustrophobia."
The banning, however, was only the beginning...

The Defiance Campaign

In response to the new National Party government's legislative agenda, the African National Congress launched
an effort to turn itself into a mass organization. The cornerstone of this effort was the Youth League's Program of
Action, which called for boycotts, strikes, and passive resistance. This became known as the Defiance Campaign.

On July 30, 1952, at the height of the campaign and prior
to his banning, Nelson Mandela was arrested for a violation
of the Suppression of Communism Act. Around the same
time, twenty others were also arrested. These included the
presidents and general-secretaries of the ANC, the South
African Indian Congress and ANC Youth League, and the
Transvaal Indian Congress.

The trial was expected to be an occasion for solidarity.
Nelson Mandela described how it was "sullied" by his colleague, Dr. Moroko, the president of the ANC. Dr. Moroko
was worried he would lose his medical practice. He chose to
make what Mr. Mandela referred to as a "humiliating plea"
to save his medical license. He took the witness stand to
renounce the very principles on which the ANC had been
founded. For Nelson Mandela and his colleagues, Dr. Moroko had committed the cardinal sin of putting his own interests ahead of those he represented. *This was the same cardi-*

nal sin that the scammers induced their surrogates to commit years later.

On December 2, 1952, all accused were found guilty of "statutory communism." The judge acknowledged that this was different to what was commonly considered "Communism." He also agreed that the accused had told their followers to avoid violence "in any shape or form." All were sentenced to nine months' imprisonment with hard labor—suspended for two years.

The attempt to revoke his law license

In 1954, the Law Society argued that Mr. Mandela's conviction in the defiance case constituted unprofessional and dishonorable conduct and applied to have his law license revoked.

Mr. Mandela later described his defense, which highlighted another consistent technique used by him throughout his life—that of positioning his argument in a manner that would better resonate with the person with whom he was negotiating. He argued that he had an inherent right to fight for his political beliefs and that this was the legal right of anyone in a state where the rule of law applied.

His team prepared well. They found a case that they were sure would resonate with the judge. That case concerned an Afrikaner who was detained during the Second World War for his pro-Nazi sympathies. Following a failed escape attempt, he was found guilty of car theft. After he was released from prison, he applied for admission as a lawyer. Despite his conviction and over the strong objection of the Law Society, the court decided he should be admitted because his crimes were political and that a man should not be barred from practicing his profession because of his political beliefs.

The case did indeed resonate with the judge. The court upheld Nelson Mandela's argument that he had the right to campaign for his political beliefs and dismissed the Law Society's application. It also took the highly unusual position

that the Law Society should pay Mr. Mandela's attorneys'
fees and costs.

Another lesson: the Sophiatown removal

The government's planned Sophiatown removal provided him with yet another invaluable lesson of the danger of
creating unreasonable expectations.

Africans had lived and owned property in Sophiatown
for over fifty years. The government was planning on relo-
cating all Sophiatown's African residents to another black
township. The removal was to take place even before houses were built to accommodate the evacuated people.

Through 1954 and 1955, rallies were held twice a week
to protest the removals. Nelson Mandela acknowledged that
mistakes were made and that unrealistic expectations were
created during those rallies. Their slogan "Over Our Dead
Bodies" created unrealistic expectations that they would
fight to the death to resist the removal. In fact, the ANC was
not prepared to do that.

The government carried out the removal on February 9,
1955: From that time on, Mr. Mandela was acutely sensitive
about raising unrealistic expectations. He would never fall
into this trap again.

> *This raises the Power of Truth and Fairness. If expectations
> you raise are unrealistic, it might seem you are not being
> truthful, and your moral authority will erode.*

THE FREEDOM CHARTER

In 1954, Professor Z. K. Matthews presented an idea in
a speech at the ANC annual conference. He asked whether
the time had come for the African National Conference to
consider convening a meeting:

> *"a national convention, a congress of the
> people, representing all the people of this*

country irrespective of race or color, to draw
up a Freedom Charter for the democratic
South Africa of the future."

Nelson Mandela remembered the regent's tribal meetings and the importance of consensus being reached by as
wide a diversity of organizations and peoples as possible.
He thought the creation of a Council of the Congress of the
People could accomplish this.

He wasn't disappointed by the people's response for in-
put. Suggestions came in from many diverse groups from
sports and cultural clubs, church groups to trade union
branches. He was amazed at the value of the suggestions of
ordinary people. Almost all demanded one-man-one-vote.

ANC leader Chief Albert Luthuli explained its historical
context:

"For the first time in the history of our mul-
tiracial nation its people will meet as equals,
irrespective of race, color and creed to for-
mulate a freedom charter for all the people
of our country."

The charter, which became known as the "Freedom Charter," was drafted by a small committee of the National Action
Council and reviewed by the ANC's National Executive Committee. It was presented at the Congress of the People, and
three thousand delegates approved each of its elements.
The significance of the charter was enormous. It defined the
goals of the South African liberation movement and became
an enduring document in South Africa's history. Mr. Mandela described the Charter as a mixture of practical goals and
poetic language that embraced the abolition of racial discrimination and the achievement of equal rights for all. The
Charter opened the door to anyone seeking a democratic,
nonracial South Africa.

The government recognized the danger the Congress and
Freedom Charter represented and set about to intimidate
its leaders.

TREASON

In March 1956, a year after the Congress, Nelson Mandela received his third ban—this time restricting him to Johannesburg for five years. It also prohibited him from attending meetings for the same period.

On December 5, 1956, the government made its next move. It arrested and charged him and all of the leaders of the Congress Alliance with high treason and with an alleged conspiracy to overthrow the state. High treason was defined as a hostile intention to disturb, impair, or endanger the independence or safety of the state. *The punishment was death.* A total of 156 leaders were arrested. They included the entire executive leadership of the ANC.

Monty Python would have been delighted by the unintended consequences of the government's next move.

The government placed all those arrested in two cells with cement floors and no furniture. Prior to their arrest, Nelson Mandela and many of his colleagues had been banned and therefore were not permitted to meet with those with whom they now shared two cells. The government had thus provided them with the very opportunity to meet and plan that the banning order was meant to prevent. Nelson Mandela and his colleagues in those two cells made good use of this time together.

A prosecution overreach

At the preliminary hearing, the government took two days just to read the charges. The prosecutor said that he would prove to the court that the accused, with help from other countries, were plotting to overthrow the existing government by violence and impose a Communist government on South Africa. This was the charge of high treason.

The government then made a critical mistake when it cited the Freedom Charter as proof of Communist intentions and evidence of a plot to overthrow the existing authorities. By doing so, the law of unintended consequences reared its head. The government's strategy unintentionally shifted the focus of the trial from the accused to the Freedom Charter. *The defense pounced.*

On January 9, 1957, through its lead counsel, Vernon Berrangé, the defense team set forth its argument:

> *"The defense will strenuously repudiate that the terms of the Freedom Charter are treasonable or criminal. On the contrary, the defense will contend that the ideas and beliefs which are expressed in this charter, although repugnant to the policy of the present government, are such as are shared by the overwhelming majority of mankind of all races and colors, and also by the overwhelming majority of the citizens of this country."*

In asserting that the accused intended to replace the existing government with a Soviet-style state, the prosecutor relied on the evidence of Professor Andrew Murray, head of the Department of Political Science at the University of Cape Town. Professor Murray labeled many of the seized documents, including the Freedom Charter itself, as communistic. What followed was high theater and another example of the importance of thorough preparation and careful positioning.

Mr. Berrangé began his cross-examination by asking Professor Murray to read a number of passages and then label them Communistic or not. The first passage addressed the need for workers to cooperate with each other and not exploit one another. "Communistic" was Professor Murray's opinion. Mr. Berrangé revealed that none other than former Prime Minister Dr. Malan made the "Communistic" statement.

It was Professor Murray's opinion that the next two passages Mr. Berrangé read were "Communistic," too. Berrangé then revealed these were statements made by none other than American presidents Abraham Lincoln and Woodrow Wilson.

The highlight of the cross-examination came, however, when Berrangé read a passage that Professor Murray unhesitatingly described as "Communism straight from the shoulder." That was a statement that Professor Murray himself had written some years earlier.

Mr. Berrangé conducted the cross-examination in a respectful manner without humiliating Professor Murray. This was only a preliminary hearing, and the defense anticipated having to rely on the professor's opinion during the upcoming trial. There was no reason to antagonize him—so they did not.

The preliminary part of the case had lasted a year. Court adjourned in September, and the defense began reviewing the evidence. Three months later, without explanation, charges against sixty-one of the accused were dropped.

In January, the government brought in a new prosecutor, Oswald Pirow, who would change the atmosphere of the trial. He was described as a pillar of National Party politics—and a longtime Afrikaner nationalist. He was also an outspoken supporter of the Nazi cause and once described Hitler as the "greatest man of his age." He was a virulent anti-Communist. The government was clearly worried about the upcoming trial.

The judges

The trial was to start in August 1958. The government set up a special high court, consisting of Mr. Justice F. L. Rumpff, president of the three-man court, Mr. Justice Kennedy, and Mr. Justice Ludorf.

Nelson Mandela was not optimistic about the makeup of the court. Justice Rumpff was rumored to be a member of the Broederbond, a secret Afrikaner society whose aim was to solidify Afrikaner power. Justices Ludorf and Kennedy were well-known members of the National Party. Justice Kennedy had a reputation as a hanging judge, having sent a group of twenty-three Africans to the gallows for the murder of two white policemen. Again, consistent with their problem-solving approach, Nelson Mandela and his defense team came up with a strategy to address the problem.

To everyone's surprise, their lawyers applied for the recusal of Justices Ludorf and Rumpff on the grounds that both had conflicts of interest that prevented them from treating the case fairly. This was an audacious strategy, but one that was carefully thought through.

They felt that Justice Rumpff, as the judge at the 1952 Defiance Trial, had already ruled on certain aspects of the case and therefore it was not in the interests of justice that he try this case.

They argued that Justice Ludorf was prejudiced because he had represented the government in 1954 as a lawyer in a case in which the plaintiffs sought to eject the police from a meeting of the Congress of the People.

How would the judges respond? Justice Ludorf announced that he would withdraw, adding that he had completely forgotten about the previous case. Justice Rumpff refused to recuse himself and instead offered the assurance that his judgment in the Defiance case would have no influence on him in this one.

The government appointed Mr. Justice Bekker, who was not linked to the National Party, to replace Justice Ludorf.

Mr. Mandela's team had solved the immediate problem.

The defense strategy

As a result of endless legal maneuvering, the trial only started on August 3, 1959—a little more than two-and-a-half years after their arrests. During the first two months of the case, the prosecutor entered over two thousand documents into the record. He called 210 witnesses, 200 of whom were members of the government's Special Branch—its secret police. On October 11, Oswald Pirow died suddenly from a stroke. The prosecution ended its case on March 10, 1960.

The defense strategy provided yet another object lesson for the importance of preparation and positioning. In this case, the defense was focusing on the judges. Justice Kennedy was from Natal. The defense team knew that people from the Natal province were noted for their loyalty to the region—and that this loyalty sometimes transcended race. The defense also knew that all of the judges were religious men.

The government expected the defense's first witness would be Chief Luthuli, the ANC president. Its attorneys prepared themselves for his cross-examination. Instead, the defense decided to call Dr. Wilson Conco as its first witness.

Dr. Conco was the son of a Zulu cattle farmer from the beautiful Ixopo district of Natal. He was a practicing physician and had been one of the founders of the Youth League and an active participant in the Defiance Campaign. He was also the treasurer of the ANC.

The defense team began Dr. Conco's testimony by asking him about his academic record at the University of the Witwatersrand, where he graduated first in his medical school class. The defense team thought this would resonate with Justice Kennedy, who, like Dr. Conco, was from Natal. They wanted to show him that Dr. Conco was the face of the ANC and was not a rabble-rouser. They succeeded. At the end of his testimony, after Dr. Conco had disclosed another medical achievement, Justice Kennedy said in Zulu: "Sinjalo thina maZulu," which means, "We Zulus are like that." This was an important start to the defense's case.

Chief Luthuli was the next witness. It was his job to position the ANC as striving for nonviolent racial harmony. He testified simply and with dignity and sincerity. He outlined the evolution of the ANC's policy. His background as a former teacher and chief added authority to his testimony. Also, as a devout Christian, he was able to relate to the judges. He testified about his views of the innate goodness of man and how this might lead to a change of heart on the part of white South Africans towards nonwhites. He thereby appealed directly to the religious convictions of the judges.

He also testified about the ANC's policy of nonviolence. He explained the difference between nonviolence and pacifism. He explained that while pacifists might refuse to defend themselves even when they were violently attacked, nonviolent people sometimes had to defend themselves when they were attacked.

An interruption

On March 21, 1960, the trial was interrupted. In the preceding months, there had been anti-pass demonstrations throughout the country. On March 21, there was another anti-pass demonstration, this time at Sharpeville—a small township about thirty-five miles south of Johannesburg. Several thousand unarmed demonstrators surrounded the local police station. The crowd was orderly and controlled.

The police force of seventy-five—many of whom were young and inexperienced—panicked. No one heard warning shots or an order to shoot. Suddenly, the police opened fire. As the demonstrators turned and ran in fear, the police continued to shoot. When the dust had settled, sixty-nine Africans lay dead. It was a massacre. Most had been shot in the back as they were fleeing. Four hundred people, including dozens of women and children, were wounded.

The next day press photos displayed the carnage on front pages around the world. The Johannesburg Stock Exchange plunged. South African whites began making plans to emigrate. The U.N. Security Council blamed the government for the shootings. Liberal whites urged Prime Minister Verwoerd to offer concessions to Africans. The government dug in its heels. It insisted Sharpeville was the result of a sinister Communist conspiracy.

In the face of mounting demonstrations, the government declared a state of emergency. It suspended habeas corpus. It assumed sweeping powers to act against all forms of subversion. South Africa was now under martial law. The country edged closer to the precipice.

The trial resumes

The trial labored on for another nine months until March 29, 1961. On March 29, 1961, Judge Rumpff announced that the three-judge panel had reached a verdict:

"On all the evidence presented to this court and on our finding of fact it is impossible for this court to come to the conclusion that the African National Congress had acquired or adopted a policy to overthrow the state by violence, that is, in the sense that the masses had to be prepared or conditioned to commit direct acts of violence against the state."

The court said the prosecution had failed to prove that the ANC was a Communist organization or that the Freedom Charter envisioned a Communist state. After speaking for forty minutes, Justice Rumpff said:

"The accused are accordingly found not guilty and are discharged."

The verdict was greeted with celebration, but there was also an ominous government reaction. The court had made the government look foolish in the eyes of the world. The government would never let this happen again. It would not again allow judges or "legal niceties" to deter it from its path. During the treason trial, there were no examples of anyone being beaten and tortured for information. This was to change.

The manner in which the government and the prosecution team approached the trial serves to emphasize the importance, in preparing for a trial or a negotiation, of putting yourself in the other side's shoes—something the government and prosecution team failed to do first. They considered neither the consequences of putting Nelson Mandela and his colleagues in a cell together nor their decision to frame the prosecution in the context of the Freedom Charter.

The manner in which Nelson Mandela and his defense team prepared for the trial proved in stark contrast to the government's and prosecution team's approach. Using prosecution witnesses' prior statements to contradict their testimony was a tribute to Mr. Mandela's and his team's lawyering skills. And they did so without humiliating them, but rather to show how different statements were susceptible to different conclusions.

THE RIVONIA TRIAL

After the verdict, the ANC knew that it would only be a matter of time before Mr. Mandela was banned or arrested again. It was decided that he would go underground.

The Black Pimpernel

Forced to live apart from his family, he moved from place to place to evade detection. He disguised himself. Sometimes he appeared as a common laborer. At other times he was a chauffeur. The police referred to him as the Black Pimpernel and he captured the imagination of his people. Thus began the period that only Hollywood screenwriters could have imagined.

He became a creature of the night travelling secretly around the country. Much to the delight of his followings, he began to taunt the police. He would call newspapers to alert them to what he was doing to highlight the ineptitude of the police. The police would lie in wait for him in one city only for him to appear in another city far away.

It was at this time that he began to believe the ANC's tactics had to change. While he fully endorsed the ANC's strategy, he had to recognize the reality that the government was using increased violence to crush the ANC's nonviolent protests. He realized that the ANC had to reconsider its commitment to nonviolence. There was disagreement within the ANC. At the treason trial, the ANC had contended that nonviolence was an inviolate principle of the movement, not simply a tactic. He also knew that Chief Luthuli's commitment to nonviolence was deeply moral and feared his opposition. However, Luthuli was ultimately persuaded and said:

> *"If anyone thinks I am a pacifist, let him try to take my chickens, and he will know how wrong he is!"*

It was also during this time that plans for an armed struggle began to take shape. A military wing of the ANC was formed. Mr. Mandela described how the campaign would start with sabotage against non-civilian targets. They would target military installations, power plants, telephone lines, and transportation links. The strategy was to undermine the military effectiveness of the state and undermine the economy. The sole goal was to bring the government to the bargaining table. There was to be no loss of life.

A farm in Rivonia on the outskirts of Johannesburg became the headquarters of those planning the armed struggle. The farm was later raided and an enormous number of documents were seized—some in his handwriting. Many of these were devastating in that they laid out plans for the armed struggle. This would be the foundation of the case against him and his colleagues.

His capture and trial

After his capture, Mr. Mandela and his colleagues were charged with sabotage and conspiracy. Under the Sabotage Law, the burden was on the defense to prove the accused innocent. The penalty was death by hanging.

The trial opened in Pretoria in October 1963. The judge was a respected Afrikaner. Based on the overwhelming nature of the evidence, there was never any doubt that the accused would be found guilty. The only question was whether they would escape the death penalty.

The defense was convinced that the fate of the accused would be decided outside the courtroom. Attorneys knew the Western governments were watching the trial closely. They knew these governments recognized Nelson Mandela's leadership qualities and had to be concerned at the possible consequences of his execution and martyrdom. This was yet another example of the necessity of focusing on the other side's position in deciding on a strategy for action.

As to the impression Nelson Mandela made during this time, one of his lawyers, Joel Joffe, explained:

> *"Nelson Mandela emerged quite naturally as the leader. He has, in my view, all the at-*

tributes of a leader—the engaging personal-
ity, the ability, the stature, the calm, the di-
plomacy, the tact and the conviction. When
I first met him, I found him attractive and
interesting. By the time the case finished I
regarded him as a really great man. I began
to notice how his personality and stature
impressed itself not just on the group of the
accused, but on the prison staff themselves."

After the prosecution completed its case, Nelson Mandela
decided that he would open the defense case with a statement from the dock. Under this procedure, he could not
be interrupted and could not be cross-examined. For four
hours, he explained his beliefs and political ideas. He provided an overview of South Africa:

"South Africa is the richest country in Africa,
and could be one of the richest countries in
the world. But it is a land of extremes and re-
markable contrasts. The whites enjoy what
may well be the highest standard of living in
the world, whilst Africans live in poverty and
misery...

Poverty goes hand in hand with malnutrition
and disease. The incidence of malnutrition
and deficiency diseases is very high amongst
Africans. Tuberculosis, pellagra, kwashior-
kor, gastroenteritis, and scurvy bring death
and destruction of health. The incidence of
infant mortality is one of the highest in the
world...

The complaint of Africans, however, is not
only that they are poor and the whites are
rich, but that the laws which are made by
the whites are designed to preserve this situ-
ation."

He retraced his conversion to multiracialism. He admitted that he was the leader of the armed wing of the ANC and
that he had planned sabotage. He described the indignity
of Africans' daily lives and the erosion of their family life.
He explained why this was breaking down moral standards

and generating violence. He showed how nonviolent protest had yielded no results. He denied that he was a Communist, but he recalled how Communists were the only political group who were prepared to treat Africans as human
beings and equals. He made a point of highlighting the distinction between the two organizations:

> *"The ANC, unlike the Communist Party, ad-
> mitted Africans only as members. Its chief
> goal was, and is, for the African people to
> win unity and full political rights. The Com-
> munist Party's main aim, on the other hand,
> was to remove the capitalists and to replace
> them with a working-class government. The
> Communist Party sought to emphasize class
> distinctions whilst the ANC seeks to harmo-
> nize them. This is a vital distinction."*

He then pointed out that cooperation between two
groups with different ideologies was not unusual:

> *"It is true that there has often been close co-
> operation between the ANC and the Commu-
> nist Party. But cooperation is merely proof
> of a common goal - in this case the removal
> of white supremacy - and is not proof of a
> complete community of interests.*
>
> *The history of the world is full of similar
> examples. Perhaps the most striking illus-
> tration is to be found in the cooperation
> between Great Britain, the United States of
> America, and the Soviet Union in the fight
> against Hitler. Nobody but Hitler would
> have dared to suggest that such coopera-
> tion turned Churchill or Roosevelt into Com-
> munists or Communist tools, or that Britain
> and America were working to bring about a
> communist world."*

He referred to the lack of dignity that Africans experienced:

> *"The lack of human dignity experienced by
> Africans is the direct result of the policy of
> white supremacy. White supremacy implies*

black inferiority...Because of this sort of attitude, whites tend to regard Africans as a separate breed. They do not look upon them as people with families of their own; they do not realize that they have emotions—that they fall in love like white people do; that they want to be with their wives and children like white people want to be with theirs; that they want to earn enough money to support their families properly, to feed and clothe them and send them to school."

He spoke about the pass laws:

"Pass laws, which to the Africans are among the most hated bits of legislation in South Africa, render any African liable to police surveillance at any time. I doubt whether there is a single African male in South Africa who has not at some stage had a brush with the police over his pass. Hundreds and thousands of Africans are thrown into jail each year under pass laws. Even worse than this is the fact that pass laws keep husband and wife apart and lead to the breakdown of family life."

Nelson Mandela finished with what his biographer, Anthony Sampson, describes as "his own apologia":

"During my lifetime I have dedicated myself to this struggle of the African people. I have fought against white domination, and I have fought against black domination. I have cherished the ideal of a democratic and free society in which all persons live together in harmony with equal opportunities."

He paused and looked at the judge:

"It is an ideal which I hope to live for and achieve."

Then, dropping his voice, he concluded:

"But if needs be, it is an ideal for which I am prepared to die."

What followed was thirty seconds of silence that seemed to many as the silence that preceded enormous applause— but there was no applause.

A co-defendant, Dennis Goldberg, described the moment:

> *"It was terribly moving. Nobody said anything. Even the judge didn't know what to say. I knew it was a moment of history. He emerged then as a great leader."*

Mr. Sampson describes his speech as being the most effective of Nelson Mandela's entire political career.

On June 11, 1964, the verdict was announced. With one exception, all of the accused were found guilty of sabotage. When the judge entered the court to announce the sentence, Nelson Mandela noted that the judge seemed more nervous than the accused. Mr. Mandela and his colleagues were sentenced to life imprisonment on Robben Island. The only white defendant, Dennis Goldberg, was sent to a white prison to serve his life sentence.

Mr. Mandela, Walter Sisulu, and Govan Mbeki had all decided early in the trial that they would not appeal for mercy—and they would not appeal guilty verdicts. This was a political trial. They wanted to convey Nelson Mandela's message that "no sacrifice was too great in the struggle for freedom." Andre Brink, the renowned anti-apartheid author, later wrote:

> *"Without any attempt to find a legal way out, Mandela assumed his full responsibility. This conferred a new status of moral dignity on his leadership."*

Nelson Mandela had accepted responsibility—and won the enormous respect of all. His already soaring moral authority had increased. The only remaining question was how the government would respond to this—and how he would reach his goals while he was their prisoner.

CHAPTER SIX

ROBBEN ISLAND TO RELEASE

"The future belongs to those who believe
in the beauty of their dreams."

Nelson Mandela

R obben Island is only two miles long. It lies eight miles
from the mainland of South Africa. It is a cold, damp,
and lonely island. Its shark-infested waters make escape virtually impossible. During the apartheid years, it was
reestablished as a prison designed to hold South Africa's
political and common prisoners.

From 1962, it had become markedly more brutal. It was
designed to humiliate and demoralize the prisoners—and
crush their morale. Men were forced to eat on their haunch-
es. Guards were instructed to beat anyone who sat on the
ground. Deaths from starvation and disease were common.

Deaths from beatings were even higher. Its brutal and sadistic reputation was well deserved.

Nelson Mandela was returning to Robben Island. He had been there two years before. When he had arrived there that first time, he had refused an order to jog to the prison gates from the harbor, where the boat had docked. The warden in charge told him that unless he started obeying orders, he might be killed—and that no one would ever know. Mr. Mandela quietly replied:

> *"If you so much as lay a hand on me, I will take you to the highest court in the land, and when I finish with you, you will be as poor as a church mouse."*

The warden backed off.

THE EARLY DAYS AT ROBBEN ISLAND

The government had miscalculated when it decided to send the thirty new political prisoners to Robben Island. On the one hand, it understood the danger in exposing these new political prisoners and their ideas to a very large general prison population throughout the country. On the other hand, it miscalculated when it decided to keep them together. Mr. Mandela explained that, by keeping them together, they gained strength from each other. By sharing what they each learned, they reinforced their collective courage.

The government made another mistake. In its determination to break his spirit and strip him of his dignity, this actually had the opposite effect. It increased his spirit and enhanced his dignity and moral authority. It prepared him for his leadership role in the very negotiations that would dismantle apartheid. The irony was inescapable. With his imprisonment, the apartheid regime had sowed the seeds of its destruction. For example, it was at Robben Island that:

- he established himself as the leader accepted by all;

- his moral authority, courage, and dignity were enhanced;

- he came to better understand the Afrikaner mindset—which would become critical in his later negotiations;

- he tested different approaches to negotiating with his Afrikaner jailers;

- he gained the respect and support of those of his fellow prisoners who were leaders of other liberation movements;

- he gained the respect and support of the younger and more radical leaders who later arrived at Robben Island; and

- he honed and tested his people skills and political acumen in dealing with a diverse group of fellow-prisoners.

Not long into his sentence at Robben Island, he met with General J. C. Steyn, commissioner of prisons. Although the subject of their meeting was prison conditions, Mr. Mandela took the opportunity to make a request of the general. He explained that, in any war, both sides would eventually have to sit down to talk. He said that whoever was the victor, there should be mutual respect between the parties. He asked the general for the opportunity for each side to respect one another. The general ignored the request for mutual respect.

> *In looking at today's politicians, elite bankers, lawyers, accountants, and business executives, who all put their own personal interests ahead of those less fortunate than themselves, none appear to place any value on being respected by anyone with opposing views. To the contrary, they consistently act in a way that makes it almost impossible to respect them—and they don't seem to care.*

His cell was eight feet by seven feet. A small barred window looked onto the courtyard. There was a single straw mat and three threadbare blankets. It would be his home for the next eighteen years.

The prisoners' daily routine was deliberately harsh. Warders would wake them at 5:30 a.m. to clean their cells and wash and shave in cold water from an iron bucket. Their breakfast was almost inedible. They would work in silence hammering stones into gravel until noon in the courtyard while the warders watched and made sure they did not speak. Neville Alexander, a fellow-prisoner, remembered:

> "To have to sit in the sun without moving and
> (for months at the beginning) without being
> allowed to speak to one's neighbour was hell
> on earth."

A MATTER OF TRUST

From a relatively trivial matter, Mr. Mandela very soon learned not to trust his captors. Just a few weeks after arriving at Robben Island, his lawyers, Bram Fischer and Joel Joffe, visited him. A major was sitting near them to supervise the meeting.

As the meeting was ending, Mr. Mandela asked about Molly, Mr. Fischer's wife. Mr. Fischer abruptly stood up, turned away and left the room. He returned a few minutes later, but still didn't answer the question. The major later explained that Molly had died a week earlier in a car accident in which Mr. Fischer had been the driver. Mr. Mandela asked the major if he could write a letter of condolence to his friend. Much to Mr. Mandela's surprise, the major agreed. Mr. Mandela wrote the letter and handed it to the major. It was never mailed.

CHALLENGING AUTHORITY

He learned another lesson relatively soon after he arrived at Robben Island. Because of the remoteness of Robben Island, the prison officials there felt they could ignore the prisoners' complaints with impunity.

One day, Robben Island's commanding officer was visited by his own commanding officer, Brigadier Aucamp. Mr. Mandela broke ranks to approach the brigadier to discuss complaints about prison conditions. The brigadier refused to hear his complaints. Instead, he sentenced him to four days in isolation.

The lesson: a challenge to authority in public will hardly ever be successful—either in prison or elsewhere. The challenge had to be made privately. He learned that no prison official (or anyone else) liked to have his authority publicly challenged. He understood that prison officials responded much better to private overtures.

> *In the context of negotiating, it is often better to talk privately to those on the other side about sensitive issues than to do it in front of their colleagues—particularly when it relates to an issue that could affect that person's standing within his or her organization.*
>
> *This is why it is always so critical to put yourself in the shoes of those with whom you are negotiating.*

DEALING WITH THE WARDENS

He understood that a warder was the most important person in a prisoner's life. He also knew that anyone who worked for the prison service of South Africa was already extremely conservative. They were all Afrikaners who believed that the political prisoners were terrorists and Communists who wanted to drive South African whites into the sea. Many were young Afrikaners who were likely to be far less educated than the prisoners.

Mr. Mandela quickly learned how to relate to the insecure young Afrikaner warders and never lost an opportunity to explain ANC policies to them. Some of these discussions encouraged him. He realized that when an Afrikaner changes he could become a real friend.

He respected the warders as human beings, but he refused to be subservient. He understood the importance of maintaining the high moral ground and believed that, by doing so, he could actually turn some of the warders around. When Denis Healey, the British Labor politician, visited him in 1970, Healey was struck by Mr. Mandela's high morale and how surprisingly well-informed he was about the outside world. He also commented that "his moral authority, even over his warders, was immense."

The warders, however, were brutal. Because they were often rewarded by the prison administration for their bad behavior, this encouraged them to repeat that behavior. This drew attention to the fact that *the standard was always set at the top.* Bad behavior should never be tolerated—and should never be rewarded.

Mr. Mandela encouraged his fellow prisoners not to be provoked by the warders—and not to be reduced to their level. Walter Sisulu saw Mr. Mandela's interaction with warders and visiting prison officials as serving the invaluable purpose of preparing him for the inevitable negotiations with the apartheid government.

By 1969—after being at Robben Island for five years—Mr. Mandela realized that the prison authorities could not run the prison without the cooperation of the prisoners—and the authorities seemed to understand this. In some respects, conditions had improved.

PATIENCE

Nelson Mandela always understood the importance of patience. He used every opportunity to develop this skill—even in the context of playing board games. For example,

CHAPTER SIX: ROBBEN ISLAND TO RELEASE

he was described as playing a "relentless" game of chess or draughts. He apparently drove those with whom he played to distraction sometimes taking an hour to make a move. He described his style as being slow and deliberate. He would consider the ramifications of every option before he moved a piece and would take a long time between moves. He would admit that this was his preferred style in politics too.

In his negotiations with the government, he used patience as a surgeon wields a scalpel. There are numerous examples in his later negotiations with the government of how he considered every consequence of each tactical move—before he made it. There are as many examples of how the South African government did not.

Mr. Mandela understood the formidable power of patience and how it could both stimulate curiosity and invite common sense. He understood how it allowed the time for questions to be framed, asked, and answered. It allowed fundamental assumptions to be tested against the goals that have been set. Finally, he understood it allowed you to get a good look at the people with whom you are negotiating.

> *While there is often a need to move quickly in any negotiation, this must be on your terms and only after you have satisfied yourself through your preparation that you really do want to move forward.*

HOW HIS FELLOW-PRISONERS REGARDED HIM

He was always highly regarded by his fellow-prisoners. Neville Alexander was one such fellow-prisoner who was a colored academic from the University of Cape Town. He also had a PhD from a university in Germany. Mr. Alexander's comments about how Mr. Mandela handled the different groups of political prisoners in those early days at Robben Island:

*"If it hadn't been for the statesmanship and
maturity of Nelson...I think we could have
had a terrible situation in that prison."*

Alexander saw him as a political animal, not as a philosopher. He was in awe of his negotiating skills and noticed how, for example, he would concede a weakness in an argument and then turn the concession to his advantage. In terms of debating skills and logic, Alexander thought by the end, Mandela was "way beyond any one of us."

A CHANGE OF ATMOSPHERE

By 1970, he had been on Robben Island for six years. The authorities decided that they wanted a different atmosphere at the prison. They replaced the commanding officer with Colonel Piet Badenhorst.

The new commanding officer rescinded a number of the newer regulations regarding study and free time. He transferred old warders off the island and replaced them with his handpicked guards. They raided and searched cells. Books and papers were confiscated. Meals were suspended without warning. Complaints were ignored. Visits were canceled without explanation. The food deteriorated. Censorship increased.

Brutality became commonplace. Messages were smuggled out and, a few weeks later, three judges came to the island. General Steyn, the commissioner of prisons, accompanied them. The prisoners were asked to nominate a spokesman. Mr. Mandela was chosen.

When they met, the judges suggested to Mr. Mandela that they talk to him privately out of the presence of General Steyn and the colonel. He declined saying that he had nothing to hide and that he welcomed the presence of General Steyn and Colonel Badenhorst. He added that he felt they should have the opportunity to reply to his charges. The judges reluctantly agreed.

This was a style that Mr. Mandela would follow whenever he was offered the opportunity to meet privately to air his complaints. This only added to his moral authority.

In this particular case, Mr. Mandela told the judges about the complaints in the presence of Colonel Badenhorst. He described a recent particularly vicious assault on one of the prisoners. The colonel interrupted, clearly uncomfortable. He challenged Mr. Mandela and asked if he had actually seen the assault. Mr. Mandela replied that he had not, but that he trusted his sources. Badenhorst responded by warning and threatening him.

Mr. Mandela turned to the judges and pointed out that if the colonel could threaten him in their presence, they could imagine what he does in their absence. Judge Corbett then turned to the others and said, "The prisoner is quite right."

Whatever the judges said, the harshness abated. Within three months of the judges' visit, Badenhorst was transferred. His successor was Colonel Willemse. Looking back on his relationship with Mr. Mandela, Colonel Willemse recalled:

> *"Mandela had a special stature. He was experienced in the politics of change. I never felt he was waiting for revenge. I never experienced bitterness among any of them, but Mandela played a role in persuading them."*

UNDERSTANDING THE OTHER SIDE

Mr. Mandela became increasingly aware of the importance of understanding the Afrikaner mind-set and urged the other prisoners to talk with the warders in Afrikaans and to learn about their psychology and culture.

This had an important effect on other prisoners like Mac Maharaj who understood why this was so necessary:

> *"I realised the importance of learning Afrikaans history, of reading Afrikaans literature, of trying to understand these ordinary*

men...how they are indoctrinated, how they react. They all have a blank wall in their minds. They just could not see the black man as a human being...

You must understand the mind of the opposing commander...you can't understand him unless you understand his literature and his language."

In addition to his other studies in prison, Mr. Mandela made a point of reading Afrikaans books. According to Mr. Sampson, he developed an understanding of the Afrikaner that his colleagues in exile would later envy. He knew he could negotiate with them—if he understood them.

This would be an important lesson and was part of understanding the Power of the Process of negotiation. One of the greatest mistakes in negotiating—or in planning any action—is not to focus enough attention on the other side and not to understand them.

In our present culture, we are so preoccupied with ourselves that we often don't pay enough attention to those with whom we are dealing. The result is that we miss warning signs in plain sight. Had we prepared in our dealings with Enron, Ahmed Chalabi, and Bernie Madoff the way Nelson Mandela prepared for his dealings with the government, we might have been spared the carnage of those scams.

AN EXTRAORDINARY VISIT...AND SOME NEW PRISONERS

By 1976, he had been on Robben Island for twelve years. That year, he received an extraordinary visit from Jimmy Kruger, the minister of justice and prisons. Mr. Kruger was seen as playing a critical role in how the government would handle the liberation struggle. This meeting would give Mr. Mandela an invaluable insight into the mind of a prominent Cabinet member.

Prior to the visit, Mr. Mandela had an idea of what was on the government's mind. At that time, the government's showcase of separate development was the Transkei, the leader of which was Mr. Mandela's nephew, K. D. Matanzima. When Robben Island's commanding officer jokingly said to Mr. Mandela that he ought to retire to the Transkei, Mr. Mandela suspected that there something behind the "joke." He knew it would have been a great prize to the government if he would agree to retire to the Transkei. This would have clearly legitimized the government's separate development policy. If the government thought he would ever even consider this, it had no idea about the man with whom it was dealing.

Mr. Mandela presumed that Mr. Kruger's visit would be related to this, but he decided that, no matter what Mr. Kruger's agenda, he would use this visit as an opportunity to present grievances to the minister. Of particular concern was the fact that the political prisoners were being treated like other common criminals.

When the meeting started, Mr. Mandela raised that issue. Mr. Kruger scoffed at the idea and said, "Nah, you are all violent Communists!" This gave Mr. Mandela the opportunity to tell him a little about the ANC and why it had turned to violence. Mr. Mandela was quite startled by Mr. Kruger's lack of knowledge. For example, he knew almost nothing about the ANC. Mr. Kruger was quite surprised when Mr. Mandela told him that the ANC was far older than the National Party. When he said they were communists, Mr. Mandela said he should read the Freedom Charter. Mr. Kruger had never heard of the Freedom Charter.

Mr. Kruger moved on to the subject of his visit. If Mr. Mandela was willing to recognize the legitimacy of the Transkei government, he said, and was willing to move there, his sentence would be dramatically reduced. Mr. Mandela rejected Mr. Kruger's proposal—as he did when he returned a month later with the same proposal.

Not wanting to burn any bridges with Mr. Kruger, however, Mr. Mandela described Mr. Kruger as "warm, cheerful and full of humor" in a letter that he knew would be read by government censors. In fact, he regarded him quite differently.

THE NEW GENERATION—BLACK CONSCIOUSNESS

Mr. Mandela was soon to face another enormous challenge from a new generation in the liberation movement—Black Consciousness.

On June 16, 1976, fifteen thousand schoolchildren gathered in Soweto to protest the government's ruling that half of all classes in secondary schools must be taught in Afrikaans, the language of the government—the language of the oppressor. Students did not want to be taught in that language—and their parents and teachers supported them. Pleadings and petitions by parents and teachers brought no results. The police confronted the gathering. They opened fire and killed a thirteen-year-old boy, Hector Pietersen. The children lost control and killed two whites. Armored cars and helicopters were brought in.

The events of that day reverberated throughout the country in every town and township. Mass funerals for the victims became national rallying points. Protest swept the country. Students boycotted schools all across the country. The education policies of Dr. Verwoerd had come back to haunt the government. The angry students had risen against the government.

In September 1976, the first of these young men started arriving at Robben Island. Mr. Mandela described how they were quite different to any type of prisoner he had seen before on the island. He characterized them as being "brave, hostile, and aggressive." They refused to take orders. Their instinct was to confront rather than cooperate. The authorities did not know how to handle them.

Mr. Mandela recalled how, during the Rivonia Trial, he had remarked to a security branch officer that if the government did not make changes, the next generation of freedom fighters would make the government yearn for Mr. Mandela and his colleagues. *That day had arrived.* It would take the government a little more time to recognize this—but it would. This new group viewed Mr. Mandela as a moderate and they challenged him on this. He responded not by challenging them, but by listening.

In dealing with these new prisoners, he soon felt invigorated. He discovered that their presence and attitude represented a breath of fresh air for him—and a welcome injection of new energy. He provided this example of "the young lions": He explained how one of the young prisoners was told to take his cap off by the major. The prisoner turned and looked at the major, and said, "What for?" Mr. Mandela said he could hardly believe what he had just heard. The major replied that it was against regulations. The young prisoner responded, "Why do you have this regulation? What is the purpose of it?" This questioning on the part of the prisoner was too much for the major, and he stomped out of the room, saying, 'Mandela, you talk to him.'

The Black Consciousness movement advocated a nonracial society—but it rejected any role for whites in achieving that society. It stressed ethnic pride and self-reliance. He remembered that this was his own position when he had formed the ANC Youth league 25 years earlier.

He saw his role as that of an elder statesman. He recognized that they would experience frustration because Black Consciousness offered no program of action. This resulted in a decision that was both strategic and wise. He made no attempt to recruit Black Consciousness followers. He knew that any recruiting effort would only alienate them. Instead, he chose to compliment them on their achievements. The aim was to show them that they were all fighting a common enemy. They asked questions which he answered—and the vast majority joined the ANC. This demonstrated his remarkable insight and people skills. Again, his strategy in dealing with them was based on his focus on their position and mindset.

This new generation had learned not be deferential to leaders solely because they were leaders. For them, respect had to be earned. Even Mr. Mandela's own leadership was questioned when these young men arrived at Robben Island—and even he had to earn their respect.

Over the next four years, inside South Africa, there was a sense of a revived ANC. It was stepping up its sabotage campaign. Strategic sites were targeted and bombed. The government reacted.

In 1980, the defense minister, General Magnus Malan, introduced a policy of "total onslaught" to combat the liberation movement. This began a particularly brutal period for the liberation movement.

> *The lesson was straight from the Duck School. One should never assume a level of sophistication, knowledge, or legitimacy in anyone simply because of the high position he or she holds. The young prisoners would not be deferential to Mr. Mandela until he earned their deference.*

A GOVERNMENT ASSESSMENT OF MR. MANDELA

By 1981, there were no signs his stature was diminishing. To the contrary, it was increasing. There was a growing movement around the world for his release. He had been on Robben Island for 17 years. The government had no intention of releasing him, but requested reports from prison authorities about him. In February 1981, the Justice Department received a summary in Afrikaans about his record on Robben Island:

> *"He adopts a persistent attitude by making repeated representations about conditions, but in a way that no steps can be taken against him. But this should not be seen as good behavior: he gives the orders and then withdraws to regard his actions from a dis-*

tance. Mandela sticks to his chosen course
and influences everyone with him not to de-
viate from this...It is clear that Mandela has
in no way changed his position and that im-
prisonment so far has had no positive effect
on him."

This was a remarkably accurate portrayal. Mr. Kobie Coetsee, the new minister of justice, requested further background. A more detailed report was provided:

"There exists no doubt that Mandela com-
mands all the qualities to be the Number
One black leader in South Africa. His period
in prison has caused his psycho-political
posture to increase rather than decrease,
and with this he now has acquired the char-
acteristic prison-charisma of the contempo-
rary liberation leader."

The government had painted itself into a corner, and the
question was what conclusions it would reach from the
report it had received. There was no escape from the fact
that the government had added to Mr. Mandela's charisma.
The report identified eleven specific attributes that he possessed. Translated from the Afrikaans, these were the attributes that were identified:

- Mandela is exceptionally motivated and maintains
  a strong idealistic approach.

- He maintains outstanding personal relations, is
  particularly jovial, and always behaves in a friendly and respectful way towards figures of authority.

- He is manipulative, but nevertheless not tactless
  or provocative.

- There are no visible signs of bitterness towards
  whites, although this may be a fine game of bluff
  on his part.

- He acknowledges his own shortcomings, but nevertheless believes in himself.

- He is a practical and pragmatic thinker who can arrive at a workable solution on a philosophical basis.

- He has a capacity for integrated and creative thought.

- He has an unbelievable memory, to reproduce things in the finest detail.

- He has an unflinching belief in his cause and in the eventual triumph of African nationalism.

- He regards himself as called to the task and this elevates him above the average white who, according to him, has apparently lost his idealism.

- He believes in self-discipline, and continually taking the initiative, to be the prerequisites for success.

There was no way around this central conclusion: his continued imprisonment increased his moral authority, leadership and stature. Although they knew this, it would be nine years before he was released.

THE GOVERNMENT'S DILEMMA

As the government was considering the report it had commissioned on Mr. Mandela, the unrest in South Africa was growing. The Soweto uprising had been a watershed event. By 1981, historian Tom Lodge wrote that South Africa was experiencing "the most sustained violent rebellion in South African history, and all the indications are that it will continue into a full-scale revolutionary war."

Remarkably, despite the government atrocities and despite the sacrifices of the Soweto schoolchildren, the Reagan and Thatcher administrations continued their wholehearted support of the apartheid regime. The Cold War was raging. Prime Minister P. W. Botha's position was outspokenly anti-communistic, which made him a popular figure in Washington, D.C., and London. He had consistently ar-

CHAPTER SIX: ROBBEN ISLAND TO RELEASE

gued that Mr. Mandela was a communist—and he justified his continued imprisonment on this basis.

The government was in a difficult position. On the one hand, it had to deal with Mr. Mandela, whose national and global stature was increasing as his imprisonment continued. On the other hand, Western support was based on the belief he was a communist.

TRANSFER TO POLLSMOOR

In April 1982, the commanding officer of Robben Island came into Mr. Mandela's cell and told him to pack his belongings. He was being transferred off the island to Pollsmoor Prison. Although he had been on Robben Island for 18 years, he was not given the opportunity to say goodbye to many of his friends.

Three other prisoners accompanied him to Pollsmoor— Walter Sisulu, Raymond Mhlaba, and Andrew Mlangeni. The government apparently felt that Mr. Mandela and his colleagues had too much influence on the other prisoners at Robben Island. The decision was taken to isolate them from the others. They believed that their troubles were being caused by a very small group of leaders led by Mr. Mandela.

In some respects, the conditions at Pollsmoor were a significant improvement to the conditions on Robben Island. They were given meals of proper meat and vegetables. They were allowed more newspapers and periodicals. In other respects, nothing improved. Mr. Mandela complained about the cold, damp cell. There were six prisoners in one cell. Water was seeping through the cement floor. He had not seen a blade of grass since he arrived.

As the government was promising the country reforms, he was allowed to meet selected foreign visitors. He met, for example, with Professor Sam Dash of America's Georgetown University, who was expecting to meet a communist. Instead, Professor Dash said he felt "in the presence not of a guerrilla fighter or radical ideologue, but of a head of state."

He acknowledged that Mr. Mandela was critical of the government's promised reforms, including the repeal of the law against mixed marriages. Mr. Mandela told Professor Dash that these changes were inconsequential. He explained that he had no interest in marrying a white woman or in swimming in a white pool.

Mr. Mandela knew that his message would get back to the South African and American governments. He assured Professor Dash, for example, that the ANC accepted that whites would have a valued and secure place in a multiracial South Africa.

AN OFFER FROM THE GOVERNMENT

In 1984, the country was in turmoil. Mike Louw, who was then second in command of the National Intelligence Service (NIS)—South Africa's equivalent of the KGB—made this evaluation of the situation:

> *"We could see no light at the end of the tunnel. It was just a question of sooner or later, there is going to be a huge conflagration. We realized there had to be a total change of direction, otherwise we were simply going to fight to the last man, and whoever inherited this country would inherit a wilderness.*
>
> *And we knew that the longer we waited, the more difficult it was going to be to climb out of this hole—that it would be better to start negotiating while the government of the day still had some power, while South Africa was still a going concern."*

The head of NIS, Dr. Niël Barnard, in a later interview, recalled his intelligence assessments:

> *"According to our assessment, there was just no question whatsoever that the towering... personality at the time [was Mandela]... he was the symbol of keeping on with this whole*

process, of not giving up, of being a leader on the island, and taking the process forward. People released from the island like Mac Maharaj and others... and the way in which they viewed the leadership of Mr. Mandela was quite clear from a real intelligence perspective... Mr. Mandela was by any real evaluation of the facts, by far the most important leader."

Mr. Mandela commanded the immediate respect of the entire anti-apartheid movement and of all of the nonwhite peoples of South Africa. He continued to remain the government's greatest problem. He was then in his twenty-first year as a prisoner. To add to the government's problem, the worldwide campaign to release him was increasingly gaining momentum. Releasing him had become a necessity for the government. It had no choice. The only question was how it would position itself in releasing him without appearing weak.

President P. W. Botha came up with the strategy he thought was brilliant that was referred to earlier. On January 31, 1985, in a debate in Parliament, and against the advice of his minister of justice, he publicly offered Mr. Mandela his freedom if he "unconditionally rejected violence as a political instrument."

On February 10, 1985, less than two weeks after the president's offer, Mr. Mandela rejected the offer.

THE IMMEDIATE AFTERMATH OF THE REJECTION

After Mr. Mandela had rejected the president's offer, an air of defiance spread through the country. The townships were becoming ungovernable and, on July 20, 1985, the government declared a state of emergency. Police were allowed to detain and interrogate suspects without restraint.

The international media coverage of the growing defiance and unrest was relentless. The police brutality was televised and broadcast into homes around the world. The

anti-apartheid movement in the United States was galva-
nized. It escalated its protests against the banks and corporations doing business with the South African government.
Ten days later this would have an astonishing result.

CHASE MANHATTAN'S CONTRIBUTION
TO THE DEMISE OF APARTHEID

For some years, the South African government had been
relying on short-term foreign loans. One of the biggest lend-
ers was the Chase Manhattan Bank of New York, with loans
of $500 million. On July 31, 1985—less than two weeks
after the declaration of emergency—Chase Manhattan decided to stop extending the South African government any
further credit. Soon, other banks would follow its example.

Inside South Africa, this had an immediate and crippling
effect on the economy. The South African rand began to
plummet. The Reserve Bank had to renew loans at much
higher interest rates from Swiss and German banks. The
government was facing a financial catastrophe.

President Botha was in a corner—and he knew it. He had
to make political concessions to reassure the bankers—and
he had to do so quickly without appearing weak. He was
already scheduled to address the National Party Congress
in Durban a few weeks later on August 15, 1985. This would
be his opportunity to address a larger audience.

THE RUBICON SPEECH

His foreign minister, Pik Botha, immediately started work
on a draft speech. The foreign minister promised American
diplomats that President Botha was "on the verge of mo-
mentous announcements." He suggested the president was
about to dismantle apartheid and release Mr. Mandela. The
speech was to include the phrase "today we have crossed
the Rubicon." Expectations for the president's speech were
in the stratosphere. On August 15, 1985, in the blinding

glare of world media coverage, President Botha delivered his speech.

Far from being conciliatory, President Botha was defiant. He said he would not take the country "down the road to abdication and suicide." He blamed the country's unrest on "barbaric communist agitators." He was hostile: "Don't push us too far," he threatened. Finally, he warned the world about Mr. Mandela. He was a communist, he told his global audience. He reaffirmed that Mr. Mandela would not be released until he promised not to plan, instigate, or commit acts of violence. *His speech left the world stunned—and blinking in disbelief.*

In the Johannesburg Stock Exchange, foreign confidence collapsed. The South African rand plummeted. The economy, which relied on foreign investment and loans, was now crippled. The Governor of the Reserve Bank, Gerhard de Kock, toured the world's bankers to try to raise loans, but he was not welcomed anywhere. International capital now saw Nelson Mandela as its only hope as the financial crisis worsened.

Foreign bankers would never regain their confidence in South Africa's future under apartheid. President Botha later claimed his ministers (including his successor, F. W. de Klerk) had approved the new speech. No matter, the toothpaste was out of the tube—and it couldn't be put back, but more was to follow. In a scene reminiscent of Monty Python, the government, having shot itself in the foot, took careful aim and shot itself in the other foot.

Two weeks after the speech, it chose to arrest Reverend Allan Boesak, a respected preacher, who had announced he would lead a march on Pollsmoor Prison to demand Mr. Mandela's release. The already growing anger and defiance were further stoked by the latest arrest, and more riots broke out. The international community was left scratching its head in disbelief. The government appeared to be on a kamikaze mission intent on taking the country down with it.

INCREASED DEMANDS FOR HIS RELEASE

Demands were stepped up for Mr. Mandela's release—
and for increased sanctions. The pressure on the government was growing daily. American campaigners were pres-
suring pension funds to withdraw their investments in
South Africa.

In the face of all of this, the leaders of the free world,
Ronald Reagan and Margaret Thatcher, stood firm. They
resolutely resisted the popular pressure. They ignored the
moral outrage being expressed throughout the world at the
cruelty of apartheid and the viciousness of the apartheid regime. President Reagan and Prime Minister Thatcher continued to reject economic sanctions against the South African regime.

When ANC President Oliver Tambo visited London to
talk with businessmen and bankers there, Mrs. Thatcher
refused to allow anyone in her government to talk to him
or any other leaders of the ANC. She remarked that anyone
who thought the ANC could ever form a government was
"living in cloud-cuckoo land."

A SURPRISE VISIT FROM KOBIE COETSEE
—AND ITS AFTERMATH

Early in 1985, Mr. Mandela had written to Minister of
Justice Kobie Coetsee to request a meeting to discuss talks
between the government and the ANC. Mr. Coetsee ignored
the request. A few months later in 1985, while in hospital in
Cape Town, Mr. Mandela received an unexpected visitor—
Mr. Coetsee. Mr. Mandela viewed the encounter at the hospital as an olive branch.

Mr. Coetsee was quite gracious and cordial to Mr. Mandela, who saw the meeting as an acknowledgment by the
government that they had to reach some kind of agreement
with the ANC.

On his part, Mr. Coetsee was amazed to be greeted by Mr.
Mandela as an old friend. "He came across as a man of Old

World values," he said later, "an old Roman citizen with *dignitas, gravitas, honestas, simplicitas.*"

Between 1987 and 1990, he would meet twelve times with Mr. Mandela while he was in jail. Years later, Mr. Coetsee was asked about his first impression of Mr. Mandela. He said he believed immediately that he was:

> *"the leader amongst leaders...everywhere and anywhere, where people choose people, you can't help choosing Nelson Mandela...He was a born leader, he was affable. The very first time that I met him he was obviously well liked by the hospital personnel, and he was respected even though they knew that he was a prisoner. He was clearly in command of his immediate surroundings...in the hospital he was sitting in a chair in the corner in hospital attire, but even that he wore with dignity. I tried my best to create the appearance of an ordinary event, and I think he also describes that as such in his book."*

A PROBLEM TURNED INTO AN OPPORTUNITY

After Mr. Coetsee's visit, Brigadier Munro, the commanding officer of the prison, told him Mr. Mandela was to be separated from the other prisoners. By prison standards, his new living arrangements were "palatial." Mr. Mandela admitted initially being puzzled at the move, but then recognized that it might be an opportunity.

He thought that he could use this new solitude to begin discussions with the government. He knew that, unless these discussions started quickly, it might be too late. This new solitude might help avoid the kind of scrutiny that might undermine an effort to start the process.

The question that remained was how to start the process. Each side was worried that the party initiating the dialog would be seen as weak. And neither side wanted to come to the table without significant concessions being made or offered. Again, Mr. Mandela demonstrated his constructive

problem-solving approach to problems. He felt that his new
isolation from his colleagues might offer him the opportunity of taking the first step—but without binding the ANC.
As he put it:

> "There are times when a leader must move
> out ahead of the flock, go off in a new direc-
> tion, confident that he is leading his people
> the right way."

The challenge now was to break the impasse—and he
soon received an opportunity to do just that.

THE EMINENT PERSONS' MEETING

Mrs. Thatcher was swimming upstream. At the October
1985 Commonwealth Conference in Nassau, she faced a
challenge over her stubborn refusal to support economic
sanctions in South Africa. Reluctantly, she was forced to
agree to a group of "eminent persons" visiting South Africa
in search of a settlement between the ANC and the apartheid regime.

Equally grudgingly, President Botha was forced to agree
to let them in. Neither he nor Mrs. Thatcher had a choice.
The best either could hope for was the collapse of the talks
because of the intransigence of Mr. Mandela and his exiled
ANC colleagues in Lusaka.

In early 1986, the seven-member Eminent Persons Group
arrived in South Africa. General Olusegun Obasanjo, the former military leader of Nigeria, and former Australian Prime
Minister Malcolm Fraser led the Group.

The government supported the idea of the full delegation
meeting with Mr. Mandela. Shortly thereafter, the delegation was to meet with the exiled ANC leaders in Lusaka and
with the South African cabinet.

The meeting would give Mr. Mandela an important opportunity to raise the subject of negotiations. He wanted an
identical message delivered to both the ANC leadership in

Lusaka and to the South African government—and he want-ed the Eminent Persons Group to deliver it.

Mr. Mandela understood the importance of world opin-ion and the pressure this could bring to bear on the govern-ment. He particularly understood the importance of pre-paring for his meetings with the Eminent Persons Group by looking at the process through its eyes. Yet again, he would demonstrate the necessity of approaching any negotiation by focusing on the other side.

He understood, for example, that Mrs. Thatcher had con-sistently attempted to persuade the Eminent Persons Group that he was a Communist and a terrorist. Mr. Mandela un-derstood that this would place him personally under a mi-croscope. He knew he would have to stamp his own stature and dignity on the group. He would have to convince them of his ability to lead the country towards liberation—while also providing the whites with security and a role in the new country. He clearly succeeded.

THE FIRST MEETING

When the meeting began, there were two government observers present—Kobie Coetsee and Lieutenant General W. H. Willemse, the commissioner of prisons. As the meet-ing began, they rose to leave. Mr. Mandela made a point of asking them to stay, saying he had nothing to hide. This was an enormously important gesture—and a clear indication of his desire to have the government at the table in any dis-cussions about the future of the country. Mr. Mandela's un-spoken message is that there would be no secrets and no hidden agendas for his discussions with the Eminent Per-sons Group.

The two government observers decided to leave—there-by making their own unspoken statement that Mr. Mandela should feel free to discuss anything at the meeting. Before they left, Mr. Mandela told them—in the presence of the delegation—that the time had come for the government and the ANC to sit down and talk.

He began the meeting by making the clear point that he was speaking only for himself. He told them his views did not even represent those of his fellow prisoners. He knew this would allay any fears amongst the ANC leadership in Lusaka that he was binding them. He was offering them an escape route. He made clear that he personally favored the ANC beginning discussions with the government as soon as possible. He then addressed some very specific issues he knew would be of concern to the South African government. He wanted to frame these issues himself and not allow the government the opportunity to define his position:

On South Africa under ANC leadership ...

> "I told them I was a South African nationalist, not a Communist, that nationalists came in every hue and color, and that I was firmly committed to a nonracial society. I told them I believed in the Freedom Charter, that the charter embodied principles of democracy and human rights, and that it was not a blueprint for socialism."

On the issue of violence ...

> "[W]hile I was not yet willing to renounce violence, I affirmed in the strongest possible terms that violence could never be the ultimate solution to the situation in South Africa and that men and women by their very nature required some kind of negotiated understanding."

On solutions to the problems ...

> "I told them I thought many of our problems were a result of lack of communication between the government and the ANC and that some of these could be resolved through actual talks ...I suggested that if the government withdrew the army and the police from the townships, the ANC might agree to a suspension of the armed struggle as a prelude to talks. I told them that my release alone

would not stem the violence in the country
or stimulate negotiations."

He impressed them enormously. The Group reported:

"He exuded authority and received the re-
spect of all around him, including his jailers."

Lord Barber, the most conservative of the group, was impressed by Mr. Mandela's self-confidence and humor. The
whole group was impressed by his clear analysis of the impasse.

Many years later, Mr. Coetsee recalled that meeting. He
claimed that it was the strategy of the government to get Mr.
Mandela to meet with the delegation on an equal footing:

"As it turned out, it wasn't on equal footing.
He turned out to be in complete charge. And
he was immediately, the way they talked to
him, elevated to some kind of pedestal, just
slightly above their level. They may not like
to hear this now, but that was the impression
I got...

[T]he first time I met him, I already saw him
as president...I wanted them to understand
that this man is highly respected by us...
that he's well cared for, that he's valuable. As
I say to you, he took charge of the gather-
ing there. He introduced them to myself and
General Willemse. He took the initiative...it
went so well right from the beginning, that I
felt that this is of great significance."

As requested, the Eminent Persons Group delivered his
messages to the ANC leadership in Lusaka and to the South
Africa government.

THE SECOND MEETING

Three months later, on May 16, 1986, the Eminent Persons Group again visited Mr. Mandela. When he asked them
whether President Botha was taking seriously the negoti-

ating concept they had discussed, they said they were not
sure.

On May 19, the Eminent Persons Group met again with
a committee of the Cabinet. They were again told that the
ANC had to renounce violence completely. The Eminent
Persons Group explained that it understood the ANC position that it could not abandon violence if the government,
for example, walked out of the negotiations. There was obviously an impasse.

While President Botha understood he would have to release Mr. Mandela, he was concerned that this could not be
done from a position of perceived weakness. Only this could
explain why he approved a plan proposed by his minister
of defense to launch a military strike against ANC targets in
neighboring countries. Thus, at the very moment the talks
between the Eminent Persons Group and the Cabinet were
proceeding, South African forces were attacking Lusaka,
Harare, and Gabone—the very capitals the Eminent Persons Group had just visited. Even Mrs. Thatcher characterized the attacks as "an unmitigated disaster." The Eminent
Persons Group immediately left South Africa. Its report included this warning:

> "If the government finds itself unable to talk
> to men like Mandela and Tambo, then the fu-
> ture of South Africa is bleak indeed."

*What was the government thinking when it launched those
raids?*

THE AFTERMATH—ANOTHER OPPORTUNITY SEIZED

After the breakdown of the Eminent Persons Group
meetings, the ANC in Lusaka called for the people to make
the country ungovernable. And the people responded. General unrest and political violence reached new heights. The
townships were boiling over in rage. International pressure
was increasing every day.

On June 12, 1986, the government imposed another state of emergency. Conventional wisdom might have suggested that this was not the most opportune time for Mr. Mandela to open negotiations with the government, but this was no time for conventional approaches to a serious problem. As Mr. Mandela later wrote, the most discouraging moments are sometimes the best time to launch an initiative because everyone is looking for a way out of the crisis.

He asked to meet with General Willemse, the commissioner of prisons. The general agreed and, a few days later, they held their meeting at the prison. Mr. Mandela asked to arrange a meeting with Mr. Coetsee. Unknown to Mr. Mandela, at that moment Mr. Coetsee was in Cape Town. The general immediately made a call and, a few minutes later, they were en route to the minister's house in Cape Town— with Mr. Mandela still in his prison uniform. Mr. Coetsee greeted him warmly.

They spent three hours in conversation. Mr. Coetsee understood the issues that divided the government and the ANC. His questions went to the heart of the issues. When asked about the next step, Mr. Mandela said he would like to meet with President Botha.

Mr. Mandela left the meeting feeling encouraged and expecting to hear back soon from the minister. Weeks and months passed. He heard nothing from Mr. Coetsee—or anyone else.

THABO MBEKI

Around this time in 1986, a meeting was occurring in New York between the ANC and Mr. Pieter de Lange, the chairman of the Afrikaner Broederbond—the secret society of conservative and enormously powerful and influential Afrikaners. Every Afrikaner who occupied an important government position was a member of the Broederbond.

Heading the ANC delegation was Thabo Mbeki, who would later succeed Mr. Mandela as president of South Africa. Again, the ANC approached the meeting by looking at the position of those with whom they would be meeting.

Mr. Mbeki and his colleagues were convinced that the South African government could be undermined from within. In her book, *Anatomy of a Miracle*, Patti Waldmeir noted that Mbeki understood the Afrikaners' dire need to be accepted by Africa and the rest of the world. He understood the need to coddle the Afrikaner and feed his need for acceptance. Mr. Mbeki explained his strategy in this way:

> *"What you needed to do—which sometimes wasn't easy—was to start off from where they were."*

He explained later he had decided to avoid confrontation because he knew it would yield no results. He explained:

> *"They were racists, we were opposed to racism, but when we talked to them, we did not denounce them for that racism, we assumed it as given. They knew we were opposed to it. But we had to start off from where they were."*

As their discussions began, Mr. Mbeki made clear to Mr. de Lange that no rift would be too deep to heal. Like Mr. Mandela, Mr. Mbeki used charm not only as a weapon to disarm, but also as a means to mask and camouflage his feelings. He described his discussions with Mr. de Lange:

> *"We would say to them, you have fears about the future of Afrikaans and Afrikaans schools, and your land, and all of this, these are legitimate fears. We may think they are unjustified, but that does not remove them, they are there, what do we do about them?*
>
> *And they were surprised. 'You mean you recognize the fact that I have a right to my language and I can indeed take up arms to resist?' And we said, 'Ja, sure we recognize that, so let's deal with the matter.'*
>
> *So I think in the end it was really the removal of fear, and an understanding of how you*

*move people. We simply had to say, we sink
or swim together—and persuade them that
they shouldn't see change as threatening."*

Later, in August 1987, Mr. Mbeki met with fifty Afrikaner dissidents in Dakar, Senegal. He opened the meeting audaciously:

"My name is Thabo Mbeki. I'm an Afrikaner."

He assured those with whom he met that whites would not be murdered in their beds. He also assured them that the Afrikaans language, culture, and history were not threatened.

PREPARATIONS FOR RELEASE

In 1987, the government appointed a committee of senior officials to meet with Mr. Mandela. It was headed by Minister of Justice Coetsee and included General Willemse, the commissioner of prisons; Fanie van der Merwe, the director general of the Prisons Department; and Dr. Niël Barnard, a former academic who was then head of the National Intelligence Service—the equivalent of the CIA. Mr. Barnard was known to be very close to President Botha.

The first meeting with the new government committee was held in May 1988. For a few months, meetings were held every week. They were then held on a less regular basis. These were to be meetings about meetings. These would be discussions about the conditions to meeting.

THE FIRST CONDITION TO NEGOTIATIONS— THE ARMED STRUGGLE

The government's position remained that, until the ANC renounced violence, it would not agree to negotiations— and President Botha would not meet with Mr. Mandela. Mr. Mandela had already rejected this demand in 1985—three years earlier. He remained consistent: If the state renounced violence against his people, the ANC too would renounce violence.

Since it was clear that he could not be budged, the government approached the problem from another angle. It explained its dilemma. It explained the National Party had repeatedly stated in its public comments that it would not negotiate with any organization that advocated violence. How, it asked, could it suddenly announce talks with the ANC without losing credibility? Mr. Mandela acknowledged the problem and the government's dilemma. He was sympathetic. He even told the government its position was very reasonable. He also said, however, that they had to resolve their dilemma themselves. He would not negotiate against himself. He then offered some practical advice. He suggested that they should tell their followers that without sitting down with the ANC, there could be no peace in South Africa.

As he later commented, he would not offer them a way out. He knew the severe financial crisis the government was facing. He also knew that the only way out of this crisis was through a negotiated settlement with the ANC. The question was how long it would take the government to reach the same conclusion.

> *This was a profound insight into the art of negotiation that Mr. Mandela had been preaching all of his life. It would be an approach to negotiation that any serious negotiator would do well to emulate. It demonstrated the Power of the Process and the Power of Positioning—the need to look through the eyes of those with whom you are negotiating to allay their fears. This, coupled with the Power of Positioning and the Power of Dignity, Congeniality and Humor, represents a potent combination for any negotiator's arsenal.*

THE SECOND CONDITION TO NEGOTIATIONS

The Cold War was still at the center of the world stage. Neither the United States nor Britain wanted to see Communist influence extended to South Africa. They were comforted by the fact that the apartheid regime was virulently anti-Communist.

The government was concerned about the ANC's alliance with the Communist Party—and it continued to believe that the ANC was dominated and controlled by the Communist Party. In reaching this conclusion, Mr. Mandela acknowledged the government's apartheid logic seemed unassailable to them: Whites and coloreds, the government argued, would always dominate and control blacks. They believed whites were inherently superior to blacks. Because the ANC had close relationships with white and colored members of the Communist Party, those white and colored communists thereby controlled the ANC. Mr. Mandela had to undermine this fundamental flaw in the logic of the apartheid argument.

He did so by framing his argument in a way they would understand. His reply was brilliant in its logic, common sense, and flattery. He made this argument to the high-level four-man government delegation: Since the four of them were the government's choice to negotiate with him, they were each obviously intelligent, smart and persuasive. If the four of them—dealing only with him on his own—could not control him or get him to change his mind, what possibly could make them think that the communists could succeed where they had failed? They had no answer to this.

Mr. Mandela understood that, as important as any particular response he might provide to any particular issue, was the impression that he left with the government by the response.

> This provided yet another remarkable lesson of knowing how to frame the issues and how not to negotiate against yourself. It was a lesson of knowing when to compromise—and when not to. It was a lesson in being firm—no matter what your personal situation.
>
> And yet again, it was another lesson in the necessity of looking at a problem through the eyes of the other side.

Dr. Barnard, as head of National Intelligence Service, and as a trusted aide to President Botha, knew that the NIS was viewed with fear and trepidation by the liberation movement. He knew that Mr. Mandela was uncomfortable about him being in the government team.

As the leader of the government team, he believed the success of the talks might depend on him. He remembered feeling the pressure entering the meetings with Mr. Mandela, whom he had not previously met. He understood the importance of cultural differences and was worried about the thirty-two year age difference between them. He was then only thirty-seven. He understood that African culture demanded that deference be given to elders. He also worried about his lack of fluency in English. He remembered when he told Mr. Mandela that he was not comfortable in English, Mr. Mandela agreed to allow him to speak Afrikaans while he spoke English. This was a gesture that he really appreciated. When asked about his first impressions of Mr. Mandela in an interview, Dr. Barnard had very little doubt:

> *"Obviously, this man was a leader...Fairly early on, one had to realize that this man, this leader, will have to play a very fundamental role in the future of our country in some way or another.*
>
> *[H]e has this strange charisma, being a man who people want to listen to...so there was, in our minds, looking from an intelligence perspective, never the slightest doubt. This is the man—if you cannot find settlement with him, any settlement will be out."*

His intelligence assessments couldn't have been clearer:

> *"According to our assessment, there was just no question whatsoever that the towering... personality at the time [was Mandela]...he was the symbol of keeping on with this whole process, of not giving up, of being a leader on the island, and taking the process forward.*

*People released from the island like Mac Ma-
haraj and others...and the way in which they
viewed the leadership of Mr. Mandela was
quite clear...Mr. Mandela was by any real
evaluation of the facts, by far the most important leader."*

---

*Except in the context of scams, the best negotiators respect
an honest discussion of different views. They respect logic
and reason. They do not make any disagreement personal.
In the case of scams, the opposite is true. In fact, when the
other side resists the discussion of opposing views, this may
be another sign of a brewing scam.*

*Mr. Mandela understood that any negotiation process was
a layered process. It was an opportunity to probe the other side and to see what kind of people they were. How they
might respond to a particular issue was sometimes more important than the particular issue being discussed. Similarly,
how they would view you was equally important.*

CHIEF MANGOSUTHU BUTHELEZI

A diversion is needed to explain the negotiating dynamic
that was taking place at the time of Mr. Mandela's first meetings with the government team—and that would continue
for the next few years.

Chief Mangosuthu Buthelezi became an important player
on the scene—and the greatest roadblock to the liberation
movement. He was descended from the Zulu king Cetywayo,
who had defeated the British at the Battle of Isandhlwana in
1879. He had become chief minister of the KwaZulu homeland with the tacit support of the ANC. Over the years, he
had drifted away from the ANC.

Though Chief Buthelezi opposed apartheid, he also opposed the armed struggle. He criticized the 1976 Soweto
school uprising. He campaigned against international sanctions. He was the government's best friend and its only option to Mr. Mandela.

Despite all of this, Chief Buthelezi had publicly, consistently called for Mr. Mandela's release. In fact, in a shrewd political move, he refused to negotiate with the government until Mr. Mandela's and other political prisoners' release. At the same time, he had condemned the Release Mandela Campaign as a gimmick. He had also privately warned that it would be "irresponsible" to release Mr. Mandela.

In 1986, Chief Buthelezi announced that he had been given permission to visit Mr. Mandela in Pollsmoor. Mr. Mandela tactfully declined to meet with him at that time by saying that it would be best to meet after he had been released.

Inside South Africa, the government was busy building up Chief Buthelezi as a serious rival to Mr. Mandela. He was given access to television and the press. He was free to travel abroad. He hired public relations advisers. He invited conservative journalists to his Zulu capital, Ulundi. He distributed his speeches globally.

Chief Buthelezi became the favorite of Western conservatives. In the United States and Germany, he was welcomed as a much more desirable alternative to Mr. Tambo and Mr. Mandela. In February 1985, President Reagan met him. Margaret Thatcher welcomed him as a champion of free enterprise and as a "stalwart opponent of violent uprising." She was wrong. Her foreign secretary, Geoffrey Howe, thought him "extremely clear-sighted but firmly independent." He too was wrong.

In early 1986, Chief Buthelezi had selected two hundred of his soldiers for secret training by the South African army near the Caprivi Strip in the remotest part of Namibia. The army trained them there in the use of rockets, mortars, and hand grenades—and in how to terrorize communities. While the South Africa government was publicly deploring violence, its own security forces were arming and encouraging these soldiers and other Zulus to attack ANC supporters. It was yet another graphic example of the government's duplicity.

The government initially denied any involvement, but the truth later emerged beyond any doubt. Documents were discovered that confirmed the South African government had been financing, arming and training Chief Buthelezi's Zulu forces against the ANC. Twelve years later, in 1998, the Truth and Reconciliation Commission learned that Chief Buthelezi had conspired with both President Botha and his Minister of Defense, Magnus Malan, to "create an unlawful and offensive paramilitary force to be deployed against the ANC."

Remarkably, as the discussions with Mr. Mandela were taking place, the government was stoking the fires of violence in the country through Chief Buthelezi. Mr. Mandela always suspected the government's role in the violence. He had to have wondered about the role in that violence of those with whom he was negotiating.

THE MOVE TO VICTOR VERSTER PRISON

On December 9, 1988, Mr. Mandela was moved again—this time to a warder's house at Victor Verster prison. It was a large bungalow with a garden and swimming pool.

He was still pressing for a meeting with President Botha. He had prepared a memorandum for the president in anticipation of the meeting. He wanted the president to know he would not be dealing with "wild-eyed terrorists." In the memorandum, he dealt with two central issues the government had raised in the meetings to date. These were the issues of the ANC renouncing violence and the issue of the ANC's casting aside its relationship with the Communist Party. These seemed to be two impenetrable roadblocks to settlement.

Mr. Mandela argued that the issue of violence was a moot issue because the government was not yet ready for sharing political power with blacks. He said that the government's rejection of majority rule was an attempt to preserve power. He argued that majority rule and internal peace were two sides of a single coin.

He suggested that the positions of the government and the ANC be reconciled in a two-stage process. The first was to meet to discuss how the conditions for negotiation could be created. The second stage would be the negotiations themselves.

The meeting was delayed when President Botha suffered a stroke in January 1989. He resigned as the head of the National Party, but unexpectedly kept his position as state president. In the South African parliamentary system, the head of the majority party becomes the head of state. The National Party now had to elect a new leader. They chose Mr. F. W. de Klerk. His appointment gave little hope to those seeking a bold policy of change.

F. W. DE KLERK

The new leader of the National Party supported the concept of "group rights," which gave each racial group certain rights—but which maintained white power. As education minister, he had attempted to keep black students out of the white universities. He had expressed shock when Foreign Minister Pik Botha had said he was prepared to serve under a future black president. He had insisted that the foreign minister publicly retract his statement. None of this was encouraging for anyone seeking the reform of apartheid—let alone its dismantling.

Mr. de Klerk's first actions after becoming party leader seemed to confirm his conservative credentials. In a major policy speech to the House of Assembly on May 18, 1989, he rejected the idea of any system based on one man, one vote. He argued that this would be "unjust towards the electorate of this house and certain other groups and therefore totally unacceptable."

Despite this, he was a pragmatist. He understood the economic crisis the country faced. He did not appear to agree with the view expressed by Foreign Minister Pik Botha in 1974 when he addressed the U.N. Security Council that

blacks and whites were too economically interdependent to
live apart. This is what the foreign minister said:

> *"An African bishop, a wise man, once com-*
> *pared the blacks and whites in South Africa*
> *with a zebra. If the zebra were shot, it would*
> *not matter whether the bullet penetrated*
> *a white stripe or a black stripe—the whole*
> *animal would die."*

This was not a popular message within the National Party. Meanwhile, political violence and international pressure
continued to intensify.

THE MEETING WITH PRESIDENT BOTHA

During this time, President Botha was effectively being
sidelined and was politically weakened. He did not react
well to this and refused to attend a gala banquet in his honor.

It was during this uneasy time that Mr. Mandela received
the invitation he had been seeking for two years. On July 4,
1989, Mr. Mandela received a visit from General Willemse,
who told him that a meeting with President Botha would be
held the next day.

Mr. Mandela knew about the sensitive relationship between President Botha and Mr. de Klerk and that this meeting might have been a way for President de Klerk to confirm
his political relevance at that time. This did not concern
Mr. Mandela. This meeting represented something that Mr.
Mandela had sought his entire adult life—a direct meeting
with the leader of the apartheid regime. His biographer, Anthony Sampson, commented that this was the ultimate test
of his dignity. He would have to stand up to a man who was
notorious for his bullying. Somehow, the prisoner had to
stand up to the president.

The meeting was held at Tuynhuys, the official presidential office. In the lobby in front of the president's office, he
met Kobie Coetsee and Niël Barnard, both of whom had
advised Mr. Mandela extensively about this meeting. Both

had instructed him not to discuss any controversial issues. This was a get-acquainted meeting, they told him—nothing more. Mr. Mandela remembers how the president walked towards him and held his hand out as he smiled broadly. Mr. Mandela felt disarmed by the president's courtesy and friendliness.

As they sat down at the table, to Mr. Mandela's amazement, the president poured the tea himself. The talk was relaxed. They spoke about South African history and culture. They spoke about the Boer War. Mr. Mandela suggested that the Afrikaners were really "the first freedom fighters." He compared the Afrikaner rebellion against the government in the First World War to his own struggles.

Mr. Mandela explained how he had come to know the Afrikaners better in prison. The president said that Mr. Mandela could contribute to a peaceful solution, but that he should not forget the contribution Afrikaners could make. Much to the dismay of Mr. Coetsee, Mr. Mandela asked for the release of all political prisoners. The president politely refused. They both agreed about the need for peace, however, and they prepared a mutual statement.

Mr. de Klerk had not been a part of the inner Cabinet and, like the rest of the Cabinet, he did not even know the meetings were taking place until shortly before he became party leader in early 1989.

Six weeks after his July 5 meeting with Mr. Mandela, President Botha resigned. Much to the president's chagrin, Mr. de Klerk succeeded him.

MEETING THE NEW PRESIDENT

On October 10, 1989, President de Klerk released Walter Sisulu and seven of Mr. Mandela's former colleagues at Robben Island. There were no conditions to the release and no restrictions placed upon the released prisoners.

Before he met Mr. Mandela, President de Klerk began dismantling some elements of apartheid's legal structure.

He opened South African beaches to people of all colors and stated that the Reservation of Separate Amenities Act would soon be repealed. These were irritants and did not address the larger issues of the liberation struggle.

He knew he had to meet Mr. Mandela. His minister of justice, Kobie Coetsee, considered Nelson Mandela a reasonable man. He also knew that Mr. Mandela had impressed Dr. Barnard and his team.

In early December, Mr. Mandela was informed that a meeting with the new president had been set for December 11, 1989. As he had done prior to his meeting with President Botha, Mr. Mandela addressed a letter to President de Klerk in which he addressed preconditions and the ANC's commitment to peace. He said the ANC would accept no preconditions to talks, especially the precondition that the government wanted: the suspension of the armed struggle.

He met President de Klerk in the same room he had met President Botha. Also present were Kobie Coetsee, General Willemse, Dr. Barnard, and his colleague, Mike Louw.

By all accounts, the meeting was not as warm as Mr. Mandela's meeting with President Botha. Close aides to President de Klerk who spoke to him soon after the first meeting say he appeared unmoved by the encounter.

The two men were quite different. Mr. Mandela and President Botha were close in age, but President de Klerk was much younger. African culture demanded that elders be given deference and President de Klerk did not defer easily. There were other differences to explain the lack of chemistry between them. The president was a shrewd politician who was also a heavy drinker and smoker. Mr. Mandela was neither and was self-sacrificing. It was unlikely that these two would ever be best friends.

Perhaps Mandela detected some caginess about de Klerk, or even some condescension. Maybe it was just that de Klerk did not pour the tea. But everyone who knows both men says that there was never any magic between them, and that their relationship only deteriorated as time went on.

Mr. Mandela noticed that President de Klerk listened to what he had to say. He urged President de Klerk to abandon the concept of "group rights," which he saw as the government's means to preserve white domination. He pointed out that the ANC had not struggled against apartheid for seventy-five years only to yield to a disguised form of apartheid. President de Klerk said he would take all that Mr. Mandela had said under consideration.

The meeting was exploratory, but was useful. Mr. Mandela was able to assess President de Klerk face to face. He understood that at the core of the upcoming negotiations was President de Klerk's determination to retain white power. He also now understood President de Klerk's position and approach to the upcoming negotiations. This is what he concluded:

- President de Klerk refused to recognize the inevitability of black majority rule.

- President de Klerk's plan was to share power with blacks—subject to a white veto power. And he would want this enshrined in a new constitution.

- President de Klerk wanted those elements of a democratic state that would protect white interests, namely, a bill of rights to protect civil and property rights of individuals; an independent judiciary as a restraint on government power; and separation of power between legislative and executive—and between central government and the provincial governments.

- In February 1990 there was little doubt that the vast majority of Afrikaners found black rule unimaginable. If they would consider universal suffrage at all, they imagined it would occur only after a long transition period. This was President de Klerk's political base.

- President de Klerk believed that, while white domination might have a limited life, white power might not. By no stretch of the imagination was democracy a solution to white South Africa—quite the opposite.

- President de Klerk believed that he could outsmart and outmaneuver the ANC in negotiations.

- President de Klerk believed that he could outvote the ANC, by forming a coalition with moderate black leaders. At a minimum, he felt he could deny the ANC an overwhelming majority; and if all else failed, to overrule the ANC by veto in a new power-sharing government.

AT LONG LAST…!

On February 2, 1990, President de Klerk radiated confidence as he mounted the podium to address Parliament in his opening speech. He had the comfort of knowing that his military was intact and firmly under his power and control. He clearly felt comfortable that he could control the new path on which he had decided to steer his country.

His knew his audience was global and that his speech would have international repercussions. He therefore chose his words carefully. He announced the lifting of the bans on the ANC, the PAC, and the South African Communist Party. He announced the freeing of Mr. Mandela and political prisoners imprisoned for nonviolent activities. He suspended capital punishment. He also lifted various restrictions imposed by the state of emergency.

International reviewers thought he had gone from apartheid to majority rule. *He had not.* Internationally, his speech was welcomed enthusiastically. Internally, obedience was always the mantra of the Afrikaners. They trusted their president—particularly because of his impressively conservative credentials.

On February 9, 1990, Mr. Mandela was again taken to Tuynhuys. There he met President de Klerk in his office. He informed Mr. Mandela that he was going to release him from prison the following day and fly him to Johannesburg.

Mr. Mandela thanked President de Klerk. He knew he needed more time so that his friends and organization could prepare for his release. Also, he wanted to walk out of the gates of Victor Verster prison. He asked President de Klerk to release him a week from that day. His request was refused.

President de Klerk clearly was taken aback. He was not used to being challenged by black men, let alone from a prisoner. Neither saw any irony in a prisoner asking not to be released and his jailer attempting to release him.

De Klerk again excused himself and left the room. After ten minutes he returned with a compromise: Mr. Mandela could be released at Victor Verster, but the release could not be postponed.

CHAPTER SEVEN

THE RELEASE AND
ITS AFTERMATH

"If you want to make peace with
your enemy, you have to work with your
enemy. Then he becomes your partner."

Nelson Mandela

President de Klerk was a realist. He understood the
role sanctions were playing in the country's economic crisis. While he knew that the sanctioning nations
would give great deference to Mr. Mandela's wishes, he also
knew that he had an army and that Mr. Mandela did not.

The president had clear strategies in mind to undermine
the sanctions movement and Nelson Mandela's global influence and popularity. And he would lose no time in implementing them.

He knew he had to diminish Mr. Mandela's stature. Once
this was accomplished, he knew it would be easier for the

South African government to persuade the world to lift
sanctions. He firmly believed that this diminution in stature
would begin as soon as Mr. Mandela was forced to deal with
the day-to-day problems of his new life out of prison. It was
unimaginable to the president that the prisoner of twenty-
seven years could possibly live up to the larger-than-life expectations of his followers. For this reason, the government
was in no rush to start the negotiations. They wanted to give
him enough time to fall on his face.

And the president would make it even more difficult for
Mr. Mandela. He would work behind the scenes with Chief
Buthelezi to make sure that black-on-black violence would
not just end—it would escalate. The president was quite
certain that Mr. Mandela's inability to end the violence
would certainly diminish his stature.

Politically, the president would create an alliance with
Chief Buthelezi's Inkatha Freedom Party that would create
an anti-ANC voting bloc. This would be an obstacle to ANC's
majority rule aspirations.

Militarily, the president would instruct his military intelligence officers to use the same dirty-tricks tactics against
the ANC that they had successfully used against the ruling
party in neighboring Namibia. In this regard, the president
acted quickly. He started to move his intelligence officers
from Namibia back into South Africa. Years later, after intelligence officers testified before the Truth and Reconciliation
Commission, the commission's report concluded:

> *"To all intents and purposes, then, opera-*
> *tives and soldiers moved from one theatre of*
> *war to another."*

While Mr. Mandela did not know about any of this at the
time, he did understand that President de Klerk had no intention of putting himself out of power without a fight. Of
one thing he was certain: the president was not about to
negotiate the end of white rule.

THE TALKS BEGIN

A month after his release, another meeting was scheduled with President de Klerk. On March 26, 1990, however, the talks stalled when the police opened fire without warning on a crowd of unarmed ANC demonstrators in Sebokeng Township just south of Johannesburg. Twelve demonstrators were killed and hundreds were wounded. Many were shot in the back as they fled.

Neither Mr. Mandela nor the world accepted that the police feared unarmed fleeing demonstrators. Mr. Mandela announced the suspension of the talks. His message to the national and international press was that the President de Klerk could not "talk about negotiations on the one hand and murder our people on the other." Secondly, he was prepared to walk away from the negotiations.

By not controlling his police and by underestimating Mr. Mandela, President de Klerk effectively undermined his own strategy. He clearly did not anticipate that police action would result in Mr. Mandela walking away from the talks. He also did not anticipate how, by Mr. Mandela walking away from the talks, this would further enhance his already enormous moral authority both at home and abroad.

> *The Power to Walk Away is an immense power, particularly when, by doing so, you are also making a statement about your moral authority. The decision to walk away obviously requires an analysis of how the other side is viewing the process.*

The May 2, 1990, meeting

Five weeks later, on May 2, 1990, the ANC and government teams met to begin preliminary talks at Groote Schuur, President de Klerk's official residence. Again, these were negotiations about negotiations.

Each side named an eleven-person team. All members of the government team were white male Afrikaners. The ANC team included two whites, one Indian, and one colored with seven blacks. Two members were women.

Contrary to expectations, the talks were cordial and were conducted with good humor. President de Klerk was pleasantly surprised that Mr. Mandela was a good listener. This impressed him, although he would later complain that Mr. Mandela would "admonish us with long monologues full of recriminations." He also believed Mr. Mandela had been "scarred" by his experiences and had no vision of the future.

After three days of talks, President de Klerk's team agreed to work to create a better climate for negotiations. They would release political prisoners, remove repressive laws, and lift the state of emergency.

Mr. Mandela, meanwhile, faced serious problems unifying the ANC. Many in the ANC were uncomfortable about offering any compromise. Despite this, Mr. Mandela's personal leadership remained unassailable. Even on that front, his staff was worried by his determination to see the best in everyone. They felt that he could be exploited. They were forced to recognize, however, that his generosity could often make other people more generous. They saw this generosity turn hostility into loyalty. This was a lesson he had learned as a small boy many years earlier.

The government, meanwhile, and much of the white press, continued to play up the communist menace. Mr. Mandela repeatedly warned the government not to impede and stall negotiations by whipping up anti-communist hysteria. It ignored him.

The Pretoria Minute

Shortly before a scheduled meeting of the ANC's National Executive Committee in July 1990, Joe Slovo, the leader of the South African Communist Party, suggested to Mr. Mandela that the ANC voluntarily suspend the armed struggle.

The feeling was that it would create a better climate to move the negotiation process forward.

Only Mr. Slovo could have made this suggestion. His credentials as a radical were impeccable The fact that it was his idea would give the suggestion some impetus. Mr. Mandela felt it might be a good idea to take the initiative and he supported the idea. He argued that the armed struggle was always intended to bring the government to the negotiating table and that the suspension could always be withdrawn.

On August 6, 1990, the ANC and the government signed what became known as the Pretoria Minute, in which the ANC agreed to suspend the armed struggle. The agreement also set forth target dates for the release of political prisoners.

What was fascinating about Mr. Mandela's decision was that he understood so clearly the distinction between strategy and tactics. Others might have been excused for confusing the two. Mr. Mandela always understood the armed struggle was always only a tactic to help reach its goal of eliminating apartheid and introducing one-man-one-vote. *The armed struggle was not the goal itself, but only a means to help reach the real goal.*

The Power of the Process emphasizes the importance of understanding your goal in any negotiation. The goal is your destination. How you get there is a strategic decision. Nothing could be more important than understanding this distinction. Too often strategies and goals become confused.

THE THIRD FORCE

Since Mr. Mandela's release, black-on-black violence had increased. Most whites depicted the violence as a tribal conflict between the Zulu Inkatha and the Xhosa supporters of the ANC. Mr. Mandela suspected the government's involvement through some "Third Force."

Within days of signing the Pretoria Minute, Mr. Mandela complained to President de Klerk about the existence of a Third Force that was responsible for the increase in black-on-black violence. He made it clear that he believed that President de Klerk knew about the Third Force and that he was doing nothing to stop it.

He noted that, whenever there was progress in the negotiations, there was an increase in violence in the country. He argued this was not a coincidence. Nor was it a coincidence that the government used this violence to undermine Mr. Mandela's credibility as a future leader. The government was actively arguing that Mr. Mandela's apparent inability to prevent this violence demonstrated his inability to lead the nation.

It would take eight years before the truth was known about the government's role in that violence. Mr. Mandela had been correct. The South African army had secretly trained assassins for Inkatha. The police had encouraged the massacres in Sebokeng and had promoted tribal battles. And we now know that President de Klerk always knew about it—despite his denials at the time.

Outside observers recognized something was wrong: the president's highly trained and sophisticated security apparatus that was so devastatingly effective against the ANC was apparently completely ineffective and even impotent against ordinary street gangs and hoodlums that were now attacking and killing ANC supporters. Amnesty International reported:

> "The attacks were launched blatantly in full daylight and often in the presence of the police and in some cases with their active participation."

What was becoming increasingly obvious was that the government had no intention of stopping the violence. And for this, Mr. Mandela would never forgive the president...

The Sebokeng massacre

The ANC had received information that Chief Buthelezi's supporters were planning a major attack on the ANC in Sebokeng Township on July 22, 1990. Mr. Mandela notified and warned the minister of law and order, the commissioner of police, and the regional commissioner of the impending attack. They were urged to protect ANC supporters and to prevent armed Inkatha members from entering the township to attend an Inkatha rally.

On July 22, busloads of armed Inkatha members entered the township in broad daylight escorted by police vehicles. After the rally, they went on a rampage. They murdered approximately thirty people. Mr. Mandela visited the site the next day and was shocked to see bodies of people who had been hacked to death and a woman had both her breasts cut off with a machete.

The following day, Mr. Mandela met with President de Klerk and demanded an explanation for the government's inaction after they had been warned of the attack. He noted that in any other nation where there was a tragedy of this magnitude, the head of state would make some statement of condolence. The president, he noted, had yet to do so. The president provided neither an explanation nor an expression of condolence.

The squatter camp killings

The second incident occurred a few months later in November 1990. A group of Inkatha members entered a squatter camp and drove ANC supporters out, killing a number in the process. They occupied the abandoned shacks and stole all the property in those shacks. Residents of the area said that the police accompanied those Inkatha members. Once again, the government took no action.

Mr. Mandela met with President de Klerk and demanded an explanation. He pointed out that the attackers could be identified quite easily. They were now occupying the shacks of the very people they had killed. President de Klerk said he would investigate and report back. *He never did.*

During this same time, the government allowed Zulus to carry so-called traditional weapons to political rallies and meetings in Natal and elsewhere. These weapons were the very weapons with which Inkatha members killed ANC supporters.

An ultimatum

Mr. Mandela was now convinced that the Third Force inside the government security services was deliberately trying to prevent talks with the government.

On April 5, 1991, Mr. Mandela wrote an open letter to President de Klerk. He threatened to pull out of the talks unless President de Klerk dismissed the minister of defense and the minister of law and order. He also demanded the banning of the carrying of traditional weapons in public; the phasing out of the migrant-worker hostels, where so many Inkatha members lived in the townships around Johannesburg; the dismantling of secret government counter-insurgency units; and the appointment of an independent commission to probe complaints of misconduct on the part of the security forces. The government was given until May to meet these demands.

At a press conference, Mr. Mandela stated his position:

> *"In no other country would the government keep Ministers whose departments were responsible for the death of thousands of people."*

President de Klerk responded by calling for a multiparty conference on violence to be held in May. Mr. Mandela refused. He said the government knew precisely what it had to do to end the violence. In May, talks were suspended.

President de Klerk was taking a calculated gamble. *He would bet on himself.* While Mr. Mandela's image suffered at home and abroad from his apparent inability to control the violence, President de Klerk's stature was actually increasing abroad. He was seen as a statesman with growing authority. With a straight face, he could claim that he had dismantled apartheid and was in control of his country. This was the foundation upon which he would make his appeal to foreign capitalists to start investing again in South Africa.

Unfortunately for President de Klerk, however, at that very time, there were growing reports in South Africa of the government's involvement in secret conspiracies in the black-on-black violence. In June 1991, for example, an ex-military intelligence officer claimed that his former superiors had planned to destabilize the black opposition inside South Africa with violence and dirty tricks—as they had done in Namibia. He claimed that the chief of the defense forces, Kat Liebenberg, had masterminded this plan. *Remarkably, the government did not deny this.*

On July 18, 1991, the *Guardian* published a story jointly with the *Weekly Mail* in Johannesburg. It was based on top-secret documents obtained from an ex-officer in the security police. These showed that, with the knowledge of Chief Buthelezi, the police had financed Inkatha through a Durban bank. The minister of police, Adriaan Vlok, was forced to admit the payments. Ten days later, President de Klerk removed Vlok and Magnus Malan, the minister of defense, from their jobs. Strangely, he kept them in his Cabinet.

More bad news was to follow for President de Klerk. The *Weekly Mail* produced still more revelations about the defense forces' secret training of assassins for Inkatha. President de Klerk admitted his authority was weakened. He would admit that the government's credibility was seriously damaged.

Two weeks later, the government appointed a commission to examine the allegations of whether or not a Third Force existed. Judge Richard Goldstone would head the commission. The *New York Times* later described him as "perhaps the most trusted man, certainly the most trusted member of the white establishment, in a land of corrosive suspicion."

THE GOLDSTONE COMMISSION

The pressure on Judge Goldstone was enormous. The government hoped he would conclude that the black political parties were responsible for the growing violence. The ANC hoped he would blame the Inkatha Freedom Party and the Third Force for fueling the violence to preserve white dominion.

Conservative Afrikaner groups recognized the danger Judge Goldstone represented. Early on, he received death threats and he had constant protection from security officers. Over the next year, the Goldstone Commission would uncover evidence of secret conspiracies and hit squads. President de Klerk would never recover from this.

In November 1992, Judge Goldstone's investigative unit raided a Pretoria office building. There it found evidence of a secret military intelligence unit controlled by the army's top intelligence officer that ran a dirty-tricks campaign against the ANC. This provided the most damning evidence to date of a deliberate government strategy to destabilize the ANC.

The next month, in December 1992, General Pierre Steyn would report that units of the army had secretly worked to attack and disrupt the ANC. He acknowledged that these units had probably been involved in several train massacres. President de Klerk responded by purging twenty-three senior Defense Force officers, but largely left most senior officers of the military in place. He then appointed three generals to investigate, but these were the very judges General Steyn had implicated. The Truth and Reconciliation Commission would later call the appointment "a serious error of judgment."

For President de Klerk, worse was to follow. Six weeks before the 1994 elections, Judge Goldstone released another report alleging that top police officers had supplied illegal weapons, arms, and ammunition to Inkatha. In a later report, never published but leaked to the Johannesburg weekly, the *Mail and Guardian*, Judge Goldstone said that the security police have "been involved for many years in the most serious criminal conduct including murder, fraud, blackmail, and a huge operation of dishonest political disinformation."

He added that "the whole illegal, criminal and oppressive system is still in place and its architects are in control of the South African Police."

Judge Goldstone recommended that Police Commissioner van der Merwe be removed from office. This recommendation was ignored.

President de Klerk claimed he did not know about the activities of the Third Force. At the time, this was met with disbelief. When he later testified to the Truth and Reconciliation Commission, he continued to maintain his ignorance.

Almost ten years later, the commission determined that President de Klerk had lied. Despite his claims of ignorance, he had subsequently admitted that his police commissioner, General Johann van der Merwe, had been ordered to bomb Khotso House, a base for the council of churches and several anti-apartheid groups. His lawyers carefully crafted how his statement should be viewed:

> *"His statement that none of his colleagues in cabinet, the state security council or cabinet committees had authorized assassination, murder or other gross violations of human rights was indefensible."*

With President de Klerk and his government on the defensive because of the revelations of their involvement in the violence, Mr. Mandela saw the opportunity he had been seeking to resume the negotiations. Still, he had an obstacle to overcome.

The mood on the streets was angry. There were calls for revenge and retribution. Mr. Mandela understood the reality he faced: a military victory was impossible. He warned ANC militants that they could not wait for the government to fall. He warned that negotiations would require fundamental concessions. In doing so, he understood the country faced a crisis. Concessions could result in a violent backlash from either the white right extremists or the black left extremists.

He knew he was walking a tightrope. He recognized the reality he faced.

> *Part of understanding the Power of the Process is to recognize the reality you face. And reality is the way things are, not the way you want them to be.*
>
> *In a brewing scam, the best scammers will always attempt to distort reality by offering something that appears too good to be true. They will attempt to steer you away from Duck School.*

CODESA I

On December 21, 1991, the Convention for a Democratic South Africa was held in the World Trade Center near Johannesburg airport. This became known as CODESA I.

Two hundred and twenty-eight delegates assembled from nineteen political parties. The right-wing Afrikaner parties and Chief Buthelezi, however, were absent. Chief Buthelezi had demanded three separate delegations for the Zulus. This was refused. He did not attend.

The opening remarks—and the leaders of the delegations

In his opening remarks, Mr. Mandela said that progress in South Africa had become irreversible. He said that governments derive their authority and legitimacy from the consent of the people and CODESA had been assembled for that purpose. The president talked about the need for a transitional, "power-sharing" democratic government.

Mr. Dawie de Villiers was the government's chief delegate to the talks. He was chosen carefully. He enjoyed remarkable standing in the Afrikaner community. He was a member of Parliament and was the revered former captain of the South

Africa rugby team. In addressing the convention, he went further than any other members of his delegation—including his president. He offered an apology for apartheid. This was enormously significant.

Cyril Ramaphosa was the ANC's chief negotiator. His remarkable intelligence made a great impact on the Afrikaners. Other members of his team included Joe Slovo, Mac Maharaj, and Valli Moosa. Mr. Mandela was never far away and was only a phone call away.

> *In any negotiation, who you choose to negotiate on your behalf is obviously enormously important—as is the ability sometimes to keep the major decision-maker out of the nitty-gritty issues. This allows the negotiating team to position itself as having to sell a requested concession to a higher authority. It also buys time. This decision will sometimes also be based on the composition of the other team—and this will require important preparation.*

The first day ends badly

The night before the convention, President de Klerk asked Mr. Mandela if he could be the final speaker the next day—even though Mr. Mandela was scheduled to speak last. Mr. Mandela persuaded the ANC to agree.

President de Klerk later claimed he had passed a message to Mr. Mandela that he would be sharply critical of the ANC in his remarks. Mr. Mandela insisted that President de Klerk had never hinted at his intentions. On national television, President de Klerk started his speech by pointing to the historic significance of the occasion and the need to overcome mutual distrust. He then attacked the ANC for not honoring agreements with the government. On national television, he questioned whether the ANC was honorable and could be trusted to honor any agreements.

When President de Klerk finished, he assumed the meeting was over. He was wrong. The room grew quiet as Mr.

Mandela strode to the podium—visibly angry. He then did what no black man in South Africa had ever done before: He challenged a white political leader in public.

Nelson Mandela spoke to a hushed auditorium. He began by accusing the President of being "less than frank":

> *"I am gravely concerned about the behavior of Mr. de Klerk today. He has launched an attack on the ANC and in doing so he has been less than frank. Even the head of an illegitimate, discredited minority regime, as his is, has certain moral standards to uphold. He has no excuse just because he is the head of such a discredited regime not to uphold moral standards...*
>
> *If a man can come to a conference of this nature and play the type of politics he has played—very few people would like to deal with such a man."*

He then dealt with the circumstances under which the president was permitted to be the final speaker:

> *"The members of the government persuaded us to allow them to speak last. They were very keen to say the last word here. It is now clear why they did so. He has abused his position, because he hoped that I would not respond. He was completely mistaken. I respond now."*

Mr. Mandela asserted that it was unacceptable for Mr. de Klerk to speak to the ANC in such language. He reminded those present that it was the ANC—and not the government—that started the initiative of peace discussions. He reminded them that it was the government—not the ANC—that had failed to live up to its agreements. He reminded them that he had told President de Klerk that it served no useful purpose to attack the ANC publicly, yet he continued to do so.

With respect to the president's remarks about the armed struggle, Mr. Mandela noted that the government had a dou-

ble agenda. As it was negotiating, it was also secretly funding Chief Buthelezi's Inkatha Party. He pointed out that the
president claimed not to know about that funding. He asked
how a man could be head of a government who didn't know
what his government was doing. He ended by rubbing some
salt into the wound he had just created:

> *"I am prepared to work with him in spite of*
> *all his mistakes. And I am prepared to make*
> *allowances because he is a product of apart-*
> *heid. Although he wants these democratic*
> *changes, he has sometimes very little idea*
> *what democracy means."*

President de Klerk was publicly humiliated in prime time
on national television—by a black man. He was furious. Mr.
Mandela's ANC colleagues were amazed. The attack was in-
tensely personal. It directly questioned and attacked President de Klerk's integrity. Most remarkable, perhaps, is the
fact that neither President de Klerk nor any member of his
team anticipated either that Mr. Mandela would respond
immediately, or the response would be so personally directed against President de Klerk.

But whatever Mandela's personal anger, a crucial political purpose was served: he positioned the ANC as an equal
participant in the proceedings and not as a second-class citizen. Some journalists saw this as sign of the shift of power
to the ANC.

The convention convened the following day for its final
session. Both Mr. Mandela and President de Klerk tried to
show that no irreparable harm had been done by the previous evening's exchange, but trust was lost. They shook
hands and said that they would work together, but the negotiations were now in a state of disarray.

A problem revealed

Looking back, CODESA I revealed the fundamental problem the parties would face, namely, who would wield power? President de Klerk's concept and strategy were clear.

He wanted a system that would give each party an effective veto over the others. Mr. Mandela dismissed this, calling it a "loser-takes-all" system.

President de Klerk believed he held all the cards: He had unchallenged control of the police, the military, and the civil service. He wanted the ANC committed to an interim government—quickly. He reasoned that the whites would dominate this interim government because of his control of the police, military, and civil service. He believed the business community supported him overwhelmingly. He also noted the international community was treating him like a hero for his role in dismantling apartheid—although he knew this was eroding fast. He wanted CODESA to write an interim constitution and elected representatives to later write the final document.

He was therefore actually eager to get to the first elections. Based on opinion polls, he believed he could win those elections—particularly with the support of minority colored, Indian, and black homeland parties. This was pure hubris—an arrogance bred by being in power for so long. He and his fellow Afrikaners could not imagine losing this power.

Their hubris was fed by a sad reality: Despite Mr. Mandela's release and the CODESA talks, little had changed inside the country. For example, while the legislative base of apartheid might have been dismantled, segregation persisted in health, schools, libraries, and swimming pools. The Transvaal town of Bethal filled its pool with sand rather than let blacks use it. Libraries in conservative white towns would charge exorbitant fees for nonresidents to use the facilities.

Work on CODESA proceeded. The nineteen CODESA parties continued to work through the issues. They met almost constantly at the World Trade Center building outside Johannesburg. A second CODESA meeting—known as CODESA II—was to be held on May 15 and 16, 1992. There, the leaders of the nineteen parties would be asked to endorse the work of the CODESA I teams.

A by-election—and a referendum

Six weeks after CODESA I, the National Party lost an important by-election in Potchefstroom, a conservative National Party stronghold. A candidate from the right-wing Conservative Party stunned his National Party opponent in a shocking upset. This caused near panic among the National Party faithful. They feared the growing power of the right wing and its opposition to President de Klerk's policies.

President de Klerk responded to the upset with a gamble. He called a referendum of white voters on March 17, 1992. This was the question white voters were asked:

> *"Do you support the continuation of the reform process which the state president began on 2 February 1990 which is aimed at a new constitution through negotiation?"*

The government's referendum campaign was described as a "monumental deception." To secure this "yes" vote, the campaign urged voters to "Vote yes if you're scared of majority rule." President de Klerk campaigned extensively on this theme. It was successful. Of the 86% of all eligible white voters who voted, 68.7% voted "yes." The president had crushed his opposition.

Like any winning gambler, President de Klerk believed he was on a roll. He and his team entered CODESA II confidently—and with a touch of arrogance. They convinced themselves the referendum result had given them the political and the moral mandate to make their demands. The ANC noted this change in the government's attitude after the referendum. They noticed the new arrogance, which puzzled them. The government had failed to anticipate that the referendum result would embolden the ANC. Whereas before the referendum, the ANC was always sensitive to President de Klerk's problem in having to pacify those Afrikaner right-wing ideologues, now, after the referendum, it no longer had to do so. The ANC reasoned the Afrikaner right no longer significantly threatened President de Klerk.

The president had unknowingly lost an important negotiating chip.

Both sides were now playing hardball. The only difference was that the government seemed unaware of the ANC's perception of the referendum results. Again, the lesson was inescapable.

Working Group 2

Meanwhile, a working group from CODESA I was continuing its work. The mission of Working Group 2 was to decide when and how the biggest constitutional question should be settled: How would South Africa be ruled: by majority vote or by power sharing?

To decide that question, Working Group 2 would have to decide how the elected constituent assembly might operate: for example, would it take decisions simply by a majority vote, or would it need a two-thirds majority for some issues?

The parties had agreed that the nineteen CODESA parties would write an interim constitution, and that they would agree on constitutional principles to bind the elected constituent assembly. Everyone agreed that the assembly would then rewrite the interim constitution as a final constitution. The major battle was over the vote needed to make constitutional changes.

Working Group 2 had already agreed that more than a simple majority of 50 percent would be required—but it had not agreed on how much more than 50% would be required. The government was encouraged. It had as many allies as the ANC at CODESA. This would provide it with significant influence over the writing of the interim constitution. And once that constitution was in place, the government and its allies would have an effective veto over any changes. Just days before CODESA II was to convene, the government felt it was well positioned—at least until May 7 and May 8, 1992.

> *A recurrent theme is the importance of looking at the situation you face through the eyes of the other party. There is always the temptation to look at it only through your own eyes, but this temptation is fatal.*

The Toilet Town Scandal

On May 7, 1992, a scandal was revealed that involved corruption and bribery at the Department of Development Aid—the department responsible for improving black life in the homelands. The ANC used the scandal to reflect the government attitude toward black poverty.

This scandal was revealed as a result of an official investigation. The presiding judge of that investigation was harsh in his criticism of the government. He concluded that the department should be abolished. President de Klerk followed his recommendation. Unfortunately for the president and the government, the extent of the corruption was highlighted by television pictures showing hundreds of portable toilets sitting in an empty field near Letsitele, in the northeastern Transvaal. There were no houses in sight. Two employees from the Department of Development Aid had designed the toilets themselves and had sold them to the department for R15 million. As if the television coverage wasn't damning enough, the next day, on May 10, 1992, the *Sunday Times* ran a front-page picture of scores of the toilets lost in an empty field under the banner headline: "Toilet Town: A Famous Landmark of Nationalist Misrule."

Just as it seemed the scandal couldn't get much worse for President de Klerk, it became apparent that the scandal occurred under the watch of Gerrit Viljoen and Stoffel van der Merwe, two of President de Klerk's senior CODESA negotiators. Neither was fired. Both were reassigned.

The murder of four ANC activists

The second scandal was revealed on May 8, 1992, and this also served to undermine President de Klerk's authority and credibility. It was revealed that government security officials were involved in the 1985 murder of four ANC activists. A message was published between Brigadier Christoffel van der Westhuizen, then head of the government's National Security Council's Eastern Province Command, and General van Rensberg, a member of its secretariat in Pretoria. The document, which was called a "signal message," named three Cradock anti-apartheid activists—Matthew Goniwe, Mbulelo Goniwe, and Fort Calata. It proposed that the activists be "permanently removed from society as a matter of urgency"—even though they knew that the reaction would be severe both nationally and internationally. Matthew Goniwe and Fort Calata were found dead two weeks later.

The authenticity of the document was never questioned. Again, unfortunately for President de Klerk, Brigadier van der Westhuizen was at that very time serving as the chief of staff of Military Intelligence. This raised the question of the role of many other senior officers and ministers who had served on the State Security Council at that time. One such member was President de Klerk himself. He issued a statement denying any knowledge of this incident. Any suggestion that either body had "planned or approved murder" was "devoid of all truth," he said.

The ANC used both scandals to discredit the president and his government on the eve of CODESA II. It stated that the rash of scandals constituted the "symptoms of a regime in terminal moral decay."

CODESA II

The day before CODESA II was due to meet, the government set a trap for the ANC. It made some new proposals:

- A two-thirds vote would be needed to pass most constitutional clauses in the assembly.
- A three-quarters majority would be needed for clauses dealing with a bill of rights, devolution of power, multiparty democracy, and minority rights.
- A senate, representing minorities, should pass the interim constitution by a two-thirds majority.

This proposal was based on the results of government internal polls. The polls showed the ANC with 45 percent popular support and the government with 26 percent. If this held up, and if the new proposals were accepted, the government would have a veto in the new government—without the support of any other group. The ANC recognized the trap. If the government's proposals were accepted, the new South Africa would never be able to amend the interim constitution written by the unrepresentative CODESA.

The ANC's leader of Working Group 2, Cyril Ramaphosa, and his colleagues took their dilemma to Mr. Mandela. They arrived at his home after eleven o'clock at night and explained the problem to him. He told them to postpone CODESA II. Mr. Ramaphosa explained that, with the session due to open in a few hours, this was not possible. Typical of their approach to problems, he came up with a solution.

The next day, Mr. Ramaphosa agreed to a 70 percent majority for passage of all constitutional clauses except the bill of rights, where three quarters would be required. The government was delighted. Mr. Ramaphosa then added a rider: If the assembly could not agree within six months, a referendum would be held. For the referendum to pass, 50% of voters would be needed to pass a new constitution. Now the government was faced with a trap. The ANC could easily delay for six months and could then seek 50 percent support from the electorate—which it would certainly receive. CODESA II was deadlocked—and was postponed. Mr. Ramaphosa had achieved what Mr. Mandela had requested.

After the postponement, President de Klerk remained confident and optimistic. He felt that he could win 51 percent of the popular vote by leading an anti-ANC alliance. He claimed to be in no hurry to get a deal. He believed that any concessions needed to resolve the CODESA II stalemate would have to come from the ANC. Senior members of his negotiating team disagreed with him.

Meanwhile, the ANC had concluded that the government was not yet ready to do a deal. They were still too far apart. While the government wanted a slow transition to power sharing, the ANC wanted a quick path to majority rule.

The ANC knew President de Klerk was very confident. It felt it had to flex its muscles to demonstrate to the government the level of support it enjoyed.

The government still felt too strong to settle and the ANC still felt too weak. The ANC was determined to correct this.

> *Mr. Ramaphosa appeared to give the government what it wanted, but the government did not read the fine print. They did not look ahead. In any negotiation, you have to keep your eye on the ball and read the fine print carefully.*

Flexing its muscles

The ANC and its allies decided on a policy of "rolling mass action," designed to display to the government the extent of its support around the country. This would consist of strikes, demonstrations, and boycotts. The date chosen for the start of mass action was the anniversary of the 1976 Soweto revolt—June 16, 1992. It was scheduled to end on August 3 and 4. The night after the start of the mass action, a heavily armed force of Inkatha members killed forty-six people, most of whom were women and children. This was the fourth mass killing of ANC people that week. People across the country were horrified by the violence and charged the government with complicity.

Mr. Mandela addressed a mass gathering. He compared the National Party to the Nazis in Germany. He expressed his dismay that the government had done nothing to prevent the killings. No arrests were made. No investigation had begun. He expressed the country's outrage—and noted President de Klerk's silence. He also noted that, at the very time the government was blocking negotiations, it was complicit in the deaths of ANC supporters. He asked why the ANC was continuing to talk to the government.

President de Klerk asked for a face-to-face meeting with Mr. Mandela, who refused the request. He felt that there was nothing to talk about. He wanted action against the criminals and some statement of regret from President de Klerk. *Mr. Mandela made it clear that he did not need more talk on this subject.*

The mass action went ahead. It culminated on August 4, 1992. This was the largest political strike in South African history. More than four million workers stayed at home.

> *By painting the government in the same corner as the Nazis, Mr. Mandela made the amoral position of the government clear. By having the courage to stand up to the government and by being prepared to walk away, he put the world on notice that the status of the talks was fragile.*

Cyril Ramaphosa and Joe Slovo

The leader of the ANC negotiating team, Cyril Ramaphosa, believed that it was important for the ANC to maintain—but not use—the threat of the armed struggle. He also believed in the importance of establishing a personal trust with those with whom he was negotiating. His teacher was having a profound impact on him.

While Mr. Mandela and President de Klerk were trading insults, Mr. Ramaphosa and Roelf Meyer, his government counterpart, were meeting secretly looking for solutions to problems. Both were young and each trusted the other. They soon really began to understand each other. The more they met, the clearer it became to Mr. Meyer that history was not on the government's side.

Both were charming. For Mr. Ramaphosa, it was a tool to exert personal power. What made Mr. Mandela and Mr. Ramaphosa such potent negotiating partners was that both used charm to expose and exploit opponents' weaknesses—and sometimes their strengths.

Mr. Ramaphosa had an advantage over Mr. Meyer. After spending a staggering seventeen months in solitary confinement, Mr. Ramaphosa developed his negotiating skills as head of the National Mineworkers Union, the most powerful black union. He recalled how initially the mine owners outclassed the union:

> "We were not sophisticated in our approach to negotiations; all we had was just a sense of injustice and a mission to improve the lot of the workers, and the raw power [of a strike]. Intellectual persuasion was not one of our key tools."

He explained that the unionists learned to do their homework "and to present our arguments in a clear, articulate, and sophisticated way."

Mr. Meyer recognized the advantage Mr. Ramaphosa had over him. He recalled his background with envy:

> "These guys had an advantage over us, they'd been through negotiations par excellence in the mining industry...while we had to learn through experience on a daily basis—you can't read these things in books."

During the mass actions, the ANC negotiating team was analyzing the reasons for the failure of the CODESA II negotiations. Mohammed Valli Moosa, a leading ANC intellectual and aide to Mr. Ramaphosa, made this observation about the government's security forces:

> "What was clear was that the regime was not ready to settle. Why not? Because the security forces were concerned about their future—they were not going to go along with an agreement that would put them before a firing squad; why should they?"

He then looked at the government's civil servants:

> *"The civil service would not make the settle-*
> *ment happen if it meant that the day after*
> *the elections they would all lose their pen-*
> *sions and walk the streets."*

Once the problem was identified, they started discussing a solution. He stressed that the negotiations had to offer something to these two important government groups.
Once the problem was identified, they started discussing a
solution. Thabo Mbeki had actually raised a solution some
time earlier, but Joe Slovo, the leader of the South African
Communist Party, raised it again. Mr. Slovo understood that
negotiations would get nowhere until the ANC recognized
President de Klerk's goals and did something to meet them.
He suggested how this might be done. While his ideas and
argument were grounded in logic and common sense, he
presented them with a revolutionary rhetoric designed to
appeal to ANC radicals. This was how he framed his ideas:

- The government, he argued, was not a defeated
  army that could be expected to give up power voluntarily.

- The ANC and its partners therefore had to be prepared to accept a deal which was "less than perfect."

- Steps had to be taken to get white soldiers, police,
  and civil servants on board. They would otherwise
  destabilize the new order.

- He argued that the ANC should seize the initiative—and the moral high ground—with a package
  of concessions on compulsory power sharing.

The reaction was explosive, but coming from Mr. Slovo,
a Communist with impeccable revolutionary credentials, it
was considered seriously. In November, the National Executive Committee debated the approach for two days. Sixty-
two of eighty members spoke.

On November 18, 1992, with Mr. Mandela's active support, the ANC endorsed Mr. Slovo's proposals. All that was
left was to sell this to President de Klerk and his colleagues.

> *This was a remarkable example of negotiators recognizing
> the reality they faced and adapting their negotiating position
> accordingly. It was also an example of the importance in any
> negotiation of seizing the high moral ground.*
>
> *It was also an example of the importance of the background
> of the person you select to make the argument you want to
> have accepted.*

President de Klerk—after the breakdown of CODESA II

After the postponement of CODESA II, President de
Klerk's Cabinet looked different. His stature within his
party was diminishing perceptively. Many of his colleagues
were disillusioned with him. The right-wingers Magnus Malan and Adriaan Vlok had both been forced to resign. Minister of Information Stoffel van der Merwe had left. Minister
of Finance Barend du Plessis had resigned after a financial
scandal, later commenting that President de Klerk had no
strategy. Leon Wessels, the deputy foreign minister, said:

> *"He misread the Mandela situation com-
> pletely. He thought he could retain his au-
> thority, and share his power. When that
> failed, he had no fallback position. He didn't
> understand black politics."*

As the president's stature waned, Mr. Mandela's stature
continued to grow. He knew exactly what he wanted. He
knew exactly how to position himself in the negotiations. It
was clear to all in his team that he wanted one-person-one-
vote in a unitary system. He wanted to remain aloof from
the detailed negotiations, but would be available whenever
needed. Mr. Ramaphosa later commented:

> *"He sets his mind on doing something and he
> becomes unshakable. We would never have*

been able to negotiate the end of apartheid
without Mandela.'"

Mr. Mandela knew that President de Klerk was under growing pressure and that his relationship with his ally, Chief Buthelezi, was deteriorating. He knew the president would realize that he needed the ANC for peace. Both leaders knew that a continuing deadlock could ruin the economy. They each knew it was imperative to return to negotiations. And they would.

THE RECORD OF UNDERSTANDING

On September 26, 1992, Mr. Mandela and President de Klerk held their summit at the World Trade Center. The two leaders were meeting to discuss the terms upon which the next round of negotiations would occur.

The ANC had originally set fourteen preconditions for returning to talks. Mr. Mandela was convinced that the president could not afford to let the talks collapse again. As a concession to President de Klerk, however, he dropped eleven of the preconditions. Of the three that remained, the most contentious was the release of all political prisoners. The president was adamant: he would not do so, particularly in the case of Robert McBride, who was still on death row for having bombed a bar in Durban in 1986, killing three white women. The ANC negotiators, including Cyril Ramaphosa and Mac Maharaj, were prepared to concede the point, but Mr. Mandela would not. He had been tipped off: the government team was split on the question. He told the president there would be no meeting unless McBride was let out. Mr. Maharaj recalls what happened next:

"Madiba just picked up the phone and told F.
W., then there is no meeting."

President de Klerk asked for half an hour. The time expired, the president had not phoned back, and Mr. Mandela upped the stakes:

"I want McBride released before the meeting."

Mr. Maharaj then told Mr. Mandela:

"I think you have gone too far now, you are jeopardizing the whole bloody thing."

Mr. Mandela just laughed and said,

"This chap, I have had enough of him, we hold the line here today."

While the president wanted to turn Mandela down flat, his colleagues were in favor of releasing McBride. He resented his "blustering and bullying tactics," but reluctantly agreed.

Mr. Ramaphosa clearly enjoyed the spectacle that day. When he was later asked what he had learned about leadership from Mandela, he referred to that summit:

"Madiba is a very stubborn man. He has nerves of steel. Once he has decided that a particular issue has to be pursued, everything else matters very little. And he can be very harsh when dealing with an opponent who is unreasonable, very brutal in a calm and collected sort of way."

He recalled that Mr. Mandela was quite direct with President de Klerk. He recalled how, when President de Klerk had said he would "never" release the three disputed prisoners, Mr. Mandela advised him to avoid such a position. He recalled Mr. Mandela saying:

"Because you know in the end you are going to have to give in, and be humiliated, and I am trying to save you from humiliation."

The remaining two preconditions were the fencing-off of Zulu hostels and the banning of Zulu traditional weapons. The pro-Inkatha faction in the Cabinet strongly opposed this measure. President de Klerk tried to avoid dealing with this by claiming he had not yet studied the draft agreement on hostels drawn up by the two negotiating teams. Mr. Maharaj recalled Mr. Mandela's response:

*"He said in that case, when we finish this
meeting, I will have to pronounce that it has
been a total failure. And F. W. panicked."*

President de Klerk agreed to consider the document
over lunch. He met Mr. Meyer and the other young moder-
ates and, a few hours later, he was ready to sign. He was,
anyway, under tremendous pressure to curb Zulu violence.
The president then sought a clause in the Record of Understanding in which the ANC would curtail the mass action
that had kept South Africa in turmoil for months. According
to a member of the government team, President de Klerk
and Mr. Mandela met for a few minutes. The subject was not
raised again.

On September 26, 1992, the summit meeting ended with
Mr. Mandela and President de Klerk signing a Record of Understanding that accepted all three preconditions.

At the end of the day, the ANC had agreed only to restart
talks on the constitution. The document included no obvious concessions to the government. The Record of Understanding was a defining moment in South Africa's history.
By some remarkable coincidence, the signing of the Record
of Understanding resulted in a decline in the violence.

*This highlighted the importance of never saying never and,
when appropriate, of being quite firm with the other side.*

CHRIS HANI'S MURDER

In April 1993, a right-wing Polish immigrant murdered
Chris Hani in the driveway of his house. Mr. Hani was one
of the most charismatic young ANC leaders. He was a hero
of the radical youth. South Africa now held its collective
breath—awaiting the inevitable explosion and the violence
that would follow.

Within a few hours of the murder, the ANC announced that this would not affect the ongoing negotiations. The message was clear. The process would not be interrupted by acts of violence.

It was Mr. Mandela who went on television and appealed for calm:

> *"A white man, full of prejudice and hate, came to our country and committed a deed so foul that our whole nation now teeters on the brink of disaster. But a white woman, of Afrikaner origin, risked her life so that we may know, and bring to justice, the assassin."*

He pleaded:

> *"Tonight I am reaching out to every single South African, black and white, from the very depths of my being. Now is the time for all South Africans to stand together against those who, from any quarter, wish to destroy what Chris Hani gave his life for freedom for all of us."*

The explosion was avoided. There was a collective sigh of relief, but there were two major consequences flowing from the murder and its aftermath:

- The South Africa political center was shown to be strong. It held firm under threat from the right and the potential explosion from the left.

- President de Klerk's power and authority were seriously undermined. Mr. Mandela was clearly the nation's leader. It was he who made the televised appeal to the nation, not the president.

President de Klerk appeared to show little understanding of the anger of the country after Chris Hani's murder. He appeared out of touch...

FINISHING THE JOB

Meanwhile, the negotiations were progressing slowly. The ANC used Chris Hani's murder to lure the government into a trap from which it would never escape.

The ANC negotiators decided to insist that an election date be set for the first election open to all races. They did so knowing that an agreement on a constitution was far off, but they knew this did not matter. Their aim was for the elected representatives to decide on the constitution. Joe Slovo made the case that a date was needed to send a signal to South Africa that negotiations were on the "last mile."

The government found itself in a no-win corner. If it refused to set a date, its credibility and integrity would be called into question. If it set a date and if the interim constitution could not be completed in time, it was betting on the fact that the election date could be postponed.

They should have known better: once the election date was set, there would never be a postponement. There would be no turning back. Why did the government agree to put itself in this position?

Mr. Mandela lured President de Klerk into the trap by appealing to his vanity, ego, and almost insatiable need for international acceptability. On July 4, 1993, the two men were scheduled to travel to Philadelphia to receive the Liberty Medal jointly. Mr. Mandela simply said he would not attend unless the election date was set. Without him, the medals would not be awarded. On April 27, 1994, the parties reached agreement for the election date. President de Klerk and Mr. Mandela received their medals.

The chosen election date allowed a little more than nine months to prepare the country for an election in which the vast majority of voters had never before voted. Practically, the negotiators had only a few weeks to agree on a new constitution. The ANC could not have wished for a better result.

The most difficult negotiations of all

What all of the parties had already come to realize was that the most difficult negotiations they faced were with their own sides.

This was particularly the case for the government negotiators, who had established bonds with Mr. Ramaphosa and his team. These bonds were the result of the teams being closeted together and working day and night with little contact with the outside world. While they all addressed each other by first name, for example, others in the government had no similar bonds. Each side did its best to help the other win over those on its side. *To some extent, they were each fighting common enemies on each side.*

The negotiations had assumed a life of their own. Only the most difficult issues were left open. The government continued to focus on power-sharing devices. There was agreement that the constitution would protect liberal democratic values.

- There would be a separation of powers between the executive, legislature, and judiciary.

- There would be a bill of rights to protect human rights and individual property.

- There would be a constitutional court to resolve disputes and ensure that the constitution reigned supreme in the new state.

- It would assign some limited powers to provinces.

For President de Klerk, these constitutional checks and balances were all part of power sharing. The constitution included provisions aimed directly at appeasing the National Party:

- There would be guarantees for the jobs and pensions of white civil servants.

- There would be provisions for the first local government elections, which would give white voters in conservative rural areas a heavier weighting in the poll.

There were two unresolved questions relating to the issue of power sharing in the executive. The first was what position President de Klerk would occupy in the Cabinet. The second was how Cabinet decisions would be made. To answer these questions, the ANC negotiators used a negotiating and problem-solving technique that they had previously honed to a remarkable degree.

Focusing on the other side

Joe Slovo proposed an approach for dealing with President de Klerk, which Mr. Mandela endorsed:

> "We must think about de Klerk, his personal position, and if we can find a solution to that, the National Party will just collapse."

Roelf Meyer had made clear that President de Klerk wanted a position of personal power within the government. He was insisting on being the deputy-president—deputy to Mr. Mandela. His opposite number, Cyril Ramaphosa, suggested that there be two deputy-presidents. The first would come from the majority party. The second would come from the runner-up. President de Klerk was not a happy camper. He was facing the prospect of being only the third most senior member of the Cabinet, but worse was to follow...

On the question of how Cabinet decisions would be made, President de Klerk insisted that important decisions be taken by consensus—or by very high majorities. This would give him a veto. It was made clear to Mr. Meyer, however, that this was unacceptable. Mr. Meyer began to believe that a less formalistic approach was needed and that this would ultimately benefit the government. This was his reasoning:

- Only a government of national unity could rule South Africa. Without President de Klerk and his party's support, there could be no stability in the country. President de Klerk controlled all of the centers of power, and all owed him allegiance.

- The ANC should commit to a moral obligation to consult with President de Klerk and his party—no matter how small a percentage his party represented.

He firmly believed the government would have more power under a voluntary arrangement than under a statutory one. Based on his experience during the negotiations and his respect for his ANC counterparts, Mr. Meyer was convinced that the ANC was more likely to follow the spirit of national unity than it would obey a constitution it resented. He maintained that his experience showed that a culture of consensus could be developed—and that this would protect the Afrikaner more than any law. He believed the Afrikaner could become indispensable:

"The choice is between merely surviving, and making ourselves indispensable to them."

He pointed out that this would be how they would be able to secure a new base of power under black rule. Meanwhile, Mr. Mandela was sending the same message to President de Klerk. Ultimately, President de Klerk reluctantly agreed.

Mr. Mandela would not agree to anything less than a majority of 50% being required for Cabinet decisions. Mr. Maharaj recalled:

"Madiba went there not to give an inch, and he just hammered him. And in the end, he cracked him."

At midnight on November 18, 1993, the new constitution was passed. At that moment, the whites relinquished their 350-year hold over the country.

While the government team left the World Trade Center exhausted, Roelf Meyer stayed on to celebrate with his friend, Cyril Ramaphosa, and the other exhausted delegates and journalists. A new South Africa was born.

This highlights one of the most significant lessons about ne-gotiation. Whenever negotiating with more than one person, you have to understand the dynamic on the other side of the table. Sometimes, when those on the other side are speaking, they are not speaking to you. Instead, they may be speak-ing to their own colleagues to establish their position within their own organization. You therefore must let them speak—and you must listen and watch.

This highlights the Power of Observation—of listening and seeing and the Power of Patience.

THOSE POWERS OF NEGOTIATION

Throughout Nelson Mandela's life, and with respect both to negotiation and leadership, the 10 Powers of Nego-tiation—those beacons of knowledge—shine through and made him an enormously successful leader and effective negotiator:

THE POWER OF THE PROCESS

Understanding that every negotiation is an ongoing process that requires defined goals.

THE POWER OF PREPARATION

Understanding the absolute necessity of preparing thoroughly.

THE POWER OF POSITIONING

Understanding how critical it is to see the deal through the other's eyes.

THE POWER OF COMMON SENSE AND LOGIC

Understanding the teaching of the Duck School.

THE POWER OF DIGNITY, CONGENIALITY AND HUMOR

Understanding that people like to do business with people they like.

THE POWER OF TRUTH AND FAIRNESS
Understanding how people respect this.

THE POWER OF OBSERVATION
Understanding the importance of listening and seeing.

THE POWER OF MORALITY, COURAGE AND ATTITUDE
Understanding moral authority, courage, and ethics.

THE POWER OF PATIENCE
Understanding its formidable power.

THE POWER TO WALK AWAY
Understanding the ultimate leverage we all have.

Our task would be to master these Powers and apply them in our everyday lives.

None of these beacons of knowledge about negotiation and leadership were new. In fact, many are so obvious that we tend to overlook them. The greatest challenge is for us to multi-task—to understand that each of these powers must be applied simultaneously.

Our common sense mode, for example, is never turned off—nor is our observation mode. Similarly, the process continues until the deal is done or one of the parties walks away. They all exist and operate together. The challenge is to stay awake and alert and avoid temptation, ambition, or wishful thinking.

AND NOW...

So, now is the time to test these powers and see how they operated in the context of some recent high-profile scams.

What emerges in some of the recent high-profile cases is an astonishing willingness on the part of some of our finest and brightest to look the other way when they had to choose between integrity, on the one hand, and profits or political dogma, on the other.

The issues raised in the Subway Test become stark and disturbing. There is more than a passing suspicion that some of our finest and brightest were not victims of the scams as they claimed, but were rather quite complicit in making the scams successful.

What is noticeably absent in the three cases we will study is any moral authority on the part of leaders or the willingness of leaders to set a standard for integrity. Equally disturbing is the lack of courage on the part of some very close to the scammers to question some of their frankly astonishingly dubious claims.

Finally, apart from the astonishing lack of preparation of those who dealt with the scammers, what becomes apparent from the three cases is the similarity between these scams and a children's tale Hans Christian Andersen wrote in 1837. In each case, the scammers were selling *nothing*. In each case, *the emperor knew...*

Part Three:

ENRON, AHMED CHALABI, BERNARD MADOFF and the EMPEROR

*"The secret of life is honesty
and fair dealing. If you can
fake that, you've got it made."*

Groucho Marx

CHAPTER EIGHT

CANARIES IN THE
ENRON COAL MINE

To help detect poisonous gases in coal mines,
miners bring canaries down a mine with them.
If the canary dies, the miner knows it's
time to get out of the coal mine.

W hat if we had sent a canary down the Enron coal mine? Would it have survived? And if it did not, why would anyone ignore the warning?

What if we had looked at Enron with the same thoroughness that Nelson Mandela looked at the Afrikaners? What if the Duck School took a look at the company? *What would we have seen?*

And with this information, would we have bought a used car from this company?

ENRON

Enron was born in 1985. Mr. Mandela was sixty-seven and in his twenty-first year on Robben Island. Ken Lay, Enron's chairman and chief executive officer, was then forty-three years old. Arthur Andersen was its accountant and would continue in that role through 2001, the year of its implosion. Some of Enron's first directors would still be serving with Ken Lay and Jeff Skilling in 2001.

THE NATURAL GAS BUSINESS

Enron began as a natural gas pipeline company. To understand Enron is therefore to understand the natural gas business.

Natural gas lies underground. It is transparent and odorless. It is light and it burns cleaner than oil or coal. It is often located next to oil deposits. It was always the poor stepson of crude oil. Gradually, its importance grew. Petrochemical plants came to rely on it as their basic fuel—and other industries followed. Soon, it was used in thousands of homes and industrial sites across the country. It was transferred around the country in a network of buried pipes.

Those owning the pipelines would buy the natural gas from large and small oil companies and would sell it to industrial customers and to regional gas utilities.

The federal government regulated the industry, from the price the owners of the pipelines would pay for the gas to what they could charge for it.

KEN LAY'S EARLY DAYS

He was born in 1942 in Tyrone, Missouri. The young Ken always worked. His dream was to live in the world of business—far removed from his world of running paper routes and performing farm chores.

The family eventually moved to Columbia, Missouri. Ken worked and took out loans to pay his way through school. In college, he took an economics course taught by a professor named Pinkney Walker. He was fascinated by the experience and, in particular, how government could shape markets. He did well at school. In 1965, he finished school with a master's degree in economics.

For the next six years, he worked at Humble Oil in Houston as an economist. Humble Oil was later to become Exxon. During this time, he was also taking night courses at the University of Houston towards his PhD in economics.

In 1968, he enlisted in the navy ahead of the Vietnam draft. He was soon reassigned to Washington. He now found himself in the military procurement process. He was twenty-six, married with two children.

In October 1972, he accepted a position as deputy undersecretary of energy policy in the Nixon administration. In 1973, the country was in the midst of a full-blown energy crisis. There were electrical outages and natural-gas shortages. This was followed by the Arab oil embargo. Pump prices soared. Gas lines stretched for blocks. Ken Lay saw this as an opportunity to leave government and enter the private sector.

FLORIDA GAS AND TRANSCO

Neither his experience nor his academic qualifications equipped Ken Lay to run a major company. Unlike many senior corporate executives in the energy business, he had no formal training in engineering or management. All of his degrees were in economics.

Despite his lack of experience, he approached Jack Bowen, CEO of Florida Gas Company, a midsize pipeline company. Bowen offered him the position of vice president for corporate planning. His starting salary was $38,000. He also received twenty-five hundred stock options. He accepted the offer and moved to Florida. Shortly thereafter, Jack Bowen left Florida Gas to join Transco Energy, a large Houston pipeline company.

By 1976, Ken Lay was president of the pipeline division at Florida Gas. By 1979, he was president of the entire company. By 1980, he was earning $268,000. While he was at Florida Gas, the pipeline industry was in terrible shape. There were constant shortages of natural gas. Some schools and factories had to close because of the shortage of gas to heat them. Gas producers lobbied the government for incentives to encourage new exploration efforts.

In 1978, Congress responded by increasing the supply of natural gas and depressing demand by raising the regulated price that would be paid to producers. While this stimulated new exploration and increased supply, demand dropped dramatically because of increased prices. This, in turn, forced industrial customers to seek other energy alternatives.

By 1980, Ken Lay was having marital problems. He was having an affair with his secretary, Linda, a divorced mother of two, and, in 1981, his wife filed for divorce. After the divorce, he married Linda. As his marriage collapsed, he decided to leave Florida. He called Jack Bowen, who was then chairman of Transco, and asked if there might be a position for him in Houston. Bowen immediately hired the 39-year-old Lay as Transco's president.

TRANSCO

Ken Lay did very well at Transco. It was a big company that controlled ten thousand miles of pipeline. It was here that he came to be regarded as a rising star. His Washington experience was seen as an advantage in dealing with the industry crisis.

In 1984, Transco was trying to help Houston Natural Gas (HNG) repel a hostile takeover. HNG was a midsized pipeline company with annual revenues of $3 billion and modest debt. Ken Lay had met a number of times with John Duncan, a member of HNG's board who later joined the Enron board. Ken Lay had offered Transco's help by becoming a friendlier acquirer. Although Transco's help was never needed, Ken Lay obviously impressed John Duncan, who later offered him the position of HNG's chairman and chief executive officer. Ken Lay accepted the offer.

HOUSTON NATURAL GAS—AND THE MERGER

Houston Natural Gas occupied a very special place in Houston. Before his death, chairman Robert Herring was active in civic projects and charities. After his death, the company needed strong leadership, and John Duncan recognized in Ken Lay the leader he was looking for. HNG was later to morph into the modern Enron.

From the beginning of his tenure there, Ken Lay believed that deregulation in the oil industry was inevitable. He was convinced that, when it came, the companies with the biggest pipeline networks would control the market. Success, he believed, lay in getting big—quickly. In his first six months, under his direction, HNG acquired Florida Gas and Transwestern Pipeline for $1.2 billion. This gave it a presence in Florida and California. HNG raised part of the $1.2 billion by selling assets that were outside its core business. The other part was borrowed. Ken Lay was on his way...

An unsolicited call

In 1985, Ken Lay received an unsolicited call from Sam Segnar, the CEO of InterNorth, a large Omaha pipeline company. InterNorth was much larger than HNG. It had over twenty thousand miles of pipeline from Texas to Iowa and the Midwest. In earlier years, the company had little debt and a lot of cash. It paid its executives modest salaries and controlled expenses. When Sam Segnar became the CEO, however, he introduced a new corporate culture. He bought a jet and a company ranch in Colorado. He also made a lot of bad diversification decisions.

His greatest concern, however, was Irwin Jacobs, a corporate raider, who had started buying InterNorth shares.
Segnar panicked. He decided that the only way to stop Jacobs was to make InterNorth bigger *and increase its debt.*
Houston Natural Gas became a very attractive target. Also,
it seemed a good fit. InterNorth—under former CEO Bill
Strauss—was Omaha's answer to HNG in terms of civic-
mindedness.

Ken Lay assigned Harvard-educated John Wing to handle
the negotiation for HNG. Wing had worked with him at Florida Gas. He did a masterful job in the negotiations. He detected Segnar's anxiety, which he exploited ruthlessly. Wing
did not share InterNorth's view of the deal as an acquisition.
He saw it as a merger.

An important part of the deal Wing eventually struck
with Segnar was that HNG's management team would take
over the management of InterNorth over a period of time.
Ken Lay would replace Segnar within eighteen months. At
that time, Houston Natural Gas was trading at about $45 a
share. Wing negotiated that price up to $70 a share. As a re-
sult, InterNorth would acquire HNG for $2.3 billion and Ken
Lay personally would receive $3 million. The new compa-
ny—HNG InterNorth—would have 37,500 miles of pipeline
and would have the largest gas distribution system across
the country.

This new company would become Enron. As for corporate raider Irwin Jacobs, although he would have 9 percent
of the new company, the company hoped this would take
him out of the picture. The new company now had over $4
billion in debt. The first task at hand, however, was to raise
the $2.3 billion needed to close the deal.

> *Looking back, this served to emphasize the importance of
> Mr. Mandela's approach of focusing first on reaching agree-
> ment as to the goal of the negotiations before getting buried
> in the nitty-gritty of the details. The difference of approach-
> ing the transaction as a merger rather than an acquisition
> was quite significant.*

Enter Michael Milken

In 1985, Ken Lay looked to Michael Milken and his Drexel Burnham firm for help financing the merger. At that time, Milken's reputation was as a financial genius. His innovative financial structures were designed to fund almost anything. Needless to say, Milken helped Ken Lay raise the money he needed to close the merger—and continued to help him after the merger.

In her 2002 *Vanity Fair* article "The Enron Wars," Marie Brenner argues that, throughout his career, Ken Lay was always attracted to ruthless and very smart people—while ostensibly remaining above the fray. She wrote how Ken Lay greatly admired Michael Milken. Whether this contributed to the aura of fraud that came to permeate Enron remains a question.

Ken Lay and Milken continued to work together despite the growing allegations linking Milken to insider trading and arbitrageur Ivan Boesky. In 1986, there were serious questions concerning Milken's honesty that might have alarmed other CEOs or their boards. This did not seem to bother Ken Lay and his board.

After Milken was sentenced to a prison term, Ken Lay described him as a visionary who had been unfairly prosecuted. After his release, Ken Lay invited him to speak at an Enron conference, despite protests from lawyers inside the company.

The immediate aftermath of the merger

No sooner than the merger closed, InterNorth regretted the deal. It was buyer's remorse at its worst. It was angry at almost every aspect of the deal, but it directed its anger at Segnar—not at HNG. Their fury at Segnar caused them to take their eyes off the ball. There was nothing about the deal that company directors liked:

- They were annoyed that Segnar had agreed to give HNG as many as eight seats on the board, while InterNorth retained only twelve.

- They did not like the fact that their name came after HNG in the name of the new company—particularly since InterNorth viewed the deal as an acquisition with them being the acquiring company.

- They did not like Segnar giving up his job to Ken Lay after such a short period of time—and they were suspicious of the severance package Segnar would receive as a result.

- What concerned them most was the possibility of the new company moving from Omaha to Houston. The company was a cultural fixture in Omaha.

Everyone at HNG—including Ken Lay—had assured them repeatedly that the company would remain in Omaha "for the foreseeable future." Once the merger was completed, however, the board retained the management-consulting firm McKinsey & Company to make a recommendation as to whether the company should stay in Omaha or move to Houston. The McKinsey consultants included John Sawhill, a close friend of Ken Lay, and a young partner named Jeff Skilling.

Not surprisingly, McKinsey recommended the company move to Houston.

The InterNorth directors' anger towards Sam Segnar grew. Everything blew up at the next board meeting. They were so incensed with him that they demanded his immediate resignation. This left them with only one option: They had to ask Ken Lay to take over. He agreed immediately.

After taking over the top position in the new company, Lay quickly gained control of the board by winning over two InterNorth directors, Arthur and Robert Belfer. Over the next few years, he would replace the Omaha block of directors with his own supporters.

In July 1986, the new company moved to Houston. The name of the new company would be Enron.

> *The company certainly had the right to move to Houston, but considering Ken Lay's assurances that they would not move, was this the right thing to do? And was it a coincidence that McKinsey assigned a close friend of Ken Lay to the team that recommended the move? Was there a strange odor in the air that might have attracted the Duck School's attention?*

ENRON IS BORN

In 1986, Enron owned the largest gas pipeline in the United States. That year, falling oil prices drove down the price of natural gas and seriously affected Enron's earnings. In early 1986, Enron reported a loss of $14 million for its first year.

By January 1987, Moody's had downgraded its credit rating to junk status. In 1987, the company reported a loss of $29.3 million—on revenues of $5.9 billion. With no profits, Enron was unable to reduce its $4.3 billion in debt, which it had taken on to finance its acquisitions and the merger. Ken Lay began looking for ways to reduce the company's liabilities.

He still had the problem of Irwin Jacobs, who now held a 9 percent stake in the company. This—and his reputation as a corporate raider—made Ken Lay and his Enron executives quite queasy. *What they did not realize was that Jacobs never had any intention of taking over the company.* Instead, what he intended was to induce the company to buy his shares at a profit. This was popularly known as "greenmail." With his company on the brink of bankruptcy and being unable to borrow from the traditional banks, Ken Lay again turned to Michael Milken.

With Milken's help, Ken Lay paid Irwin Jacobs $240 million in "greenmail." To the absolute outrage of shareholders, he raised part of this amount by raiding the company's employee pension funds. He borrowed the balance needed to pay off Jacobs using Milken's devices. With its growing debt, the company was now in desperate need of a new source of profits and cash flow. In 1987, Enron had serious concerns about even meeting payroll. The company was in serious trouble.

> *In dealing with Irwin Jacobs, Ken Lay had to balance his personal self-interest in removing a potentially troublesome minority investor, on the one hand, and the interests of his company and its employees in having their pension funds remain intact, on the other. Ken Lay chose then as he would always choose in the future. He would always choose his own interests ahead of any others'. Raiding the company's employee pension funds had to be the mother of all red flags for anyone looking at the way Ken Lay conducted business.*

THE FOCUS ON EARNINGS

To understand Enron is to understand its total and singular focus on earnings. If the removal of apartheid was Mr. Mandela's total and singular focus, Enron's was on the issue of earnings.

Ken Lay understood that his company's stock price was dependent on Wall Street's perception of his company's performance. He understood that Wall Street rewarded companies based on their ability to produce steadily increasing earnings. He also understood that his company's banks looked to this, too. If there were rewards in being able to show steadily increasing earnings, the other side of the coin—erratic quarterly earnings—was a danger sign for Wall Street and the bankers. This had to be avoided above all else.

For Enron's bankers, erratic earnings could have immediate and catastrophic results for the company. For example:

- It could accelerate repayment of long-term loans:

  > *To avoid default under its long-term loans, Enron had to show quarterly earnings that were at least 1.2 times the interest on its*

*debt. Failure to do so would trigger repay-
ment of those loans.*

*As everyone knew, even though a company
could show earnings to protect its long-
term loans, this did not mean that it had
enough cash for its operations. To counter
any cash flow shortfalls, companies would
therefore have to seek short-term loans to
meet its immediate cash needs. This created
yet another problem tied to earnings:*

- Rolling over short-term loans could be difficult:

  *These short-term loans could only be rolled
  over or renewed if the lender could be satisfied that the companies could repay the
  loans. Again, quarterly earnings—and the
  consistent performance of the borrower—
  would be used to show this ability to repay
  the loans.*

  *In 1986, Enron had over $1 billion in short-
  term loans that matured quickly and that
  needed to be refinanced. In these early days,
  Enron was constantly on the verge of being
  in violation of its loan agreements.*

From 1986 through 2001, therefore, the focus of everyone at the company—and of everyone looking at it—would
be its earnings and whether the company could meet its
quarterly targets.

Some legal shifting of earnings

In managing these earnings targets, the company understood that *there was no benefit in exceeding* its earnings target in any quarter. In fact, *to exceed a quarterly target this
would be to create a problem.* This would raise the bar for
the next quarter since, to show steadily increasing earnings,
the company would have to exceed the previous quarter's
results.

To avoid such problems, a company could legitimately try to shift any excess earnings from one quarter into the next. This "shifting" could be accomplished legally *by timing when particular legitimate transactions could be booked.*

Some illegal shifting of earnings

What no company could do, however, was to create *a fictitious transaction* to achieve the result of shifting earnings from one quarter to another. Ken Lay knew this. Enron's internal audit team knew this. Its outside auditors knew this. And its in-house and outside lawyers knew this.

What they all also knew was that the way to test whether or not the transaction was real was quite simple. *They simply had to track down the other party to the transaction.* And, if that proved impossible, it would be back to the Duck School:

> *If it looked like a fictitious transaction and smelled like a fictitious transaction, and if nobody could establish that it was legitimate, there was a good chance we would be looking at a fictitious transaction.*

Just as a coal miner would take a canary down the mine to warn the miner against poisonous gases, the existence of a fictitious transaction is the equivalent of those poisonous gases.

Enron simply had to choose between either playing by the rules or breaking them. Breaking them would put the company, its investors, employees and bankers at risk. It seemed they just didn't care.

How Ken Lay and his team approached this in Enron's early days would be a good barometer for how they would approach the same choice in the future. Needless to say, when faced with the same choice years later, they chose the same way.

ENRON OIL

The one division of InterNorth that did not move to Houston was its oil trading business located in Valhalla, New York. Louis Borget had created the business that was later renamed Enron Oil. This was Enron's canary in the coal mine. It provided early evidence that Ken Lay and his team would always choose profits over integrity and would not play by the rules.

When InterNorth approached Louis Borget in 1984 to set up the business, they offered him a very lucrative package that included bonuses based on the profits he brought in. Unlike the other divisions, this division—now named Enron Oil—made money. But, unlike the rest of the company, it did so by trading. Its traders simply bet on the direction of crude oil prices. *This was pure speculation*—and the company's traders were very good. In 1985, the year of the InterNorth-HNG merger, Enron Oil made $10 million. The following year, 1986, it made $28 million. Its bonus pool of the few traders was $9.4 million. That year, Enron reported a loss of $14 million. *Enron Oil was therefore very important to the company.*

Louis Borget's nominal superiors in Houston were John Harding and Steve Sulentic. The treasurer of Enron Oil was Tom Mastroeni.

A call from Apple Bank

On January 23, 1987, Herb Perry—an auditor in Enron's internal audit department in Houston—described the call his boss, David Woytek, received from a security officer at Apple Bank on Forty-second Street in New York.

The caller revealed unusual cash transactions from the Isle of Guernsey from Enron in $100,000 increments. The approvals of the transactions, the caller said, were not coming from authorized corporate treasurers. They were coming from two executives in New York named Louis Borget and Thomas Mastroeni, *who seemed to be writing themselves checks.* Wire transfers of millions of dollars had flowed in from a bank in the Channel Islands. Over $2 million had flowed out to an account in Mastroeni's name. Nobody at Enron could find the Apple Bank account on Enron's books.

At that time, Enron Oil was reporting profits of more than $30 million a year—one-third of the total earnings of the company.

The explanation

On February 2, 1987, Borget and Mastroeni were summoned to Houston to meet with Mick Seidle, Ken Lay's number two. Also present were Woytek and his deputy, John Beard. The traders' superiors, Sulentic and Harding, had an explanation for the whole thing.

Apparently, the Apple Bank account was used to move some profits from 1986 into 1987. It was revealed that this had happened before using other entities named Isla, Southwest, and Petropol. Enron Oil would generate a loss on one contract and then have that loss set off against profits of the same amount from another contract.

David Woytek, the head of Enron's internal audit department, described this in a memo to Ken Lay as the creation of "fictitious losses."

In later testimony, Borget said that Harding asked him to shift profits, originally for tax reasons. For his part, Sulentic later testified that Enron Oil and other subsidiaries were *"routinely instructed by Enron senior management to shift profits from month to month and year to year."*

Sulentic defended the transactions as representing the objective of a transfer of profitability from 1986 to 1987. He did concede the methods Borget and Mastroeni had used were unacceptable. Mastroeni then presented falsified bank statements, not knowing that Enron had unaltered statements in its possession. He said that he and Borget had paid a bonus to a trader and didn't want to have to explain it to management.

> *What was remarkable was what was not asked. For example,*
> *there is no record of anyone asking who in "Enron senior*
> *management" had "routinely instructed" them to shift prof-*
> *its and what they knew of the transactions with the non-exis-*
> *tent Isla, Southwest, and Petropol. Nor is there any record of*
> *anyone asking who received those bonuses the traders didn't*
> *want to reveal to management. Perhaps, the company didn't*
> *ask because they didn't want to know the answers...*

The reaction to the explanation

Stunningly, most of the Enron executives in the room listening to Mastroeni's explanation actually accepted it. Neither Mastroeni nor Borget was reprimanded. An Arthur Andersen accountant who was involved is quoted as saying:

> *"No one pounded the table and said these*
> *guys are crooks. They thought they had the*
> *golden goose, and the golden goose just stole*
> *a little money out of their petty cash."*

The auditors later discovered there were payments of $106,500 to an M. Yass. Borget said he was an English broker. Mastroeni claimed he was a Lebanese national. Speculation was that it was an attempt at humor. M. Yass was really "my ass." Borget denied this.

When Ken Lay was told that the amount at issue in Valhalla was no more than $2 million to $4 million, he told his audit depart just to go get the money back. Perry, who went with Woytek to Valhalla to get the money back, was sternly warned, "Whatever you do, do not upset Borget." Arriving in Valhalla, Woytek, Beard, and Perry discovered that the trading operation was controlled completely by Borget and Mastroeni. One member of the Houston audit team was an Arthur Andersen partner and an expert in oil-and-gas trading. *The Houston team was not allowed to interview anyone at Valhalla.*

"Everything is proper," Borget told Perry. "We've just had an audit done." Despite this, the Houston team of auditors could find no evidence of the Isla, Southwest, and Petropol entities. They suspected those entities did not exist—or, if they did, Borget and Mastroeni had set them up. Something smelled foul in the air—and everyone there recognized the stench.

Perry and Woytek were sitting with John Beard in a trading room at Valhalla trying to unravel the fraud when they were interrupted by a call from Houston. To the team's astonishment and disgust, Rick Kinder, the company's general counsel, summoned them back to Houston. They were ordered to turn over the investigation to Arthur Andersen. It seemed Houston was worried the traders would get upset and the company would lose its trading income.

While the Arthur Andersen investigation was moving forward, Enron Oil remained the only Enron division that was making money. Because of this, there was very little chance that the Enron executives would risk offending Borget. Seidl actually sent a telex to Borget thanking him for his contributions to the company. He wrote:

> *"Your answers to Arthur Andersen were clear, straightforward, and rock solid—superb. I have complete confidence in your business judgment and ability and your personal integrity. Please keep making us millions."*

The April 29 board meeting

On April 29—three months after that call from Apple Bank—Arthur Andersen reported back to the board's audit committee. It reported that it was "unable to verify ownership or any other details" regarding Enron Oil's supposed trading partners—Isla, Southwest, and Petropol. It could find no evidence that the so-called profit-sharing transactions were legitimate and noted that the Apple Bank transactions had no purpose other than to shift earnings. Despite this, it refused to provide any opinion as to the legality of what had occurred. Nor was it willing to say whether the profit shifting had a material effect on Enron's financial statements. *Instead, Arthur Andersen took the position that Enron had to make those determinations itself.*

Needless to say, if Arthur Andersen would not make those determinations, Enron was happy to. It sent Arthur Andersen a letter from its general counsel, Rich Kinder, and another Enron lawyer stating:

> *"The unusual transactions would not have a material effect on the financial statements... and that no disclosure of these transactions is necessary."*

David Woytek recommended to Ken Lay and the board that they should fire the two traders. They did not.

At least two people at that board meeting questioned Lay's judgment. One was Ronald Roskens, then the president of the University of Nebraska. He would leave the board two years later to join the government. The other was Carolyn Kee of Arthur Andersen. Within three years she left Enron.

In her *Vanity Fair* article, "The Enron Wars," Marie Brenner writes how it was obvious at that April board meeting to both the board and to Arthur Andersen that Borget and Mastroeni had opened fraudulent bank accounts and that they would continue to do whatever they were doing. She quotes an auditor who told her "Lay read the report and he read his budget, and estimated how much they made and if they were fired what he could lose...My conclusion was that this is a guy who puts earnings before scruples, rather than reacting to the dishonesty right in front of him."

For Ken Lay, earnings trumped scruples.

Two months later, an Enron lawyer concluded that the profit-shifting deals were "legitimate common transactions in the oil trading business" and that they did not "lack economic substance." This was contrary to all of the evidence—and the fact that Enron's own in-house auditor had called the transactions "fictitious." *It also flew in the face of the small matter that nobody could find those trading companies that were a part of those "legitimate common transactions."*

As long as the traders were making money for the company, Ken Lay and his board didn't care that the "fictitious"
transactions were with entities nobody could find.

> *The performance of Ken Lay's legal and accounting team in
> ignoring the clear evidence of wrongdoing was yet another
> red flag. It was surely proof that nothing Enron's profession-
> al team said in the future could be relied upon. Certainly,
> based on their performance here, they would say anything to
> satisfy their clients—and mislead investors. What would the
> Duck School make of this?*

Enron Oil's internal controls

At that same April 29 board meeting, Arthur Andersen
also reported to the audit committee something else that
was potentially devastating.

Enron Oil was supposed to have strict internal controls
to prevent the possibility of large losses. Its open position
in the market was never supposed to exceed eight million
barrels. If losses reached $4 million, the traders were to liq-
uidate the position. When the Andersen auditors had tried
to check whether Enron Oil was complying with the policy,
they could not. Borget and Mastroeni had destroyed their
daily position reports. For those on the Enron board who
did not realize this before, they now surely had to know
they were dealing with thieves and con men.

At least one senior executive, Mike Muckleroy, the head of
Enron's liquid-fuels division, believed that Enron Oil had to
be ignoring the trading limits. He applied some Duck School
logic: he argued that the same limits that were designed to
protect the company against huge losses also had to limit
gains. It made no sense to Muckleroy that Enron Oil could
be showing the types of profits it was showing without also
exceeding its trading limits. He was right.

He complained to Seidl more than six times—to no effect.
He then went to Ken Lay, who was no more interested in

looking into it than Seidl. He apparently told Muckleroy that he was being paranoid. Muckleroy asked Ken Lay:

> *"What do I have to do to get you to understand that this could do devastating damage to our company?"*

At the company's mid-August board meeting, despite Muckleroy's persistent warnings and despite the fact that everyone knew that the two traders were crooks, the Enron board appeared unconcerned about the potential catastrophe the company was facing. Astonishingly, Ken Lay and his board instead did the unthinkable: They actually *increased* Borget's trading limits by 50 percent.

For whatever reason, Ken Lay and his board—and all their professional advisors—believed these thieves and con men would respect these new increased trading limits. *They would be wrong.*

In the end, the scam the traders were running collapsed, but not because of anything Enron's senior management did. In their book, *The Smartest Guys in the Room,* Bethany McLean and Peter Elkind explained that the traders made one mistake Enron couldn't forgive: They stopped making money.

It soon became apparent that the two traders kept two sets of books. One was sent to Houston and one tracked the real activities of Enron Oil.

They were paying huge commissions to the brokers who handled their sham transactions and who demanded kickbacks. It seems that the Enron internal audit team was correct—Isla, Southwest, and Petropol were all phony companies set up in the Channel Islands. Borget and Mastroeni and the other brokers had stolen $3.8 million from Enron.

On October 9, 1987, Seidl met Borget for lunch in Manhattan. Borget admitted that he had been betting that the price of oil was headed down. For months, the market had gone against him. As his losses had mounted, he had continually doubled his bet in the hope of recouping everything when prices ultimately turned in his direction. Borget had dug a hole so deep that there was virtually no hope for the company. Seidl understood. He called Houston frantically.

Mike Muckleroy

Muckleroy was a navy man. He took charge. He flew immediately to New York to see if he could salvage the disaster the company faced. Enron was looking to cover over $1 billion. The company was facing an abyss. Bankruptcy seemed inevitable.

Muckleroy met with Mastroeni to review Enron Oil's books—and he knew what was happening. He demanded to see the real books. It is reported that he told Mastroeni that, while in the navy, he had killed people. Apparently, he added, "I sleep like a baby." The next morning, Mastroeni produced the real books.

For the next three weeks, Muckleroy worked to reduce the company's obligation. He was a trader himself, and he bluffed the other traders. To gain time, he made them believe Enron had crude oil in hand. Within a few days, oil prices began to decline. He saved the company by reducing the damage to around $140 million.

Ken Lay's "shock"

For a year, Ken Lay and his team had overwhelming evidence that these two traders were crooks. They all knew something was wrong, but they made a conscious decision. The money the two traders were making for the company was far more important than controlling the crooks. They didn't care what these two crooks were doing—as long as they were making money. In fact, the less they knew, the better...

Now, in a scene that would be repeated years later, Ken Lay and other Enron executives professed shock at what these traders had done. These were the same traders the company had caught stealing millions of dollars and who had engaged in fictitious transactions.

The company announced that it would take an $85 million after-tax charge to 1987 earnings. It blamed it on "losses from unauthorized trading activities by two employees in its international crude oil trading subsidiary." Enron's stock began to fall. By the October announcement it was down 30 percent.

At an all-employee meeting in late October, Lay told the crowd that he had no idea what had occurred. Bethany McLean and Peter Elkind wrote that Lay told the meeting that he had been blindsided by Borget. "If anyone could say that I knew, let them stand up, he said. Apparently two people had to prevent Muckleroy from standing.

At a board meeting held to discuss the loss, Lay denied any responsibility.

At the very time Enron knew about the Enron Oil scandal and the planned $85 million charge, the company was negotiating and closing agreements with its banks. The agreements closed before the $85 million charge was announced. Needless to say, the banks were outraged. Ken Lay and his team had lied to them.

> *This would cast a bright light on the honesty and integrity with which Enron, Ken Lay and Arthur Andersen would conduct future business.*

The aftermath

As damage control, Enron filed a lawsuit against Borget and Mastroeni for fraud. There were also investigations by both the Securities and Exchange Commission and the U.S. Attorney's office, but the government chose not to prosecute the company.

In early 1988, Enron restated its financials for the previous three and a half years, blaming "unauthorized activities...designed to shift income."

In early 1990, Borget pled guilty to three felonies and was sentenced to a year in jail and five years' probation. Mastroeni pled guilty to two felonies. He received a suspended sentence and two years' probation.

After the scandal, Ken Lay found himself in an uncomfortable position. His wish had largely come true: by the end of the 1980s, deregulation was almost complete.

The question now was what business model to apply to the newly deregulated industry. And once it had decided on that new model, would the company display the same culture in moving forward that was exhibited in the Enron Oil adventure? Considering Ken Lay remained the chairman and CEO, and considering Arthur Andersen remained the company's auditors and the board was largely unchanged, this was unlikely.

> *Enron, Ken Lay, and Arthur Andersen all had a problem: Years earlier, they all knew of the criminal activities of the two traders, but had decided to look the other way. So too did Enron's board. It had chosen profits and fees over integrity.*
>
> *Was it any surprise that they would do the same years later? Why would anyone have expected anything different from this group in the future?*

JEFF SKILLING AND THE GAS BANK

In 1990, Jeff Skilling—that bright young partner at McKinsey & Company—was working as a consultant to Enron. He had identified a future business model for the company. He introduced his ideas for the Gas Bank, which proved to be revolutionary. His idea was quite simple:

> *Natural gas producers would contract to sell natural gas to the Gas Bank—and would be induced to do so by being paid in advance for some of the gas being purchased. This would*

be a means for them to fund their crude oil activities.

Customers would contract to buy from the Gas Bank—and would thus be guaranteed a long-term supply of natural gas. The Gas Bank would receive the difference between the selling and buying price.

He also had another idea: these new contracts could be traded in much the same way as other commodity contracts could be traded. No hard assets would be needed for this new business model. Other companies could provide the gas and delivery systems.

His concept was that natural gas could be referred to in the context of its financial terms. To explain this, he would compare a natural gas contract to a cow. Just as a cow had many different kinds of meat that commanded different prices, so too did a natural gas contract have different parts of different values. This was both innovative and ingenious. It was also a totally legitimate business model for which Skilling rightfully received accolades.

Bethany McLean and Peter Elkind offered another insight into Jeff Skilling, however. They wrote that he was a gambler at heart and had always been. They described this as his most dangerous blind spot.

His demand

In June 1990, Skilling agreed to join Enron to run the Gas Bank himself. His title would be chairman and CEO of a new division—Enron Finance. The agreement Skilling reached with the company allowed him to benefit directly from the economic value the new division created. Before agreeing to join Enron, however, Skilling made a demand: the company had to agree that the new division could use mark-to-marketing accounting.

Unless the company agreed, he would not join them. To understand this demand is to understand the mark-to-marketing accounting that Skilling demanded.

Mark-to-market accounting

Conventional accounting required revenues to be booked as they are generated. In the case of a twenty-year contract, for example, these earnings would be booked over that twenty-year period. This generally resulted in financial statements that reflected the precise financial condition of the company.

Mark-to-market accounting, however, allows *the estimated value* of the contract over its term to be booked *on the day the contract is signed.* If the estimated value proved to be inaccurate, the company would have to make adjustments as necessary in later years. The financial markets would not respond well to downward adjustments. *The name of the game, therefore, would be to keep these poorly performing assets off the company's books to avoid having to make these downward adjustments.*

For some industries, mark-to-market accounting is used with some comfort. For example, Wall Street brokerage firms are required to use this method—but there is a precision involved here since there is always a current market price for their portfolios. As a result, it is a precise accounting tool.

The difficulty of using this in the natural gas industry

In the natural gas industry, the mark-to-market accounting method would create insurmountable problems. This was not rocket science, and anyone would understand the problem:

> *How would you even begin to estimate the price of natural gas over a twenty-year term?*

To do so would require clairvoyant powers. Anything—a war, a natural disaster, an economic downturn, or the discovery of new energy technology—could affect the price of gas over twenty years. And there would then still be the question of how it would affect the price. Making these estimates would be pure gambling. Then again, as we know,

Skilling was a gambling man. For the gambler, there would be good and bad news.

- The good news was that, because these projections were such an imprecise science, the gambler who controlled the business could control his company's quarterly revenues.

- The bad news was that, at some time, either the poorly performing assets—or over-optimistic projections—would have to be purged from the company's books or else restated. Even with the most honest projections, this would become almost inevitable. But with the most optimistic projections that defied the laws of business gravity, this would become a certainty.

Years later, Andy Fastow—who was one of Skilling's earliest hires in 1990 and who moved through the ranks to chief financial officer in 1998—would find imaginative ways to defy those laws of gravity. And everybody—including Ken Lay, Jeff Skilling, and Enron's board—would claim *they had no idea what he was doing.* This was despite their daily meetings with him. This was reminiscent of the fictitious transactions of the Enron Oil days.

The "quality of earnings" problem that this created

When Ken Lay and his distinguished and experienced board agreed to Skilling's demand that mark-to-market accounting be used for his Gas Bank, did they understand how difficult it would be to forecast the value of long-term contracts? And did they understand the effect this would have on the company? What were these effects that they may or may not have understood?

The first direct effect of mark-to-market accounting is a "quality of earnings" problem. While the earnings of the company would certainly appear quite spectacular when the earnings from that twenty-year contract was booked on the day the contract was signed, *the company's actual cash-flow from that contract would certainly be quite modest.* This

would be the case even in the unlikely event that its projected twenty-year value was totally accurate.

The company faced the certainty of having spectacular
paper earnings, but cash that bore no relation to those earnings. This is why this has been called a "quality of earnings"
problem.

Ken Lay understood the effect of booking earnings from
a twenty-year contract immediately. He understood the
company would have to start each new quarter as a fresh
quarter—because cash coming in from the previous quarter's twenty-year contract could not be included in the new
quarter's figures. They had already been booked.

The big-picture effect

To put this into a context, this mark-to-market accounting would change *the company's primary goal* in evaluating
new transactions.

Normally, the goal in evaluating any proposed commer-
cial transaction is that it is a viable, bona fide transaction
with a sound economic objective. Now, the goal would be
solely on the effect the transaction would have on the company's financial statement. Now, the goal was to sign *new
contracts* every quarter so that the projected revenues
could be booked *immediately*.

Once the company's goal had changed from business vi-
ability to the *number of contracts* signed, this would result
in many transactions that were neither viable nor bona
fide—and many with no sound economic objectives. *And all
of this occurred...*

And most remarkable of all...

As remarkable as Ken Lay and Enron's board of directors
agreeing to allow Jeff Skilling to use the mark-to-market accounting method, was the fact that Arthur Andersen apparently did not warn the company of the fundamental gamble—and huge risk—involved in having to predict the value
of long-term gas contracts. *Or did they?* But Skilling, as we

now know, was a gambler. Also, we now know that Arthur Andersen would deliver whatever advice Ken Lay wanted.

If this was remarkable, this didn't hold a candle to the Securities and Exchange Commission permitting the use of mark-to-market accounting for the Gas Bank. Initially, the SEC did focus on the obvious issue: how would Enron estimate the value of energy prices in long-term contracts? The agency suggested that additional disclosures be made to investors, but Skilling thought this perfectly reasonable suggestion was unreasonable. He responded by claiming that mark-to-market earnings would be calculated based on "known spreads and balanced positions." He further claimed that Enron's numbers would not be "significantly dependent on subjective elements." *Remarkably, the SEC bought his nonsensical arguments.*

It has been reported that when Skilling heard the news that the SEC would not object to the use of the mark-to-market method of accounting, he brought in champagne to toast the accounting change. And he had good reason. He had gambled—and won.

While his innovative new business model was brilliant, he apparently had no idea of what was happening around him in the manipulation of earnings—if you could believe him. There is no dispute that Jeff Skilling, Ken Lay, and Andrew Fastow met regularly to brainstorm solutions to the problems caused by the quality-of-earning problem in particular and by the earnings problem in general.

Andrew Fastow confirmed this when he testified before the House Energy and Commerce Oversight Committee on his many conversations with Jeff Skilling about the off-the-books partnerships. In his testimony, however, Jeff Skilling told the committee:

> *"I was not aware of any financing arrangements designed to conceal liabilities or inflate profitability...I do not believe the company was in any imminent financial peril."*

THOSE QUESTIONS

Winston Churchill once wrote that the farther backwards you can look, the farther forward you are likely to see.

We began by asking some questions: We asked, what might have happened had anyone looked back? If anyone had studied Enron, its culture, and its leaders in the same way Nelson Mandela studied the Afrikaners, their culture, and their leaders, what would he or she have seen? And would it have warned us of the looming disaster in 2001?

Looking at Enron, Ken Lay, Arthur Andersen, and those who were with Enron from its formation through its implosion, could anyone have been surprised that the way they acted in response to the Enron Oil saga was repeated? Or could anyone have been surprised by the consistent refusal to accept responsibility for their actions and inactions that led to the implosion?

And what can one say about the company's auditors and accountants—Arthur Andersen? In Enron's earliest days, they witnessed dishonesty, fraud, and money being shifted to nonexistent companies—yet they refused to report what they saw. They claimed they could find no evidence that the so-called profit-shifting transactions were legitimate, yet the firm's own investigation revealed that it could find no evidence that any of the profit-shifting transactions were real.

In a nutshell, Arthur Andersen showed a blind loyalty to Enron and offered the company what it requested—no matter what it requested. It could therefore never have been a surprise to anyone that Arthur Andersen would display these same traits in events that led to the 2001 implosion of the company.

So, what are the lessons from Enron's early years? The facts were there for anyone to see. As presidents and Wall Street honored Ken Lay and his company, astonishingly either nobody bothered to look or nobody cared...And which was worse

.

CHAPTER NINE

HOW THEY SOLVED
THEIR PROBLEMS

*"Out of intense complexities,
intense simplicities emerge."*

Winston Churchill

At the end of each business day, Enron would have to come up with the cash necessary to settle the energy contracts traded on its online system. With insufficient cash reserves, it would need to access cash through lines of credit or investment capital. And this would create a problem.

To access those lines and any investment capital, Enron would need a favorable credit rating. And for this, Enron would need to show steady growth, consistent earnings, cash flow, and no increase in debt. And this would bring us back to the ever-present problem Enron faced:

How could Enron reflect consistent earn-
ings if there were fluctuations in its trading
business?

Anyone who understood the Duck School could answer
this: Enron had a big-time problem, and the choices it made
in addressing this problem resulted in the company's implosion. One example follows.

By the end of 1999, Enron's year-end financials were not
looking good. Because cash flow for 1999 was dwarfing the
huge earnings for that year, this would clearly concern Wall
Street and Enron's bankers and investors. The Enron brain
trust knew time was running out before the end of the financial year, which was now only a few weeks away. Was
there anyone within the upper echelons of management
who was not aware of this potentially devastating problem?
Was there anyone on Enron's board or at Arthur Andersen
who was not aware of the projected year-end financials?
What would they do?

Coincidentally, it was October 1999 when Enron awarded
Nelson Mandela its prize and extolled his virtues. It was then
that Enron, too, claimed to share those values. So, shortly
after it honored him for his moral authority, Enron was con-
sidering embarking on a series of transactions. The facts
would speak for themselves as to the ethical propriety of
those transactions.

PROJECT NAHANNI

Weeks before the 1999 financial year end, the company
was in desperate straits. All eyes were on what the company's year-end financials would look like. If the singular and
sole focus throughout the end of the year was on the company's financial performance, the year-end numbers were
front and center stage.

Clearly, the company's huge reported earnings were out of sync with its cash reserves. This would not impress Wall Street or Enron's bankers. Faced with this huge and rapidly looming problem, Enron's top guns came up with a transaction they called "Project Nahanni" that was built on a lie:

- Two weeks before the year's end, the company borrowed $500 million—*but it would not call it a loan.* The Duck School would inevitably rear its unpopular head, but nobody at Enron cared.

- With that money, Enron bought Treasury securities, which it then sold.

- Enron then characterized the $500 million received from the sale as part of Enron's 1999 operating cash flow—which was *exactly* what the company needed to reflect in its 1999 financials. In fact, the sudden infusion of $500 million represented 41 percent of the entire reported 1999 cash flow from operations.

- A week after the 1999 financial year's end, Enron repaid the loan in the 2000 financial year.

Enron Bankruptcy Examiner James Batson confirms this:

> *"To mask the fact that Enron's earnings were artificial, the company was apparently forced to come up with schemes to generate cash flow. One was a 1999 deal codenamed Project Nahanni. Enron, weeks away from the year-end, borrowed $500 million in treasury securities from Citibank, sold them immediately and reported the proceeds as operating cash flow. That represented 41% of the total cash flow from operations recognized by Enron in 1999. The firm swiftly repaid the loan without it ever showing up as debt on its financial statement. In effect, just this one transaction represented a $500 million scam."*

So, how did this deal happen? How was Project Nahanni approved? Who approved it? Who persuaded whom to do this deal? How could a last-minute transaction that accounted for 41 percent of the company's total cash flow from operations go undetected and unquestioned? Where were the analysts whose job it is to analyze? Where were the financial media?

THE BLOCKBUSTER DEAL

On July 19, 2000, the company made a dramatic announcement of a ground-breaking agreement with Blockbuster. It announced "a 20-year, exclusive agreement to deliver a Blockbuster entertainment service, initially featuring movies-on-demand, via the Enron Intelligent Network.

There were only two slight problems with Enron's announcement. Bankruptcy Examiner Batson described what Enron *failed* to mention in its announcement:

> "This agreement reflected nothing more than an aspiration. Enron did not have the technology to deliver VOD [video on demand] on a commercially viable basis and Blockbuster did not have the rights to movies to be delivered."

Where was Enron's board when this announcement was made?

Where were its lawyers and accountants?

Its new broadband business

As background to the Blockbuster announcement, towards the end of 1999, Jeff Skilling was preparing for a presentation of his new broadband business to Wall Street. Enron's plan was relatively simple. It would provide bandwidth and switching capacity to distribute video and other content at reasonable prices. Within two years, it promised to create a market in bandwidth trading.

In January 2000, at a meeting with analysts, Ken Lay would claim that the new broadband business would easily surpass Enron's gas and power trading businesses. Skilling went further. He explained that Enron would capture at least 20 percent of the projected $68 billion U.S. bandwidth market in 2004. He predicted operating income of more than $1 billion by 2004. He predicted $11.7 billion in revenues from content services by 2008. He predicted these broadband businesses were worth an additional $37 per share that was not accounted for in Enron's then share value.

Although the new company had no business, the stock jumped after that meeting. *Skilling had sold Wall Street something that did not exist.* And it was not just that it didn't exist, it was anyway a seriously flawed business model at that time. Perhaps given six or seven years development, it might have worked. So, what were these flawed business concepts in Enron's model?

THE TECHNOLOGY DID NOT EXIST

As Bankruptcy Examiner Batson confirmed, the technology required to implement its broadband trading model did not exist at that time.

CONSUMERS WOULD NEED HIGH-SPEED CONNECTIVITY

To implement the model that would deliver video into television sets, consumers would need the required high-speed connectivity to allow for delivery of this video-on-demand. At that time, many homes did not have this connectivity— and those that did have this connectivity were connected to computers. This made Enron's predictions of quick results a fantasy.

THE COMPETITIVE DISADVANTAGE

The cable television industry enjoyed a huge competitive advantage. It was already in millions of homes across the country. On the other hand, for customers to participate in Enron's new model, Enron had to persuade them to buy a special box for their televisions—at a cost of around $500. Again this would take time—and patience. No quick results.

Time and patience were luxuries Enron could not afford. Despite this, Ken Lay and Jeff Skilling made extraordinary promises to Wall Street that would require them to generate revenues virtually immediately. Ken Lay promised that it would lose no more than $60 million in 2000. This was an impossible target that required them to start showing quarterly results immediately.

Not surprisingly, the company actually honored its earnings promises to Wall Street—despite the *absolute impossibility of being able to do so legitimately.* How did they do this?

FIRST QUARTER

The company announced $59 million in revenues by exchanging surplus strands of fiber on its networks for fiber of its competitors. (Enron could book the fiber it sold as an immediate gain, while the fiber it was buying could be depreciated over twenty years. No cash passed hands.)

SECOND QUARTER

The company announced a $53 million pretax gain by doing a deal with Andrew Fastow's partnership, LJM2, whereby it would hold the fiber until Enron could find a buyer. (Fastow, who was still Enron's CFO, agreed to pay Enron $100 million—$30 million in cash and $70 million as a note. Ken Lay personally approved this deal.)

THIRD QUARTER

The company booked $35 million in profits based on an investment it made in a technology start-up called Avici Systems.

By the end of the third quarter there was still virtually no cash being generated. The Blockbuster deal was already on its deathbed. A major part of the deal was Enron's obligation to negotiate deals with the phone companies that provided local DSL access around the country. If Enron had not secured these phone agreements by December, *Blockbuster had the right to walk away from the agreement.*

When it became clear Enron could not meet this deadline, it negotiated an extension until March. And even though Enron could not meet this extended deadline, Enron found a way to monetize the Blockbuster deal in a scheme called "Project Braveheart."

In doing so, one can only wonder if it could do so without a broad grin.

> *This raises the question of why nobody uncovered the brazen lies that Ken Lay and Jeff Skilling told. This broadband scam was quite detectable if anyone took the trouble to probe the premise of the model. Most did not. Jim Chanos of Kynikos Associates did.*
>
> *Nobody asked the most obvious of questions. Nobody conducted the most elementary due diligence. And those responsible for asking the questions and conducting the due diligence were amongst our finest and brightest...*

PROJECT BRAVEHEART

It was a remarkable series of transactions:

- Enron contributed the Blockbuster agreement that was on life support to a subsidiary, Enron Broadband Services, Inc. ("EBS").

- It then sold a 45 percent interest in EBS for $115 million to a second investment vehicle called Hawaii 125-0, which was funded with $115.2 million from the Canadian Imperial Bank of Commerce.

Of course, Canadian Imperial Bank of Commerce wasn't interested in investing in Braveheart. What it was interested in, however, was becoming one of Enron's preferred banks. EBS executives promised the bank that its investment would be repaid in early 2001. *This could not be committed to writing because this would not allow Enron to book revenues from the transaction.*

By the end of the quarter, EBS claimed a $53 million gain on Braveheart. This represented 84 percent of the broadband division's revenues.

Some at Arthur Andersen registered their disapproval of Enron's plans to book profits from the transaction. One of their accountants, Carl Bass, wrote an e-mail in August 2001:

> *"Help me out here. How do you sell an asset and generate operating cash flow?"*

Mr. Bass was ignored.

TERMINATING THE BLOCKBUSTER DEAL AND EBS

On March 9, 2001, just months after booking $53 million in profits, Enron terminated the Blockbuster deal with this announcement:

> *"Enron intends to initiate discussions with various content providers for delivering their content over the Enron platform."*

Carl Bass at Arthur Andersen noted that, with the termination of the Blockbuster deal, Enron should be reporting a loss. He apparently had not noticed that Enron had long ago tumbled down that rabbit hole and was now living in Wonderland. In fact, the company *increased* its value to $58 million. Bankruptcy Examiner Batson noted:

> *"Apparently, Enron's 'intention to initiate discussion' was even more valuable than it 'exclusive relationship with Blockbuster.' "*

By late summer of 2001, Enron recognized the inevitable and closed down the business. Within about a year, EBS went from reporting $111 million of gain to being worthless.

> These transactions could never have occurred without the bank funding the EBS acquisition of the worthless contract. Everyone involved with the transaction knew the bank would never have funded this transaction on its merits. The bank was not scammed.
>
> When the real transaction could not be committed to writing because Enron could not book revenues from the transaction, everyone knew that when Enron booked those revenues, it was not entitled to them. Those involved were not scammed. They participated in a scam.

THOSE EXPLANATIONS

Project Nahanni occurred at the end of the 1999 financial year, so how would Ken Lay position the company in Enron's 1999 Annual Report to preempt the seemingly inevitable questions that might strike a little too close to home? In his letter to shareholders that accompanied Enron's 1999 Annual Report, he attempted to address the problem with this gem:

> "Enron is moving so fast that sometimes others have trouble defining us. But we know who we are."

That the company knew who it was had to be an enormous relief to everyone. It did acknowledge, however, that some people were having trouble "defining" the company. So what might be an example of the trouble people were having?

Wholesale services

"Wholesale services" accounted for more than 90 percent of Enron's revenues, but what were they? This is how its 2000 Annual Report describes that activity:

> *"Enron builds wholesale businesses through the creation of networks involving selective asset ownership, contractual access to third-party assets and market-making activities."*

If you had no idea what this meant, you would be in good company. Here's how Andrew Fastow, Enron's chief financial officer, explained Enron's business model:

> *"We create optionality. Enron is so much more valuable—hence our stock price—because we have so much more optionality embedded in our network than anyone else."*

Presumably, he thought this would be helpful—or maybe not. He went on to say:

> *"Our disclosure is more complete than anyone's...We don't want to tell anyone where we're making money."*

No kidding...And when Fastow was challenged that Enron's made its money speculating, he insisted it did not: *"It's not trading. It's optimization."* There were few in the financial media who could understand any of this.

Enron's description of its finances

In January 2001, Dan Ackman, a reporter for *Forbes,* amusingly characterized Enron's explanation of its finances as reading like "something written in German, translated to Chinese and back to English by way of Polish."

The next month, much to the irritation of the Enron senior management, Bethany McLean, a reporter for *Fortune,* reached the same conclusion writing that the company was "largely impenetrable to outsiders." She asked how Enron made its money? She noted that analysts didn't "seem to have a clue."

The response of Enron's senior management was not difficult to anticipate. It responded the way all scammers respond—it attacked. Managers ridiculed and denigrated Ms. McLean personally. They called her unethical. They said she was ignorant and inexperienced. They did everything but address the substance of her argument—and the reason was clear. Faced with a challenge, a logical rational discourse on the subject was the last thing Enron's scammers wanted—because that would have unraveled the scam. They refused to participate in a discussion. They exhibited a style and culture that would give them away as scammers.

ENRON AND NELSON MANDELA

The story of Enron is a story of choices. It is how some of the smartest people in the world chose not to look and see and, instead, how they chose to do nothing. The story is about a determination to avoid asking questions. It is about their fear that the answers might kill the goose that was laying those golden eggs. It is a story about their all-consuming fear of common sense—and the Duck School.

The greatest disappointment perhaps was the performance of Enron's star-studded board of directors. *Business Week* published one of the most articulate statements outlining the importance and role of a board of directors. This came from an executive *Business Week* named as one of the top 25 managers in the world. This is what the executive wrote about his own board—

> *"A strong, independent and knowledgeable board can make a significant difference in the performance of any company. Our corporate governance guidelines emphasize the qualities of strength of character, an inquiring and independent mind, practical wisdom and mature judgment.*
>
> *Like any successful company, we must have directors who start with what is right, who do not have hidden agendas and strive to*

*make judgments about what is best for the
company and not what is best for themselves
or some other constituency."*
The executive was Ken Lay.

Looking back to that 1999 October evening at Rice University when Ken Lay announced with pride that Nelson Mandela epitomized the ideals upon which that prize was established, one had to wonder whether even the self-delusional Mr. Lay really ever believed that. Certainly, he had no idea of the man Enron was honoring that evening.

The only remaining question was the culpability of those who saw what was happening and who did nothing. Fortunately for us all, on that count, the criminal and civil justice systems have spoken with a rare clarity...

CHAPTER TEN

CANARIES IN THE
CHALABI COAL MINE

"Ahmed Chalabi may go down as
one of the great con men in history."

Newsweek—May 31, 2004

Y ou couldn't have made this up. Could a convicted
embezzler really have scammed a nation's finest and
brightest? Could he have outwitted the nation's su-
perspies with their space age technology and unlimited re-
sources? Could he have scammed the intelligence agencies
of our allies? And what about our media establishment? If
so, surely this would be the stuff of John le Carré, the British
spy novelist. *Surely this could never have happened in real
life, right?*

Well, apparently it did happen...

What if we had sent a canary down the Ahmed Chalabi coal mine? *Would it have survived?* And what if our finest and brightest had studied Mr. Chalabi the same way Mr. Mandela studied the Afrikaners, their culture, and their leaders? What if our finest and brightest had applied the teachings of the Duck School? And what about the Subway Test? *What would they have found?* And would they then have bought a used car from him?

"A WILLING SUSPENSION OF DISBELIEF"

There was something not quite right about this picture of an embezzler scamming a nation. Had anyone looked, they would have seen that all was not well in the land of Chalabi. *But the CIA and the State Department had looked. And they had each decided that he could not be trusted.*

After the CIA and State Department had taken him off their payrolls and severed their ties with him, the finest and brightest in the Pentagon and in the Vice President's office publicly embraced him with apparent sincerity. In observing this, *Newsweek* made this comment:

> "When it served their own ideological agenda, his neocon sponsors engaged in a willing suspension of disbelief. The ideologues at the Defense Department were warned by doubters at the State Department and CIA that Chalabi was peddling suspect goods. Even so, the Bushies were bamboozled by a Machiavellian con man for the ages."

But were they really bamboozled? Why wasn't this just another case of a guy in a subway selling us a fake Rolex with us knowing it was a fake? Can you really be scammed if you knew what you were buying was a lie?

A clue to this question might have been buried in the Bush administration's response to an interview Mr. Chalabi gave to a London newspaper. After his lies had finally been exposed, he was challenged about them. He was unapologetic—even defiant. If he had embarrassed his friends in the Bush administration, he appeared unconcerned. He had not lied, he claimed. At worst, he said, he had erred:

> *"We are heroes in error. As far as we're con-*
> *cerned, we've been entirely successful. That*
> *tyrant Saddam is gone and the Americans*
> *are in Baghdad."*

How did the Bush administration respond? *They did not.* Where was the outrage or anger one would have expected after such a public embarrassment? *There was none.*

His allies responded by simply repeating his lies. Undeterred by the lack of weapons of mass destruction as the coalition forces swept through the country, the Bush administration simply continued to assert that they were there somewhere. And it would keep looking, until its own search team, the Iraq Survey Group, finally concluded that no weapons existed.

If Mr. Chalabi was indeed a scammer, the inevitable and uncomfortable question was whether his Washington allies were co-conspirators or victims. Did they really believe him or did they simply use what he was telling them to pursue their own agenda?

To answer this, we would have to send our canary not very deep down into the Chalabi coal mine. We would need to focus on the man: who he was and what he wanted and needed to accomplish his goals. We would need to see what the Bush administration saw when they decided to hitch their wagon to his star.

> *We would need to see whether, like the Imperial Weavers in*
> *Hans Christian Andersen's immortal tale about the Emper-*
> *or's New Clothes, Mr. Chalabi had achieved his goals simply*
> *by giving the emperor the magical invisible cloth he wanted*
> *so desperately.*
>
> *And how would Mr. Chalabi persuade the emperor's clos-*
> *est and most trusted advisors to confirm that the magical*
> *invisible cloth he had weaved was actually real and beauti-*
> *ful—when it was neither? He didn't have to because the em-*
> *peror's closest and most trusted advisors wanted to believe*
> *as desperately as the emperor...*

As head of the major Iraqi opposition group in exile, Ahmed Chalabi wanted to be the next president of Iraq. *This was no secret.* Even his most ardent detractors would admit that he was a remarkably astute businessman. He recognized the economic perks that the presidency would bring. He also recognized that he would not have to wait until he became president for some of those economic perks to start kicking in.

The Bush administration had no problem with any of this—provided he could deliver what it wanted. *And what did the United States want?* It wanted a friendly post-Saddam Iraq.

For the Americans the logic was unassailable: Chalabi was a Shiite and was close to the Shiite leadership—both in Iraq and Iran. The Iraqi Shiites hated Saddam Hussein—for good reason. The Shiites were therefore seen by the Bush administration as an indispensable ally in any post-Saddam Iraq.

If Ahmed Chalabi could persuade his Washington allies that he could deliver the support of the Iraqi Shiites, he would be on his way to achieving his goal. So, he set about persuading them that he could. He did so knowing they could never conclusively disprove he had that support. What made this even easier for him was that President Bush and his advisors really wanted to believe he indeed had that support. Even though there were many experts who believed he did not, *their views were apparently ignored.*

Mr. Chalabi also knew what he did not want. A military coup against Saddam would not help him, since it would surely have resulted in a senior military officer of the regime replacing Saddam Hussein—thereby leaving Mr. Chalabi out in the cold. In *Rise of the Vulcans*, Richard Perle, one of Ahmed Chalabi's closest neocon friends in Washington, is quoted as saying:

"It would be a tragedy if Saddam is removed only to be replaced by another tyrant."

Clearly, a best-case scenario for the United States and Mr. Chalabi would be for Saddam Hussein's successor to come from a pro-United States Iraqi opposition group in exile. And the largest such group was the Iraq National Congress, led by none other than Mr. Chalabi.

LUCK ARRIVES

Luck arrived for Ahmed Chalabi with the September 11, 2001, attacks, which would jolt the United States and the world. Long before September 11, President Bush and Vice President Cheney had announced to the world exactly what would make them attack Iraq. They stated quite clearly that if Saddam Hussein were shown to be reconstituting his weapons of mass destruction program, they would consider military intervention. In a *News Hour* interview with Jim Lehrer during the 2000 presidential campaign, candidate Bush stated his position:

> *"I will tell you this: If we catch him developing weapons of mass destruction in any way, shape, or form, I'll deal with that in a way that he won't like."*

To emphasize this point, candidate Bush said that if, as president, he found that Saddam was manufacturing weapons of mass destruction, he would "take him out." In the vice presidential debate, candidate Dick Cheney was asked whether he agreed. He replied:

> *"We might have no other choice...If in fact Saddam Hussein were taking steps to try to rebuild nuclear capacity or weapons of mass destruction, we'd have to give very serious consideration to military action to stop that activity."*

Ahmed Chalabi was listening. He now had a road map—a blueprint for American military intervention in Iraq. He would need some professional help that could probably only have come from a foreign intelligence agency—but this would be no problem. It would come from a Shiite nation that Ahmed Chalabi had courted for years and that unashamedly wanted to exert more influence in post-Saddam Iraq. That nation was Iran.

Mr. Chalabi went to work, and he succeeded brilliantly. In an article in *Salon*, John Dizard set forth the common perception at the time that Mr. Chalabi had succeeded brilliantly in inducing the United States to intervene militarily in Iraq and depose Saddam Hussein. He wrote that it was Chalabi who provided crucial intelligence on Iraqi weaponry to justify the invasion, almost all of which turned out to be false. He noted that it was Chalabi who led America's leaders to believe that they would be greeted as liberators.

In *America's Secret War*, George Friedman listed the intelligence and command failures of the Iraq campaign. Ahmed Chalabi featured prominently. Friedman claimed that Chalabi was actually an Iranian agent and that the intelligence he and his Iraqi National Congress provided was designed to clear the way for a Shiite-dominated government under the influence of Iran.

He also claimed that America's leaders were unaware that Iranian intelligence had organized the Shiites in Iraq after Desert Storm. Chalabi persuaded America's leaders that the Shiites would be happy to see the Americans and be ready to be organized by them. In fact, the Ayatollah Ali Sistani had already organized them.

So, who was this man that America so relied on?

WOULD YOU BUY A USED CAR FROM THIS MAN?

In 2000, Max Singer, the co-founder of the conservative Hudson Institute, summed up the high regard in which Ahmed Chalabi, the leader of the Iraq National Congress, was held:

"Ahmed Chalabi, a person of extraordinary integrity, competence, and stature...He's a rare find."

He came from a prominent family in Iraq. He spoke excellent English. He had spent his younger days at boarding school in England, after which he then spent several years studying in America. He earned an undergraduate and a master's degree in mathematics from M.I.T. He earned a PhD in mathematics from the University of Chicago in a branch of geometry known as knot theory.

Most significantly, he had used his time in the United States to study American politics. After completing his degree in Chicago, he returned to the Middle East and became a math professor at the American University in Beirut.

His first business experience was in the banking business in Jordan. In 1992—years before his neocon friends in America embraced him—the Jordanian banking authorities closed his bank. That year, he was sentenced in absentia to 22 years of hard labor on 31 charges of embezzlement, theft, misuse of depositor funds, and speculation with the Jordanian dinar. The Jordanian Central Bank governor, Mohammed Said Nabulsi, commented:

"Chalabi was one of the most notorious crooks in the history of the Middle East."

In the early 1990s, he became close to Richard Perle, who was an assistant secretary of defense in the Reagan administration. In 1992, in the wake of the first Gulf War, he founded the Iraqi National Congress, an organization of Iraqi opposition groups in exile.

By the mid-1990s, he attended conferences on a post-Hussein Iraq organized by Perle and sponsored by the American Enterprise Institute. It was here that he first met a group of neoconservative and conservative intellectuals who had served in the administrations of Ronald Reagan and George H. W. Bush. These included Dick Cheney, Donald Rumsfeld, and Paul Wolfowitz. By 1993, Ahmed Chalabi was receiving CIA funding for providing intelligence on Iraq.

Robert Baer, a veteran case officer in the CIA's Directorate of Operations in the Middle East, commented on the quality of the intelligence Mr. Chalabi was providing:

> *"He was reporting no intel; it was total trash. The I.N.C.'s intelligence was so bad, we weren't even sending it in."*

When the CIA tried to check Mr. Chalabi's assertions about troop movement or palace plans, Robert Baer said:

> *"There was no detail, no sourcing—you couldn't see it on a satellite."*

Pat Lang, who headed counterterrorism in the Middle East and South Asia for eight years at the Defense Intelligence Agency, had this opinion about Mr. Chalabi:

> *"He's a fake, one of the greatest frauds ever perpetrated on the American people."*

As for Mr. Chalabi's capacity to head a new government in Iraq, Robert Baer offered this opinion:

> *"If we pulled out he wouldn't last two hours."*

Despite this, his Iraq National Congress received covert funding from the CIA and about $33 million from the State Department during the 1990s. This funding was cut off after he fell out of favor with the CIA and the State Department. Undaunted, the Pentagon stepped in. It paid him $340,000 a month for providing intelligence in the period preceding the war. It only stopped paying him after the war when it became apparent that the information he provided was largely false. Until then, however, the vice president and Pentagon continued to see him as a future ruler of a friendly Iraq. They saw him as an Americanized Iraqi who understood Arab politics and how to talk to Arab leaders. Max Singer wrote:

> *"He has such a unique degree of Iraqi support, despite the strong and well-funded efforts of the State Department and the CIA to find and promote an alternative leadership, because Iraqis recognize his integrity, loyalty, and ability."*

What might have been clear to Mr. Singer was not that clear to many others who did not believe that Iraqis held him in esteem. This was particularly the case regarding the claim that Ahmed Chalabi had widespread support among *all* Iraqis, not just the Shiite community. Although his followers claimed he had support amongst the Sunni, Kurd, and other minorities, there was no evidence of this support. To the contrary, most evidence appeared to support the position that he was not highly regarded by these groups. Mr. Chalabi himself was unconcerned by the skeptics. *He had already won over President Bush's most trusted and loyal advisors.*

The 2005 Iraqi election results told the story. Baghdad was where Ahmed Chalabi saw his major support residing. His Iraq National Congress obtained 0.36 percent of the vote in Baghdad. To put this into perspective, out of almost 2.5 million voters in Baghdad, only 8,645 voted for Mr. Chalabi. He fared no better in the Shiite city of Basra, where he obtained an equally dismal 0.34 percent of the vote. In the violent Sunni province of Anbar, a mere 113 people voted for him.

The election was a personal rebuke for Mr. Chalabi, but not for his former colleagues. The new Iraqi government contained many of his old colleagues, many of them members of the exile alliance he once led. Jalal Talabani was its president. Adil Abdul Mahdi, his boyhood friend, was vice president. Barham Salih, comrade of many years, was deputy prime minister. The people rejected him.

So much for the widespread support he claimed to have among *all* Iraqis and not just the Shiite community.

A PERFECT LEADER OF THE OPPOSITION

Robert Baer, that veteran case officer in the CIA's Directorate of Operations in the Middle East, in describing his first meeting with Ahmed Chalabi in Washington in 1994, wrote that his first impression was that it was difficult to imagine someone less likely to unseat Saddam Hussein. He described Chalabi as looking more like a banker than someone who was going to ride into Baghdad on the top of a tank. He noted that outside Iraq, Chalabi was regarded as a felon. Inside Iraq, he was largely unknown.

Even though the Saddam Hussein regime never appeared to take him seriously, Ahmed Chalabi's neocon allies in Washington did. He had spent more time in London than Baghdad, and, although he had plotted for years to overthrow the regime, Saddam Hussein made no effort to eliminate him. Deputy Prime Minister Tariq Aziz is reported to have told NBC's Tom Brokaw:

> *"You guys can have Chalabi! You can keep feeding him all the prime rib and expensive Scotch. He doesn't know anyone here. He hasn't been to Iraq in twenty-five years."*

THE GOVERNMENT'S POSITION ON WMD—BEFORE CHALABI

Prior to September 11, neither Secretary of State Colin Powell nor National Security Advisor Condoleezza Rice offered any hint that the Bush administration regarded Saddam Hussein as posing any imminent threat against the United States.

As for Saddam Hussein's military capability, the impression conveyed by the Bush administration at that time was that Saddam Hussein was under control. They even noted that, far from representing a destabilizing influence in the area, *his military capability was actually degrading.*

On February 24, 2001, at a news conference in Cairo, Egypt—less than six months before the September 11 attacks—the secretary of state was asked about Saddam Hussein's military power:

> *"He has not developed any significant capability with respect to weapons of mass destruction. He is unable to project conventional power against his neighbors. So in ef-*

*fect, our policies have strengthened the se-
curity of the neighbors of Iraq."*

He went further, however. He said: "he threatens not the
United States." This had to have been bad news for Ahmed
Chalabi, but worse was to follow. A few months later, on May
15, 2001, Secretary Powell testified before the Foreign Operations, Export Financing and Related Programs Subcom-
mittee of the Senate Appropriations Committee:

> *"The Iraqi regime militarily remains fairly
> weak. It doesn't have the capacity it had 10
> or 12 years ago. It has been contained. And
> even though we have no doubt in our mind
> that the Iraqi regime is pursuing programs
> to develop weapons of mass destruction—
> chemical, biological and nuclear—I think
> the best intelligence estimates suggest that
> they have not been terribly successful."*

In an interview on CNN on July 29, 2001—six weeks before the attacks, Ms Rice suggested that Saddam Hussein
was under control:

> *"But in terms of Saddam Hussein being there,
> let's remember that his country is divided,
> in effect. He does not control the northern
> part of his country. We are able to keep arms
> from him. His military forces have not been
> rebuilt."*

Despite this, less than two months later, on September 17,
2001—six days after the attacks on New York and Washington—something changed. President Bush signed a directive
ordering the Pentagon to begin preparing military options
for the invasion of Iraq. *This was without any evidence of a
connection between Iraq and the September 11 attacks—or
without any evidence of a connection between Saddam Hussein and Osama bin Laden or Al Qaeda.*

What had suddenly prompted President Bush to call
upon the Pentagon to start preparations for war against
Iraq? What had suddenly prompted the Bush administration to start talking about the growing threat of Saddam's
weapons of mass destruction?

Presumably, there had to have been new intelligence that had emerged over the past few months that revealed an imminent threat posed by Iraq. *There could be no other conclusion*—unless Secretary of State Powell and National Security Advisor Rice were each out of the loop, which was unlikely. It now seems clear that the new source of intelligence was none other than Ahmed Chalabi and his friends.

He knew he was holding all the cards. The Bush administration had no way to confirm what he was telling it. He knew how weak the administration's intelligence capacities were in the region. In fact, this was precisely why it was paying him to provide them with information. As CIA agent Robert Baer wrote in *See No Evil*, the CIA apparently didn't have a single source in Iraq or in neighboring countries.

So, with nobody on the ground in Iraq to provide vital intelligence, Ahmed Chalabi stepped forward. He claimed his sources had penetrated Saddam Hussein's inner circle. The Bush administration enthusiastically embraced and accepted his offer—and paid him handsomely for doing so. It was willing to take the chance that he would be honest with it.

HIS MANIPULATION OF THE MEDIA

He disseminated the "evidence" of those weapons of mass destruction brilliantly. He repeated the lies until he knew they would eventually be believed. His "evidence" was showing up in foreign intelligence agencies and in the press around the world. One former United States intelligence official is reported as saying:

> *"We had a lot of sources, but it was all coming from the same pot. They were all INC guys. And none of them panned out."*

He used the print media brilliantly. Again, he used the power of repetition. On June 26, 2002, for example, Entifadh Qanbar, an INC official, sent a memo to the Senate Appropriations Committee. He revealed 108 English language news stories that appeared between October 2001 and May 2002 that relayed INC information collected from "defectors, reports, and raw intelligence" about Iraq. Everyone believed that because the stories were being so widely disseminated, they had to be true. *Newsweek* offered details about how he manipulated the press and foreign intelligence agencies. It reported how he began coming up with Iraqi defectors who told reporters stories of Saddam working with terrorists and stockpiling weapons of mass destruction. Chalabi would then pass on the defectors to American intelligence agencies.

In December 2001, for example, Chalabi produced a defector who told the *New York Times* that he had seen biological and nuclear-weapons labs hidden around Baghdad, including one underneath a hospital. The defector later became a source for the Defense Intelligence Agency.

To *Vanity Fair*, Chalabi peddled another defector, a supposed former general in the Iraqi secret police, who told of terrorists in training, practicing to hijack passenger aircraft at a secret base near Baghdad. (The defector, Abu Zeinab, was dismissed by the CIA as a "bullsh----er," according to an intelligence source. He then went back to the CIA and was again rejected.)

He also produced for the German intelligence agency a source code named "Curveball" who told of Saddam's building mobile bioweapons labs. He then sent in another defector to the Defense Intelligence Agency to corroborate Curveball's information. So what did the DIA think about all of this? They labeled this defector a "fabricator" and attached a warning notice to his report. Then, as only Monty Python's writers could have imagined, access to the notice was so highly restricted that other intelligence officials never saw it. As a result, both defectors' reports—which were judged by the DIA to be pure fiction—actually worked their way into official pronouncements that became part of the Bush administration's building case for war. To put the cherry firmly atop the cake, Secretary of State Powell actually relied on these discredited defectors' reports.

These claims of the existence of mobile labs would offer a window into how Mr. Chalabi plied his trade. Scott Ritter, a former weapons inspector for the United Nations, knew Ahmed Chalabi. In 1998, Mr. Ritter was working as a liaison for the U.N. program. At the time, the United Nations had been unable to account for a number of suspected Iraqi weapons—and U.N. inspectors had exhausted other sources of intelligence. Mr. Chalabi had offered to help. He again claimed to have operatives who had penetrated Saddam's circle.

On January 27, 1998, Mr. Ritter met with Mr. Chalabi in London. At their meeting, Mr. Ritter admitted making a mistake:

> "I should have asked him what he could give me. Instead, I let him ask me, 'What do you need?' "

The result of his mistake was to identify all of the United Nations' gaps in intelligence. Over the next several hours, Mr. Ritter outlined most of the U.N. inspectors' capabilities and theories, telling Mr. Chalabi how they had searched unsuccessfully for underground bunkers with ground-penetrating radar. He also told him of his suspicion that Saddam may have had mobile laboratories. Mr. Ritter then made an admission:

> "We made that up! We told Chalabi, and, lo and behold, he's fabricated a source for the mobile labs."

In the months before the invasion of Iraq, the Bush administration referred constantly to these mobile weapons laboratories. On February 5, 2003, Secretary of State Colin Powell addressed the United Nations and spoke of an unnamed eyewitness who had supplied "firsthand descriptions of biological weapons factories on wheels and rails."

Ahmed Chalabi understood the tension between the Pentagon and the CIA, and he exploited it. The Pentagon perceived the CIA as being overly conservative. Mr. Chalabi therefore fed the Pentagon's hunger for raw intelligence that might support its position. Again, *Newsweek* reported how Chalabi fed the neocons' hunger for raw intelligence. For this, he found a receptive audience in the office of the vice president and at the Pentagon. I. Lewis (Scooter) Libby, the Vice President's chief of staff, and Wolfowitz were eagerly looking for links between Saddam and Al Qaeda.

In this regard, and to provide more weight to that raw intelligence, Mr. Chalabi gave his neocon allies what they so desperately wanted. He offered a story about a secret meeting in Prague between Muhammad Atta, the leader of the 9/11 hijackers, and a high-level Iraqi intelligence officer. This story was repeated for years by Vice President Cheney and his neocon allies. This was despite the fact that we know from photographic evidence that, at the very date and time of that alleged meeting, Atta was in the United States.

Was the vice president scammed by Chalabi or did he knowingly promote a story he knew to be false?

IRANIAN FINGERPRINTS

Ted Galen Carpenter, the vice president for defense and foreign policy studies at the Cato Institute, asked this haunting question:

> *"Is it possible that Iran used Chalabi and his organization to lure the United States into invading and occupying Iraq?"*

He then listed three motives for Iran doing this. The first was a historical hatred of Saddam Hussein:

> *"First, Iranians regarded Saddam Hussein as more than just an adversary; they viewed him with the same kind of fear and loathing that Russians in the 1940s viewed Adolf Hitler. Saddam had invaded and ravaged their country in a war that lasted nearly a decade, and he had used chemical weapons against Iranian troops and possibly Iranian civilians. Washington did Iran a gigantic favor by eliminating a man that Iranians regarded as a demonic enemy."*

The second was the elimination of Iran's only strategic counterweight in the region:

> "A united Iraq was the principal obstacle to Iranian preeminence. A U.S. occupation of Iraq (especially the disbanding of the Iraqi army, which Chalabi strongly advocated) significantly advanced Iran's interests. The possible destabilization of Iraq arising from the elimination of a strong central government in Baghdad—and the possible emergence of a friendly, Shiite-led successor government—was a potential bonus for Tehran."

The third was Iran's need for the United States to be distracted:

> "Finally, the Islamist regime had an incentive to distract the United States. Washington was beginning to pay an extensive amount of attention to Tehran's nuclear ambitions. Tying down the U.S. military in a nation-building quagmire in Iraq might reduce the likelihood that Washington would be able to take preemptive action against Iran. Notably, the loose talk in some hawkish American circles about the Iraq war being merely the first stage of a campaign of forcible regime change throughout the Middle East has subsided greatly as the difficulties of the Iraq occupation have mounted."

The idea of Iran being an active player in persuading the United States to launch its war was indeed haunting. Maybe the United States knew the role it played—then again, maybe not. And maybe the United States used Iran and Ahmed Chalabi to justify a war it wanted. Maybe the United States was not fooled at all—then again, maybe it was...

However one looks at this, it is impossible to escape the irony. Like the United States, Iran was only too happy to see Saddam Hussein deposed. Like the United States, Iran wanted him to be replaced by its man in Baghdad. So, here were two competing nations that, as far as the world was concerned, hated and mistrusted each other, each wanting the same result: Saddam Hussein deposed and replaced by its man in Baghdad.

Leaping from the pages of a John le Carré novel, Ahmed Chalabi would offer each nation the prospect of being its man in Baghdad. *Did either nation understand this?* Certainly Iran did. And just imagine its glee at the prospect of the United States doing the dirty and expensive work of deposing Saddam Hussein and then rebuilding Iraq. This must have seemed too good to be true. Whether the United States suspected any of this remains an open question.

It now appears that, just as the CIA had previously offered Ahmed Chalabi its help, Iran too appears to have offered him its help. It appears that they worked together to create and distribute any misinformation they thought would feed new urgency in the United States to intervene militarily in Iraq. His Iraq National Congress would effectively become a front for the Iranians. It was the view of many respected commentators and analysts that they succeeded brilliantly together.

A year after the war started, on May 25, 2004, the London newspaper the *Guardian* reported:

> " 'It's pretty clear that Iranians had us for breakfast, lunch and dinner.' said an intelligence source in Washington yesterday. 'Iranian intelligence has been manipulating the US for several years through Chalabi.' "

Larry Johnson, a former senior counterterrorist official at the State Department, said: "When the story ultimately comes out we'll see that Iran has run one of the most masterful intelligence operations in history. They persuaded the U.S. and Britain to dispose of its greatest enemy.' "

There was one example offered of Iran's fingerprints on Mr. Chalabi's intelligence offerings. Early in 1995, a team of inspectors from the International Atomic Energy Agency found a 20 page document that apparently originated from inside "Group 4," the department that had been responsible for designing the Iraqi bomb. The question the team faced was whether or not this document was authentic.

They found that the stationary, page numbering, and stamps all appeared authentic. It appeared to be a progress report on the results of their continued work after 1991. It referred to experiments on the casting of the hemispheres (i.e. the bomb core of enriched uranium). There were some crude diagrams attached. The document appeared to be damning evidence that Iraq was successfully pursuing a nuclear bomb in defiance of sanctions and the inspectors.

There were just a few slight problems with the document: It appeared to the experts that the document was originally written in Farsi by an Iranian scientist and then translated into Arabic. Some of the technical descriptions in the document used terms that would only be used by an Iranian. For example, for the term "dome," the document used "Qubba," which was an Iranian term. Instead, it should have used the term "hemisphere" which was "Nisuf Kura" in Arabic.'

Tom Killeen, of the Iraq Nuclear Verification Office at IAEA headquarters in Vienna, effectively confirmed this account of the incident.

> "After a thorough investigation the documents were determined not to be authentic and the matter was closed."

When asked how the International Atomic Energy Agency (IAEA) had obtained the document, it was disclosed that Khidir Hamza had provided it. Hamza was the former member of the Iraqi weapons team who briefly headed the bomb design group. His effectiveness as a nuclear engineer was limited by his fear of radioactivity and refusal to enter any building where experiments were underway.

It turns out that the year before the document was presented to the IAEA, Mr. Hamza started working with none other than Ahmed Chalabi. Despite the fact that Mr. Hamza's document was totally discredited, he and Ahmed Chalabi's representative were briefing Deputy Defense Secretary Paul

Wolfowitz on details of Saddam Hussein's nuclear program. We now know that program did not exist.

Pat Lang remarked on the quality of the work of the Iranian intelligence agencies. He said he had been told by colleagues in the intelligence community that Mr. Chalabi's program to provide information about weapons of mass destruction and insurgents was effectively an Iranian intelligence operation. He said:

> "They [the Iranians] knew exactly what we were up to. [It was] one of the most sophisticated and successful intelligence operations in history. I'm a spook. I appreciate good work. This was good work."

It seemed that many in America's intelligence agencies saw those Iranian fingerprints. It is hard to imagine that those in the Bush administration did not.

A PARTING THOUGHT

Did Ahmed Chalabi really scam a nation's finest and brightest? Can you be scammed if you still do the deal even though you have recognized the lies the scammer is selling? Did the Bush administration recognize the lies? If not, should it have?

And who used whom? Did the Bush administration use him to further its own agenda—or was it used? When the administration repeated his lies to sell the war—without acknowledging its own reservations—did it become the scammer?

Whatever the answers, what about the principles of the Duck School? And what about Nelson Mandela's lessons?

The lessons learned only served to confirm what we already knew about the need to ask:

- If lousy questions were asked, if facts were ignored and common sense was abandoned, lousy decisions would follow.

- If you start the decision-making process with the decision you want to reach—and then start asking questions to justify the decision you have already made—this will also lead to lousy decisions.

It is difficult to avoid the conclusion that the Bush administration also ignored the famous teachings of the Duck School. For example:

- Choose reality—the way things are, not the way you want them to be.

- If you smell something unusual in the air, don't turn away—just breathe deeply and brace yourself.

- Start with an open mind—free yourself from your assumptions.

- Understand that nothing is ever quite what it seems.

- Those apparently clear and simple choices are rarely clear and simple.

- Be honest with yourself.

- Remember that, for every plausible explanation, there might be another plausible explanation that might lead us in another direction.

As with the previous chapter about Enron, we began by asking some questions. We asked what might have happened had anyone studied Ahmed Chalabi in the same way Nelson Mandela studied the Afrikaners, their culture, and their leaders. And had someone studied him, what would he have found? Well, some had studied him...

It is difficult not to conclude that those who embraced him were really akin to those who encountered that person in a subway tunnel offering fake Rolexes. They desperately needed to show someone that they had something that looked like a Rolex. It didn't matter to them that they knew or suspected that what they had bought was fake...

ELEVEN

BERNARD MADOFF

"Judge not the horse by the saddle."

"Take a second look. It costs you nothing."

Chinese proverbs

A s Jeff Skilling was selling Wall Street his broadband illusion, Enron's stock soared, but, as reality reared its ugly head, the stock corrected itself. Because the market is reactive to news and rumors, it is often unpredictable—unless, of course, we are clairvoyant.

If Enron, WorldCom, or HealthSouth stock were in your portfolio prior to their implosions, you were in good shape—and in good company. They were the darlings of Wall Street. You would have needed a crystal ball to avoid your portfolio going into the tank when those companies imploded. Bernard Madoff apparently had a crystal ball.

If you were holding stock whose fortunes were tied to the 1997 Asian currency crisis and the 1998 Russian debt crisis, you would have needed that same crystal ball to have anticipated those crises. Then there was the long-term management crisis, to say nothing of the subprime mortgage crisis. The crystal ball you would need would be one similar to Bernard Madoff's.

To believe Bernard Madoff, his crystal ball remained in fine shape for fourteen and a half years. Despite the events that gave rise to such market volatility over those fourteen and a half years, he was able to avoid them all and save the value of his portfolios.

During this time, there was one certainty that emerged in the financial markets: *funds managed by Bernard Madoff experienced no volatility of any kind.*

Not only was the performance of his portfolios consistent for all of these years, he consistently generated 12 percent per annum for those whose funds he managed. And this was after the hedge funds had taken an average of 4 percent in fees. Bernard Madoff, therefore, had to generate *at least a 16 percent return* consistently over fourteen and a half years to get his investors their 12 percent average annual return. *There was a strong whiff of too-good-to-be-true in the kingdom of Madoff.*

This was not an after-the-fact expression of wisdom. Skepticism was first voiced in two articles that were published in May 2001—a decade before he was sentenced to serve 150 years in prison. On May 7, 2001, Erin E. Arvedlund wrote an article in *Barrons* entitled "Don't Ask, Don't Tell—*Bernie Madoff is so secretive, he even asks investors to keep mum.*" In the May 2001 edition of *MAR/Hedge (RIP)*, Michael Acrant wrote an article entitled: "Madoff tops charts; skeptics ask how." Over the next nine years, many on Wall Street shared this skepticism. Many suspected fraud. Many could not believe the SEC had not yet stepped in. One was Harry Markopolos.

The Duck School would be proud of Harry Markopolos, a mild-mannered fraud investigator from Boston. He is a derivatives expert who has either traded or assisted in the trading of several billion dollars in option strategies for hedge funds and institutional clients. He has also had experience managing split-strike conversion products using both index options and individual stock options. As he has somewhat immodestly written of himself:

> *"Very few people in the world have the mathematical background needed to manage these types of products, but I am one of them."*

In 1990, he was working for a Boston investment firm when the head of the firm told him about a huge unregistered hedge fund run by Bernard Madoff. The fund was producing simply incredible returns based, in part, on the very split-strike conversion products with which Harry was quite familiar. He was asked to reverse-engineer Madoff's trading strategy so that the firm could duplicate Madoff's revenue streams. *He could not.*

When asked in a *60 Minutes* interview how long it took him to figure out that something was wrong, Harry Markopolos said:

> *"It took me five minutes to know that it was a fraud. It took me another almost four hours of mathematical modeling to prove it was a fraud."*

One question was whether or not one needed to be a math genius to know something was wrong. Clearly there were enough warning signs to put anyone on notice that all was not quite kosher in the Bernard Madoff kingdom. *His results were literally too good to be true.* Harry Markopolos put it this way:

> *"As we know, markets go up and down, and his only went up. He had very few down months. Only 4 percent of the months were*

down months. And that would be the equiva-
lent to a baseball player in the major leagues
batting .960 for a year. Clearly impossible.
You would suspect cheating immediately."

Harry Markopolos discovered that, despite these phenomenal results, none of the major firms on Wall Street had
money with him. Harry had traded with some of the largest
equity derivative firms in the world. *He could not find any-*
one who had traded with Bernard Madoff.

There were also a few logical problems he found that
anyone conducting any due diligence could have found: for
example, for Madoff to execute the trading strategy he said
he was using, he would have had to buy more options on the
Chicago Board Options Exchange than actually existed.

To add to this particular problem that Bernard Madoff
faced was the fact that, if he was using the OTC OEX index
put options every month, as he claimed, the Wall Street
firms on the other side of those trades would have had to
be laying off a significant portion of that risk. But there is no
evidence that they ever did—and we now know why. *Ber-*
nard Madoff never conducted a single trade in fourteen and
a half years.

What made this scam challenging to detect for those
unfamiliar with the Duck School was that the players surrounding Madoff were all distinguished and quite respectable, as was he. One of the teachings of the Duck School is
that it doesn't matter how distinguished and well respected
the messenger is who tells us that the duck is a swan. Until
we are satisfied the duck is a swan, it will remain a duck.
Fortunately, Harry Markopolos understood this.

What made this even more difficult to detect was that his
scam was the classic "affinity scam." This is a scam in which
the scammer preys on groups of which he is a member. Because he is a member, others in the group are more likely
to trust him. After all, he was one of them. And once prominent, respected, wealthy, and well-connected members of
the group started to do business with him, others followed

suit. Their logic was that if these prominent folks were satisfied, that was good enough for them.

So, because he was Jewish, he focused initially on the Jewish community in the United States and overseas. He soon
attracted some of the most prominent in the Jewish community. These included, for example, the charitable founda-
tions of Nobel Laureate Elie Wiesel, movie director Steven
Spielberg, Jeffrey Katzenberg, Sen. Frank Lautenberg of
New Jersey, and New York publisher Mortimer Zuckerman.

He then became an equal-opportunity scammer extending his reach beyond the Jewish community to thousands
of victims that included banks, financial institutions, insur-
ance companies, and individuals around the world.

HIS BUSINESS MODEL

Bernard Madoff managed what was apparently one of the
largest hedge funds with estimated assets of perhaps $60
billion. What he created was not his own hedge fund. Instead, what he created was a private label hedge fund that
was broadly set up as follows:

- He would allow third-party Fund-of-Funds to operate a private label hedge fund under their own
  name, but with him managing the funds.

- In return for the equity funding they provided
  from their customers, he managed the funds *as
  their agent* using his trading strategy. The returns
  from this strategy would flow through to the third-
  party hedge funds and their investors.

- The third-party hedge funds would charge their
  investors for their services. The normal rate in the
  industry was a management fee of 1 percent and
  a profit share of 10 percent. Madoff allowed them
  to charge a management fee of 1 percent and 20
  percent of profits. According to Harry Markopolos's calculations, the total fees to the third-party
  hedge funds represented 4 percent of the investment made.

- He claimed he would earn his fees by charging commissions on all of the trades done in their accounts.

- In return for managing their clients' funds, these third-party firms were not allowed to name Bernard Madoff as the actual manager either in their performance summaries or marketing literature. This was despite the fact that his performance was phenomenal.

His positioning

Madoff positioned himself brilliantly. He claimed he only managed the money of a small and exclusive group. Becoming his customer was treated as akin to a membership in an elite club.

Once accepted as a client, he followed standard account opening procedures. Customers then gave him all investment authority over their funds. They retained only the authority to deposit cash and request withdrawals. All other rights associated with their accounts were ceded to him.

Next steps

He struck deals with large investment firms that provided him with billions of dollars of their clients' money to manage. In return, he agreed to allow these firms to charge a fortune in annual fees. For example, the largest of these groups was the Fairfield Greenwich Group. It made hundreds of millions of dollars each year from its relationship with Madoff.

The money he managed for these third-party firms averaged 12 percent per annum for the investors for years. In fact, over fourteen and a half years—or 174 months—he showed only seven down months, with his largest monthly loss being -0.55 percent.

How he claimed he did it

Madoff attributed his unusual success to the "split-strike conversion strategy." Under this strategy:

- He claimed he invested in a "basket" of Standard & Poor's 100 Index ("S&P 100 Index") common stock. He would make money for his investors by buying stock before price increases and selling after the price increases. He claimed that, several times a year, he moved investor funds entirely "out of the market" to invest in United States Treasury Bills, money market funds, and cash reserves until the next trading opportunity. This occurred at the end of each quarter. This allowed Madoff to avoid disclosure of the stock in the basket required by SEC Form 13F.

- He then claimed he devised a hedging strategy to buy and sell S&P 100 Index option contracts corresponding to the stocks in the baskets. This allowed him to appear to manage the downside risk associated with inevitable price fluctuations of the stock in the baskets.

AN UGLY DUCK OR A BEAUTIFUL SWAN?

Bernard Madoff was selling his ugly duck to the financial community as a beautiful swan. Many of the most prominent Wall Street firms and financial experts around the world did not buy this. Some did.

On November 7, 2005, Harry Markopolos submitted to the SEC a seventeen-page document that outlined his opinion regarding Bernard Madoff's activities. It was ignored. In total, he made over five written submissions between May 2000 and April 2008. He argued that what Bernard Madoff was selling was a scam. In his November 7, 2005, document, he raised the following questions to the SEC:

A PROBLEM WITH THE MATH

If Bernard Madoff allowed the third party hedge fund to charge 4 percent, and if his annual return to the investor was 12 percent per annum, this required him to provide a return of 16 percent consistently year after year. *How could anyone generate so high a return so consistently over fourteen and a half years?* It defied common sense.

THE NUMBER OF AVAILABLE CONTRACTS

Based on the third-party hedge funds marketing literature, *there were not enough index option put contracts available* to implement Bernard Madoff's hedging strategy. This was a fatal flaw to his model and provided yet further cause to believe that the 12 percent annual average return was impossible to attain over many years. This alone should put the world on notice that the smell in the air was growing worse.

THE COST OF THESE CONTRACTS

These put options *are extremely expensive and could cost in excess of 8 percent.* Moreover, their cost would have been even higher than 8 percent during past stock market crises. This would make the consistent 12 percent return even more problematic—if not impossible. This too was worthy of further inquiry.

ENRON, WORLDCOM, HEALTHSOUTH

Bernard Madoff's strategy was to own only index put options and not single stock put options. This meant that *if one or more stocks in the basket were to collapse, the index put option would offer little protection* and the value of the whole basket would drop. Considering that Bernard Madoff never had more than a one-month loss in a row—and even then no more than one-half of 1 percent—you have to assume that no Enron, WorldCom, or HealthSouth stock ever filled his baskets at the time of their totally unexpected implosions.

HOW COULD HE BE SO MUCH BETTER?

Could Bernard Madoff have had perfect knowledge of the market's direction because of his access to customer order flow into his broker-dealer business? Considering he posted monthly losses only once every few years and that every major Wall Street firm does significantly worse, *how could he be so much better than everyone else?* This seemed highly unlikely.

WHY WERE HIS FEES APPARENTLY SO LOW?

Why would Bernard Madoff charge only undisclosed commissions when he could have earned standard hedge fund fees? These were 1 percent of the amount being managed plus a fee of 20 percent of the profits. This represented 4 percent of the amount being managed.

WHY THE SECRECY?

Why would Bernard Madoff not want even his investors to know that he was managing their money? Was it to avoid the attention of the regulatory agencies? And why weren't investors entitled to know who was managing their money? Something did not smell well...

WHAT ELSE WAS HIDDEN?

If people invested because of Bernard Madoff, but knew, for example, that the marketing material of the fund into which they were investing had failed to

disclose who was managing their portfolio, *what were the chances of other
pertinent facts also not being disclosed?*
And how could anyone trust who those
who were ostensibly managing the
fund?

What is remarkable about these questions is how many
were so obvious. The questions represented nothing more
than a Duck School inquiry.

SO, WHAT ACTUALLY HAPPENED?

In his March 1, 2010, ruling, United States Bankruptcy
Judge Burton R. Lifland set forth what happened:

> *"Rather than engage in legitimate trading
> activity, Madoff used customer funds to sup-
> port operations and fulfill other investors'
> requests for distributions of profits to per-
> petuate his Ponzi scheme. Thus, any pay-
> ment of 'profit' to a [Madoff] customer came
> from another [Madoff] customer's initial in-
> vestment."*

He then addressed the customers' account statements
and the collapse of the scheme:

> *"Given that in Madoff's fictional world no
> trades were actually executed, customer
> funds were never exposed to the uncertain-
> ties of price fluctuation, and account state-
> ments bore no relation to the United States
> securities market at any time. As such, the
> only verifiable transactions were the cus-
> tomers' cash deposits into, and cash with-
> drawals out of, their particular accounts.
> Ultimately, customer requests for payments
> exceeded the inflow of new investments, re-
> sulting in the Ponzi scheme's inevitable col-
> lapse."*

THE POWER OF COMMON SENSE: THE DUCK SCHOOL

What Nelson Mandela and the Duck School teach is to focus on what we are being sold—and not on the messenger.

APPLYING THE SUBWAY TEST:

A guy in a subway approaches you and offers to manage your money.

He tells you that he has managed other folks' money for over ten years, yielding them an average of 12 percent per annum without ever showing two consecutive months of losses.

And even then, he tells you, the losses have never been more than a half of 1 percent even through every single financial crisis and major company implosions over the past ten years.

The only condition to him handling your money is that you tell nobody that he is handling it.

Assume too that none of Wall Street's finest and brightest firms have ever come close to matching these results and that many have expressed skepticism about our man's results.

Finally, assume the size of the transactions he claims he does on a regular basis are so large that major Wall Street firms would necessarily have to be involved in the other side of these transactions. Assume you can find no evidence of them ever being involved in any such transactions.

QUESTION:

Would you *even consider* giving this guy your money to manage?

And why would your answer be any different if the guy you met was a former chairman of the board of directors of NASDAQ?

This example assumes you meeting the money manager directly and he wants to manage your money. How is the situation any different if you are a financial institution responsible for investing your clients' funds?

ASSUME THE FOLLOWING SCENARIO:

You are a financial institution with hundreds of clients looking to you for investment advice. They want you to handle the investment of their money.

The same guy in the subway approaches your financial institution with essentially the same deal.

The only tweak is this: He says that, if you give him your clients' money to manage, and if you set up a private label hedge fund for this purpose, he will allow you to charge your clients and receive a fee equal to 4 percent of the amount he will manage. And he will do all of the work. You will collect the fees.

The only condition is that you tell nobody that he is managing your clients' money and that his name is not to appear on any of your marketing literature or reports.

Assume too that none of Wall Street's finest and brightest firms have ever come close to matching these results and that many have expressed skepticism about our man's results.

Finally, assume the size of the transactions he claims he does are so large that major Wall Street firms would necessarily have to be involved in the other side of these transactions. Assume you can find no evidence of them ever being involved in any such transactions.

QUESTION:

Would you *even consider* giving this guy your money to manage?

And why would your answer be any different if the guy you met was a former chairman of the board of directors of NASDAQ?

Finally, could Bernard Madoff's scam ever have succeeded without everyone looking the other way? And how could those who chose to look the other way and who refused to ask questions now claim to be victims of a scheme so implausible as to defy belief?

CHAPTER TWELVE

THE EMPEROR'S NEW CLOTHES

"A child of five would understand this.
Send someone to fetch me a child of five."

Groucho Marx

Who would have thought that a child's tale written in 1837 would provide some insight about the modern scam? And who would have thought that the same tale might have been a hidden handbook for scammers?

In 1837, Hans Christian Andersen wrote *The Emperor's New Clothes.* His tale was about swindlers who understood the emperor's love of fine clothes. It was about the emperor's advisors, who were afraid to tell him the truth—and how, even when the emperor himself finally realized the truth, he refused to admit his mistake. It is about how they all refused to acknowledge that they were really buying nothing at all.

The tale was also about a small child in a crowd who recognized what the emperor's closest advisors would not recognize, namely, that the magical clothes did not exist. Perhaps this was the child Groucho was looking for.

Hans Christian Andersen's tale has stood the test of time.
It has cast a remarkable light on the modern scam—and
how we make choices. In each of the three adventures we
have discussed, the scammers also sold the emperor something that didn't exist. But, before we are reminded of the
tale, and before we reveal the hidden handbook for scammers that is contained in the story, we need a casting call to
remind ourselves who the players in the tale might be if we
applied it to the Enron, Ahmed Chalabi, and Bernard Madoff
adventures.

A CASTING CALL

As you re-read the tale in the context of the Enron, Ahmed
Chalabi, and Bernard Madoff adventures, imagine the players:

THE EMPEROR AND HIS LOVE OF CLOTHES:

- Enron and its love of meeting quarterly
  earning targets so that its executives
  could become very rich.
- The Bush administration and its love of
  finding evidence of weapons of mass destruction to justify an invasion of Iraq.
- The third-party private label hedge funds
  and their love of receiving huge fees and
  achieving 12 percent annual returns for
  their investors.

THE SWINDLERS:

- Enron's Ken Lay and Jeff Skilling.
- Ahmed Chalabi.
- Bernard Madoff.

THE ILLUSORY MAGIC CLOTH

- *Enron:* illusionary transactions that would make it appear that it was meeting its quarterly targets.

- *Chalabi:* illusionary evidence of weapons of mass destruction.

- *Madoff:* illusionary annual returns of 12 percent.

THE ADVISORS WHO DID NOT WANT TO UPSET THE EMPEROR

- *Enron:* its board members, its lawyers, and Arthur Andersen.

- *Chalabi:* everyone in President Bush's inner circle and the media.

- *Madoff:* everyone in the inner circle of the third-party private-label hedge fund and all of the individual investors' professional advisors.

THE CROWD

- *Enron:* the financial media and analysts.

- *Chalabi:* the media and Congress.

- *Madoff:* the financial media, analysts, and the SEC.

EXAMPLES OF THE CHILD IN THE CROWD

- *Enron:* Bethany McLean and James Chanos.

- *Chalabi:* the CIA and State Department.

- *Madoff:* Harry Markopolos.

The obvious question is whether the emperor in the tale and in each of our adventures is delusional. Does he know that what he is buying doesn't exist—or is he just pretending it exists as a means to an end. In the case of the Enron and Madoff adventures, do the emperors simply want to buy what doesn't exist as a means to get quite rich? In the Chalabi adventure, does the emperor want to buy what doesn't exist simply as an excuse to attack Iraq.

In each adventure, however, can there really be any doubt that each emperor really knew that he was buying nothing?

THE TALE

"Many, many years ago lived an emperor, who thought so much of new clothes that he spent all his money in order to obtain them; his only ambition was to be always well dressed."

Hans Christian Andersen

Two swindlers, who knew about the Emperor's love of clothes, came to his city and quickly made people believe that they were weavers. They claimed they could make the finest clothes imaginable with cloth that had magical qualities. It was invisible, they said, to anyone who was unfit for his office or who was unpardonably stupid.

Word of the magical cloth quickly reached the emperor, who was very wise. He realized that if he was dressed in clothes made from this new magical cloth, he would easily be able to learn who in his empire was unfit for office—and who was clever and who was stupid. He quickly ordered his new suit of clothes. He even paid the swindlers in advance so that they could start work immediately.

The swindlers set up two looms in another part of the city and pretended to be hard at work. They demanded the finest silk and the most expensive gold cloth. And everything they received, they kept for themselves. For days and nights on end, they pretended to work away tirelessly at their empty looms. People in the city could see the candles in their room burning late into the night. As the new clothes had to be nearing completion, excitement grew.

The emperor was growing impatient. He decided to send one of his trusted advisors, an honest old minister, to see how work on the new clothes was progressing.

When the minister visited the swindlers, he saw nothing at all on their looms. The swindlers beckoned him to come closer. They pointed to the looms and asked him to step even closer to admire the wonderful pattern and beautiful colors of the new cloth, which they described in exquisite detail. Try as he might, the old minister could see nothing:

> *"Oh dear," he thought, "can I be so stupid? I should never have thought so, and nobody must know it! Is it possible that I am not fit for my office? No, no, I cannot say that I was unable to see the cloth."*

> *"Now, have you got nothing to say?" said one of the swindlers, while he pretended to be busily weaving.*

> *"Oh, it is very pretty, exceedingly beautiful," replied the old minister looking through his glasses. "What a beautiful pattern, what brilliant colors! I shall tell the emperor that I like the cloth very much."*

The swindlers continued to demand more money, silk, and gold cloth. Again, they continued to pretend to work at the empty looms.

As the emperor grew more impatient, he sent another trusted and wise old counselor to report on the progress of the new clothes. Like the old minister, he looked at the looms, but could see nothing. Again, the swindlers invited him to step closer, and again they explained in the minutest detail the fine pattern and beautiful colors.

> *"Is it not a beautiful piece of cloth?" asked the two swindlers, showing and explaining the magnificent pattern, which, however, did not exist.*

> *"I am not stupid," said the man. "It is therefore my good appointment for which I am not fit. It is very strange, but I must not let anyone know it"; and he praised the cloth, which he did not see, and expressed his joy at the beautiful colors and the fine pattern. "It is very excellent," he said to the emperor.*

*Unable to contain himself, the emperor now need-
ed to see the new clothes himself. He visited the
swindlers with his two advisors who had previously met them.*

> *"Is it not magnificent?" said the two old
> statesmen who had been there before. "Your
> Majesty must admire the colors and the pat-
> tern." And then they pointed to the empty
> looms, for they imagined the others could
> see the cloth.*

*The emperor was uncomfortable. He could not
see anything. Was he stupid? Was he unfit to be
emperor? This was terrible!*

> *"Really," he said, turning to the weavers,
> "your cloth has our most gracious approval"
> and nodding contentedly he looked at the
> empty loom, for he did not like to say that
> he saw nothing.*

*And, of course, none of his other attendants could
see anything at all. Despite this, they all said how
beautiful the new clothes were. Like the emperor,
they too could not admit what they could plainly
see—nothing! In fact, they all advised him to wear
the wonderful new clothes at a great procession
that was soon to take place. The emperor was
delighted and appointed the two swindlers "imperial court weavers." When the new imperial court
weavers later announced that the new clothes
were ready, the emperor and his entourage came
into the hall where the swindlers were waiting.
As the emperor entered, the swindlers held their
arms up as if they were holding the clothes.*

> *"Does it please your Majesty now to gra-
> ciously undress," said the swindlers, "that
> we may assist your Majesty in putting on the
> new suit before the large looking-glass?"*

*The emperor undressed. The swindlers pretended
to dress him in the new clothes—first the trou-
sers, then the coat, then the cloak, one piece after another. They were ecstatic and explained to
the emperor:*

> *"They are all as light as a cobweb, and one
> must feel as if one had nothing at all upon the
> body; but that is just the beauty of them."*

The procession was about to begin.

> *"I am ready," said the emperor. "Does not my suit fit me marvelously?" Then he turned once more to the looking glass, that people should think he admired his garments.*

The chamberlains, who were to carry the train, stretched their hands to the ground as if they lifted up a train, and pretended to hold something in their hands; they did not like people to know that they could not see anything.

As the emperor began his march in the procession under the beautiful canopy, people rushed into the street to see him. Nobody wanted to admit that they could not see his new clothes—for this would have been admission that they were either stupid or unfit for office. So they all admired his new clothes and they all complimented him on how well they fitted him. Never had the emperor's clothes been more admired.

And then from the crowd there was a cry from a small child who couldn't have been more than five years old:

> *"But he has nothing on at all," said a little child at last. "Good heavens! Listen to the voice of an innocent child," said the father, and one whispered to the other what the child had said. "But he has nothing on at all," cried at last the whole people.*

That made a deep impression upon the emperor, for it seemed to him that they were right; but he thought to himself, "Now I must bear up to the end." And the chamberlains walked with still greater dignity, as if they carried the train that did not exist.

THE ADVENTURES

Hans Christian Andersen's tale corresponds diabolically with our three adventures. For example:

THE EMPEROR WANTED TO BELIEVE...

In all three adventures, each emperor really wanted to believe that the nonexistent products existed—even though they each must have had their doubts. And his advisors knew this.

THE SWINDLERS PRETENDED TO CREATE SOMETHING

In all three adventures, the modern scammers each claimed to have created or found something for their particular emperor that didn't exist.

THE SWINDLERS' HUBRIS

In all three adventures, the scammers' hubris intimidated their emperor and his advisors into refusing to admit that he did not see the products.

THE SWINDLERS WERE WELL PAID

Like the weavers, the scammers in our three adventures were all extremely well paid for spinning their nonexistent products.

THE OLD ADVISOR WHO WENT TO INSPECT THE ILLUSORY CLOTH

The scammers assured all the advisors in the three adventures that the nonexistent products were real. The advisors were afraid to admit they saw no products.

THE WEAVERS CONTINUED TO DEMAND MORE MONEY

Like the weavers, the scammers in the three adventures continued to demand money as they were creating their nonexistent product.

THE EMPEROR SENT MORE ADVISORS TO INSPECT THE CLOTH

The emperors in our three adventures also sent other advisors to inspect the nonexistent product. They too could not bring themselves to tell the emperor that the product did not exist.

THE ADVISORS WERE WORRIED ABOUT THEIR JOBS

The advisors in our three adventures, like the tale's emperor's advisors, were all worried to deliver news to their emperors that the products didn't exist. They worried that they would upset the emperors and would lose their jobs. The scammers repeated the lies so often that it became increasingly difficult for the advisors to admit there was nothing there.

THE EMPEROR NEEDED TO SEE THE CLOTH HIMSELF

The emperors in our three adventures also wanted to see the products for themselves. When they went to see them, their advisors and the scammers assured them the products were there, even though the emperor too could not see them. He too did not want to admit that they were not there—or maybe he didn't care.

THE EMPEROR SHOWS HIS NEW CLOTHES TO THE CROWD

The emperors in our three adventures also displayed their nonexistent product to the crowd that included all the major media outlets. Nobody in the crowd would admit that the products didn't exist.

THE EMPEROR AND HIS ADVISORS ALL KNEW...

The emperors and their advisors in our three adventures all knew the products didn't exist. They were not scammed.

THE CHILD IN THE CROWD

It took a child in the crowd to point out that the products didn't exist, but by then it was too late. The damage was done.

THE SUBWAY TEST REVISITED

The swindlers and the scammers played the role of the guy in the subway with a fake Rolex to sell. The emperor and his advisors all knew what they were buying, but still bought it. The fact that nobody had the courage to admit that what they bought was fake didn't change the fact that they knew it was fake. And the fact that they may not have trusted themselves to see what was in front of them doesn't change the fact that they suspected that what they were asked to buy was fake.

THE HIDDEN HANDBOOK FOR SCAMMERS

So, what about that imaginary scammers' handbook—the gem that lay buried deep within Hans Christian Andersen's tale? What advice and guidance would it offer aspiring scammers about the art of the scam? And what warnings would it offer us that a scam might be brewing? Whether or not scammers over the years had read Hans Christian Andersen's tale, they all seemed to follow the advice contained in that imaginary handbook.

The first part of the handbook would reveal the art of the scam itself—ten gems of advice for generations of scammers, both born and yet unborn. The second part would focus on those the scammers should target.

The Handbook: Part One

THE SIZE OF THE LIE:

> *Being caught in any lie is always bad, so why bother with a small lie? The larger the lie, the more tempting it will be and the more likely it will be believed. The emperor is greedy. His greed is your best friend.*

THE TARGET OF THE LIE:

The target of the lie must be the emperor or someone so close to him that he will follow his advice. There is no point in targeting anyone else.

DON'T FORGET THE FLUFF:

Offer the emperor much more than he actually wants—more than he can imagine. If the emperor loves clothes, offer him clothes with magical qualities. If he loves money, offer him more than he can possibly imagine. If he wants evidence of weapons of mass destruction, don't hold back.

FOCUS ON THE ADVISORS:

To win over the emperor, first win over his advisors. All advisors worry about losing their jobs—so remind them.

THE FALSE LOYALTY:

Concentrate on those advisors with false loyalty—those who will offer the emperor only the advice he wants. Remind them what he wants.

REPEAT THE LIES:

The more lies are repeated, the more they will be believed. They will soon assume a life of their own. Nobody wants to be out there on his own. As you repeat them, so will others. Soon, by repetition the lies will become self-evident truths.

FRAME THE QUESTIONS AS SIMPLE CHOICES:

Always seize the initiative by framing the question carefully. Then offer simple and obvious answers to your questions.

ALWAYS OFFER COVER:

People never want to admit a mistake, so always offer them the cover to avoid having to admit a mistake. The cover they want is for other advisors to agree with them.

DON'T NEGOTIATE:

Offer the swindle on a "take-it-or-leave" basis. Don't get into a negotiation except on issues you don't care about. Once there is a sense that there is a negotiation occurring, you are potentially doomed. When this happens, kick in the need for speed.

PATIENCE AND COMMON SENSE ARE THE ENEMY:

Never allow anyone the time to apply common sense or to encourage discussion. Only deliver the clothes on the day of the procession. Time is your enemy. Generating the need for speed is critical.

The second part of my imaginary handbook would contain another six gems. This time, the focus is on the characteristics of those who would be the easiest to scam.

The Handbook: Part Two

LOOK FOR THE SOLE DECISION-MAKER:

Why? *Because everyone around him will focus on keeping him happy—and bad news is rarely delivered to a sole decision-maker.*

LOOK FOR FEAR AND INTIMIDATION:

Why? *Because fear and intimidation tend to discourage those who might otherwise offer the emperor advice they think he might not want to hear.*

LOOK FOR THE STIFLING OF DISSENT:

Why? *Because dissent encourages discussion—and discussion always generates questions, and this is always bad news for the scammer.*

LOOK FOR A LIMITED EXCHANGE OF VIEWS:

Why? *Because any exchange of views encourages discussion—and we've just learned about the perils of discussion. The less that views are exchanged, the better for the scammer.*

LOOK FOR THE EMPEROR BESTOWING POWER ON OTHERS:

Why? *Because everyone wants more power. If the emperor is likely to offer more power as a reward for giving him what he wants, this will increase his advisors' determination to give the emperor what he wants.*

LOOK FOR A REFUSAL TO ACCEPT OR DEMAND RESPONSIBILITY:

Why? *Because the scam is always easier to sell to people who are not held responsible for being scammed. Emperors and their closest advisors historically rarely take responsibility. If they are not personally at risk, they have nothing to lose. They can always blame someone else.*

NELSON MANDELA'S GIFT

If Hans Christian Andersen's tale tracks the recent high-profile scams, and if the tale also offers a handbook for scammers, then it also offers a validation of Nelson Mandela's gift of the Ten Powers of Negotiation and his other life-lessons.

A parting question is whether any of the scammers in any of the Enron, Ahmed Chalabi, or Bernard Madoff adventures would have survived the questions asked by anyone with a moral compass who had also mastered those Ten Powers of Negotiation and who had summoned the courage to apply the teachings of the Duck School.

Whatever your conclusion, we face some undeniable realities in confronting future scams.

The first is that *we live in a cheating culture.* The sooner we recognize it for what it is, the better...

The second is that *we can no longer trust our finest and brightest* to help us expose scams simply because they are our finest and brightest. Too often, they choose profits and fees over integrity and scruples...

The third reality is that *our schools refuse to step up to the plate in a meaningful manner.* Not only do they often remain thunderously silent at the sometimes outrageous behavior of their alumni, they steadfastly refuse to accept responsibility for their failure to focus enough attention on teaching acceptable ethical standards. By failing to require their students to study inspirational leaders like Nelson Mandela, academia's ivory towers fail miserably in their larger mission. If we can't trust even our best schools to turn out graduates with greater ethical sensibilities, the schools become complicit and nothing will change...

The fourth reality is that *we have to trust ourselves* to recalibrate our own moral compasses—and demand the same of everyone we live and work with. Until we are prepared to distinguish between what we have the right to do and what is the right thing to do, we will continue to slide backwards into an ethical abyss. Until we are prepared to walk away from something that is not the right thing to do—even though we have the right to do it—we will continue to slide towards that abyss.

The fifth reality is that, until our leaders demonstrate they have *moral authority* and show that they lead by example and demand ethical standards of which we would be proud, we have little hope to expect more ethical behavior. Until those leaders exude moral authority and don't reward bad behavior, the slide will continue.

There is hope, however. If we can lead our lives in the spirit of the lessons of Nelson Mandela's life and if we can apply the common sense approach of the Duck School, there is hope that we might be better positioned to detect the next scam and avoid the temptations of the next generation of scammers. If we can draw on the inspirational man and his life experience, we will see what is possible. If we can muster up the courage and moral authority to act in the way we know we should, we can do it. And for that we can thank a quite remarkable man's gift...

INDEX

A

African Mine Workers Union: 57

African National Congress (ANC)
Government's enemy: 39

Alexander, Neville: 86–126, 89–126, 90–126

Andy Fastow: Enron CFO

Apartheid
Generally: 38
Implementing apartheid: 58
Pass laws: 79
South Africa's Truth and Reconciliation Commission: 38
The Suppression of Communism Act: 63

Aucamp, Brigadier: 87–126

B

Badenhorst, Colonel Piet: Robben Island commanding officer: 90–126, 91–126

Baer, Robert: Case officer in the CIA's Directorate of Operations in the Middle East. *See* Chalabi, Ahmed: Baer, Robert: case officer in the CIA's Directorate of Operations in the Middle East

Barnard, Niël: the head of the National Intelligence Service, South Africa's equivalent of the KGB
Description of Nelson Mandela: 40
Intelligence assessments: 100
Leader of the government team in meeting Between President Botha and Nelson Mandela: 116

Batson, James: Enron Bankruptcy Examiner: 199–208

Bizos, George: Nelson Mandela's friend and attorney: 48–82

Boesak, Reverend Allan: 103

Boesky, Ivan: Arbitrager: 173

Borget, Louis: Creator of Enron Oil
1987, Feb meeting with Mick Seidle, Ken Lay's number two: 180
Admission to Seidl, October 1987: 186
Apple Bank: 180
Destroyed daily position reports: 184
Explanation: 180
Nominal superiors: 179
Pled guilty to three felonies: 188

Botha, Pik: South African apartheid-era foreign minister
Insight into how Nelson Mandela approached his epic negotiations: 42
U.N. Security Council address in 1974 - Zebra analogy: 121
Upset president when he said he was prepared to serve under a future black president: 120
Worked on drafting of Rubicon speech: 102

Botha, President P. W.
Conspired with Buthelezi to create unlawful paramilitary force against ANC: 119
Forced to agree to Eminent Persons Meetings: 106
January 1985 tactical gambit in: 32
Nelson Mandela's response to 1985 tactical gambit: 33
Preconditions to negotiating with Nelson Mandela: 113
The Rubicon speech: 102

Bowen, Jack: CEO of Florida Gas Company: 169

Brink, Andre, anti-apartheid writer: 81

Bush, President George W.

Administration had no way to confirm what Chalabi was telling them: 220

Administration has no problem with Chalabi being next president of Iraq: 212

Administration's response to an interview Mr. Chalabi gave to a London newspaper: 210

Announced prior to 9-11 what would make USA attack Iraq: 213

Immediately after 9-11, Bush administration prepares for Iraq war: 219

Prior to 9-11, Bush administration did not regard Saddam as an imminent threat: 218

Was administration really scammed by Chalabi?: 227

Buthelezi, Chief Mangosuthu

Conspired with president Botha to create unlawful paramilitary forces: 119

Creates militia: 119

Favorite of the West: 118

Mandela declines to meet with him in 1986: 118

Roadblock to the liberation movement: 118

C

Chalabi, Ahmed

2005 Iraqi election results: 217

Administration's position on weapons of mass destruction before Chalabi: 218

Aziz, Tariq: "You guys can have Chalabi!": 218

Background: 215

Baer, Robert: case officer in the CIA's Directorate of Operations in the Middle East

Chalabi's capacity to head a new government in Iraq,: 216

Described first meeting with Chalabi: 217

No CIA human sources in Iraq: 220

Quality of the intelligence Mr. Chalabi was providing: 216

CIA

Baer, Robert: Case officer in the CIA's Directorate of Operations in the Middle East. *See* Chalabi, Ahmed: Baer, Robert: case officer in the CIA's Directorate of Operations in the Middle East

Chalabi on the CIA payroll in 1993: 215

Chalabi understood the tension between CIA and Pentagon: 222

CIA opinion of Abu Zeinab who was offered by Chalabi: 221

Taken him off payroll: 210

Warned Defense Department: 210

Curveball: 221

Duck School and Chalabi: 227

Hamza, Khidir: former member of the Iraqi weapons team: 226

"Heroes in error": 211

Iran

Iranian fingerprints: 223

Larry Johnson: Iran has run one of the most masterful intelligence operations in history: 225

Three motives for helping him: 223

Was his Iraq National Congress a front for Iran?: 225

Iraq Survey Group: 211–228

Johnson, Larry: former senior counterterrorist official at the State Department: 225

Knew what it would take for US to invade Iraq: 213

Lang, Pat: headed counterterrorism in the Middle East and South Asia for eight years at the Defense Intelligence Agency

Opinion of Chalabi: 216

Quality of Iranian intelligence agency: 227

le Carré, John: spy novelist: 209

Manipulation of the media: 220

Muhammad Atta meeting: 223

Nabulsi, Mohammed Said: Jordanian Central Bank governor: 215

Neocons: 210–228

Perfect leader of the opposition: 217

Powell, Colin secretary of state, opinion on Iraq before 9-11: 218

Ritter, Scott: former weapons inspector for the United Nations: 222–228

Saddam Hussein: 212

Singer, Max: co-founder of the conservative Hudson Institute: 214

Subway Test: 210

Succeeded brilliantly: 214

Understood the tension between the Pentagon and the CIA: 222

What he did not want: 212

What he wanted: 212

Willing suspension of disbelief: 210

Chanos, Jim: the president of Kynikos Associates, a short-selling hedge fund

Broadband industry: 23

Concerned about Enron's financial disclosures: 24

Congressional testimony: 23

Chase Manhattan's contribution to the demise of apartheid: 102

Cheney, Vice President Dick

Chalabi finds receptive audience: 223

Say Chalabi as future president of Iraq: 216

Vice presidential debate: 213

Willing suspension of disbelief: 210

CODESA I

1991: Convened on December 21: 138

Absentees: 138

ANC's chief negotiator and team.: 139

A problem revealed: 141

Nelson Mandela did what no black man in South Africa had ever done: 140

President de Klerk believed he held all the cards: 142

President de Klerk was publicly humiliated in prime time on national television by a black man: 141

The first day ends badly: 139

Working Group 2: 144

CODESA II

1992: November 18 - Mr. Mandela and ANC endorse Joe Slovo approach: 152

ANC negotiating team analyzed the reasons for the failure of negotiations: 150

Early government trap: 146

Joe Slovo addresses the problem and proposes a solution: 151

Postponement: 147

President de Klerk's diminished stature after the breakdown of CODESA II: 152

Coetsee, Kobie: South African minister of justice

1985 visit with Nelson Mandela: 104

Attended first Eminent Persons Meeting: 107

Demands background on Mr. Mandela: 97

Led committee of senior officials to meet with Mr. Mandela in 1987: 113

Recollection of first Eminent Persons Meeting: 109

D

de Klerk, President F.W.

Announces Nelson Mandela's release on February 2, 1990: 125

Appoints Goldstone to lead commission in August 1991: 135

Believed he could win the first elections: 142

Chosen as leader of National Party in January 1989: 120

Credibility

1991 Revelations: 135

Appoints judges implicated in scandal: 136

Claimed no knowledge of the Third Force: 137

First day of CODESA I: 136. See Truth and Reconciliation Commission

Ignored Judge Goldstone's recommendation that Police Commissioner van der Merwe be fired: 137

No response to mass killings in June
    1992: 149
Sebokeng massacre: 129–132
The murder of four ANC activists: 146
The Toilet Town Scandal: 145
Third Force. See Third Force
Truth and Reconciliation Commis-
    sion. See Truth and Reconciliation
    Commission
First actions as new leader in 1989: 120
First meeting with Nelson Mandela prior
    to release: 123
Loses by-election and calls for referendum
    March 1992: 143
May 2, 1990 meeting: 129
Nelson Mandela would never forgive him.:
    132
Pretoria Minute - August 6, 1990: 131
Record of understanding 1992: 153
Referendum results in 1992 embolden
    ANC: 143
Squatter camp killings 1990: 133
Strategies to undermine Nelson Mandela's
    global influence and the popularity
    of the ANC: 127
Succeeds P.W. Botha as president in 1989:
    123
Summary: 41–42
The new president's position on taking
    office: 124
Third Force. See Third Force
Upon release, strategies to undermine
    Nelson Mandela's global influence
    and the popularity of the ANC.: 127

**de Lange, Pieter: the chairman of the
Afrikaner Broederbond**
Discussions with Mr. Mbeki: 112
Meeting with the ANC: 111

Duck School
Ahmed Chalabi: 228
Common sense and Madoff: 238
Enron and the Duck School: 21
Enron illegal shifting of earnings: 178
Harry Markopolos and Madoff: 231
Its teachings: 16

Mick Muckleroy and Enron Oil trading
    limits: 185
Overcoming our flaws: 17
Project Nahanni: 199
Ten Powers: 161
That sense of smell and sight: 20
Those surrounding Madoff: 232

E

Emperor's New Clothes
Casting call: Enron, Chalabi, and Madoff:
    244
Connection with Enron, Chalabi and
    Madoff: 249
Hans Christian Andersen: author: 243
Hidden handbook for scammers: Part
    One: 252
Hidden handbook for scammers: Part
    Two: 254
Subway test: 252
The tale: 246

Enron
Arthur Andersen: 183–196
Bass, Carl: accountant at Arthur Ander-
    sen: 204–208
Batson, James: Enron Bankruptcy Exam-
    iner: 199–208, 200–208, 201–208,
    204–208
Blockbuster: 200
Broadband business
    Flawed business concept: 201
    Generally: 200–208
Canadian Imperial Bank of Commerce:
    204
Citibank: 199
Code of Ethics: 29
Duck School: 15–25, 18–25, 21–25, 22–25,
    25, 96, 138, 161–163, 167–196,
    178–196, 179–196, 184, 185, 198–
    207, 199–207, 231–241, 232–241,
    238–241, 256–257
Enron Bankruptcy Examiner: 199
Enron Oil. See Enron Oil
Enron Prize for Distinguished Public
    Service: 27
Enron's description of its finances: 206

Importance of Enrol Oil: 179

Jeff Skilling: Enron CEO. *See* Skilling, Jeff

Ken Lay: Enron Chairman. *See* Lay, Ken: Enron Chairman

Mark-to-market accounting: 190

Arthur Andersen's failure to warn: 193

Generally: 190

The big-picture effect: 192

The difficulty of using this in the natural gas industry: 190

Merger: HNG and InterNorth

Generally: 171

The aftermath: 174

Mike Muckleroy: head of Enron's liquid-fuels division. *See* Muckleroy, Mike: head of Enron's liquid-fuels division

Natural gas pipeline business: 168

Project Braveheart: 203

Project Nahanni: 198

Quality of Earnings problem: 191

Enron Oil

Aftermath: 188

Apple Bank: 180

April 29 board meeting: 183

Beard, John: deputy head of Enron's internal audit department: 180

Borget, Louis: creator of Enron Oil: 180–196

Earnings

Danger posed by not meeting targets: 176

Enron focus on earnings: 176

Illegal shifting: 178

Legal shifting: 178

Explanation: 180

Explanation: Reaction: 181

Greenmail

Irwin Jacobs: 176

Raiding company's employee pension funds to pay Jacobs: 176

Harding, John: one of Louis Borget's nominal superiors in Houston: 179–196

Internal controls: 184

Ken Lay's "shock": 186

Lay challenges employees at all-employee meeting: 187

Losses in first two years: 175

Mastroeni, Thomas: treasurer of Enron Oil: 180–196

Muckleroy, Mike: head of Enron's liquid-fuels division. *See* Muckleroy, Mike: head of Enron's liquid-fuels division

Questions not asked: 178

Seidle, Mick: Ken Lay's number two: 180–196

Sulentic, Steve: one of Louis Borget's nominal superiors in Houston: 179–196

Those explanations: 205

Two sets of books: 185

Woytek, David: head of Enron's internal audit department: 180–196

F

Fastow, Andrew: Enron CFO: 202

Defied laws of business gravity: 191

Fastow's partnership LJM2: 202

His explanation of Enron's business model: 206

Met regularly with Ken Lay and Jeff Skilling: 193

G

Gibran, Kahlil, philosopher: 20

Goldstone Commission

Damning evidence uncovered: 136

Found security police involved in criminal conduct: 137

New York Times assessment of Goldstone: 135

Pressure from all sides: 136

H

Hani, Chris's murder: 155

Harvard: 5, 8, 28

Healey, Denis: British Labor politician: 88

Houston Natural Gas: 171

Humble Oil: 169

Hussein, Saddam: 218, 225, 227

I

InterNorth: 172, 174

Iraq Survey Group: 211–228

J

Jacobs, Irwin: a corporate raider:
    172–196

Jongintaba, Regent: 46, 49
    Guarding minority's rights: 50
    How he conducted and approached those
        meetings: 49
    Tribal meetings: 49

K

Katzenberg, Jeffrey: movie executive: 233

Kee, Carolyn: Arthur Andersen accoun-
    tant: 183

Kinder, Rich: Enron's general counsel:
    183

L

Lautenberg, Frank: US senator: 233

Lay, Ken: Enron Chairman: 29
    Accepted position as HNG's chairman and
        chief executive officer: 171
    Attracted to ruthless and very smart
        people: 173
    Early days: 168
    Florida Gas Company: 169
    Key to the candy store: 31
    Line of credit: 31
    Muckleroy asks Ken Lay to act agaoinst
        the traders: 185
    Transco Energy: 170
    Withdrew $77 million: 31

le Carré, John: spy novelist: 209, 225

Lewinsky, Monica: White House intern: iv

Lies generally
    the brazen lie: 19
    The lies of omission: 20
    The shaded lie: 20

Lincoln, Abraham: 15

Louw, Mike: then second-in-command of
    the National Intelligence Service:
    100

M

Madoff, Bernard
    2001, May - First skepticism expressed:
        230
    Business model: 233
    Claimed to create "basket" of Standard &
        Poor's 100 Index ("S&P 100 Index")
        common stock: 235
    Classic "affinity scam.": 232
    Crystal ball: 229
    Duck School: 238
    Fairfield Greenwich Group: 234
    How he claimed he achieved such remark-
        able returns: 235
    Katzenberg, Jeffrey: 233
    Lautenberg, Frank, Senator: 233
    Lifland, Burton R.: 238
    Markopolos, Harry
        Background: 231
        Found a few logical problems: 232
        How long it took him to find some-
            thing was wrong,: 231
        Submissions to SEC: Between 2000
            and 2008 five written submis-
            sions: 235
        Submissions to SEC: Details of Novem-
            ber 7, 2005 submission: 235
    No volatility in any funds managed: 230
    Offered a private label hedge fund: 233
    Positioning: 234
    Prominent Wall Street firms and financial
        experts did not buy his scheme: 235

Spielberg, Steven: 233
Subway test: 239
United States Bankruptcy Court Ruling: 238
Wiesel, Elie: 233
Zuckerman, Mortimer: 233

Maharaj, Mac: prisoner on Robben Island with Mr. Mandela: 91-126, 101-126, 117-126, 153

Malan, Dr. D.F., former South African prime minister: 38

Mandela, Nelson
After release, talks begin: 129
ANC: Joining: 56
ANC: problems unifying the ANC: 130
Black Pimpernel: 75
Charged with treason in 1956: 68
Chase Manhattan stops extending credit to government on July 31, 1985: 102
Chris Hani's murder: 155
Consequences of Chris Hani murder: 156
Dash, Sam: 99
Defiance Campaign: 64
Denied he was a Communist: 78
Early formal schooling: 52
Early lessons
    Avoid humiliating anyone: 47
    Generally: 47-52
    Importance of virtue and generosity: 48
    Knowledge through listening and observing: 49
    Tribal meetings. See Jongintaba, Regent
Eminent Persons' Group
    1985 Thatcher forced to agree: 106
    1986 First meeting: 107
    1986 second meeting: 109
Father, his: 46
February 1990 release: 126
First meeting President P.W. Botha: 122
First meeting with President de Klerk: 123
Freedom Charter

Response from the government: 68
Response from the people: 67
Goldstone Commission: 136. See Goldstone Commission
Government assessment of Nelson Mandela in 1981: 96
Government attempt to revoke his law license in 1954: 65
Government conditions to negotiations
    second condition to negotiations: ending ties to the communist party: 115
    The first condition: ending the armed struggle: 113
He and ANC support Joe Slovo's proposals re CODESA II on November 18, 1992: 152
Kobie Coetzee's visits him in 1985: 104
Lawyering Skills
    Defending revocation of law license: 65
    Treason Trial - Analysing the make-up of the court: 71
    Treason Trial - An audacious strategy: 71
    Treason Trial - A surprise first witness: 72
Leadership and democracy
    Early lessons: 50
    Like a shepherd: 51
Lessons: Avoid creating unreasonable expectations: 66
Luthuli, Chief Albert: ANC leader: 67-82
Maharaj recollection about negotiations regarding McBride: 153
Matthews, Professor Z. K.: 67
McBride, Robert: convicted murderer: 153
Moral authority: 46-82, 47-82, 48-82, 53, 53-82, 68-82, 81-82, 129-164, 162-164, 163-164, 256-258
Moroko, Dr. former president of ANC: 65
Negotiations about negotiations in 1990: 129
New constitution signed 1993: 160
President Botha's offer to release him and the rejection of the offer in 1985
President de Klerk lured into a trap 1993: 157

Qualities/10 Powers

Power of Truth and Fairness: 68

Qualities: Moral authority: 27–34, 34, 43–44, 84–126, 88–126, 91–126, 98–126

Qualities/Ten Powers

Identifying three indispensable attributes for a freedom fighter: 54

Patience: 88

Power of Morality, Courage and Attitude: 59

Power of the Process: 92

Power to walk away: 59

Recognized reality: 137

Understanding that every negotiation was a series of negotiations: 55

Understanding the concept of "positioning": 56

Understanding the distinction between strategy and tactics: 131

Understanding the importance of meticulous preparation: 57

Understanding the other side: 91

Understood the importance of defining goals: 55

Using a solution-oriented approach: 56

Walking away after Sebokeng massacre: 129

Record of Understanding signed 1992: 153

Rivonia trial

Defense speech: 77

Generally: 75

Robben Island. See Robben Island

Rolling mass action June 16, 1992: 148

September 1952 bannings and arrests: 64

Sharpeville massacre: 73

Sisulu, Walter: old friend: 54

Slovo, Joe, head of South African Communist Party: 130–164

Third Force: 131–164, 132–164, 134–164, 135–164, 137–164

Those honoring him: A delicious irony: iv

Transfer to Pollsmoor: 99

Transfer to Victor Verster prison: 119

Treason Trial

A government mistake in putting them

in two cells?: 69

The government overreach: 69

The verdict and its aftermath: 74

Understanding President de Klerk's position and approach to the upcoming negotiations: 124

University of Fort Hare: 52

University of the Witwatersrand: 54–82, 72–82

Markopolos, Harry: fraud investigator. See Madoff, Bernard: Markopolos, Harry

Marx, Groucho: 243

Marx, Groucho: comedian: 4, 15

Matanzima, K.D.: leader of Transkei and Mr. Mandela's uncle: 93–126

Mbeki, Govan: co-defendant in Rivonia trial and fellow-prisoner on Robben Island: 81

Mbeki, Thabo: would succeed Mr. Mandela as South Africa's president: 111–126

Meyer, Roelf: leader of government negotiating team

Leader of government negotiating team: 149

Recognized advantage Mr. Ramaphosa had over him: 150

Milken, Michael: convicted financier: 173–196

Mqhekezweni, provisional capital of Thembuland: 49

Muckleroy, Mike: head of Enron's liquid-fuels division: 185–196

Applied some Duck School logic:: 185

Muckleroy asks Ken Lay to act against the traders: 185

N

National Intelligence Service: 40–44, 100–126, 113–126, 116–126

National Party: 38–44, 64–82, 70–82

Implementing apartheid

Classifying the races: 59

Creating separate areas, amenities, and facilities: 60

The problem of education: 62

The problems posed by Cupid: 61

The problems posed by literature: 62

Not a popular message within the party: 121

The Suppression of Communism Act: 63

Wanted to enter World War II on side of Nazi Germany: 54

Winning the 1948 election: 58

P

Pentagon: 223

Perle, Richard: neocon supporter of Chalabi: 212, 215

Pollsmoor Prison

1982: April - arriving at Pollsmoor: 99

1984: An assessment of Mr. Mandela by NIS: 100

Ponzi, Carlo: creator of Ponzi scheme: 3

R

Ramaphosa, Cyril: ANC's chief negotiator

Advantage over his counterpart, Roelf Meyer: 150

Enjoyed McBride negotiations between Mandela and de Klerk: 154

Leader of ANC negotiating team: 149

Reagan, President Ronald

Administration's whole-hearted support for the apartheid government: 98

Rejected economic sanctions against government: 104

Welcomed Chief Buthelezi: 118

Robben Island

A government assessment of Mr. Mandela in 1981: 96

Approach: Dealing with the wardens: 87

Approach: Understanding the Afrikaner mind-set: 91

Approach: Using the power of patience: 88

Brutality had become common place 1970: 90

Conditions make escape impossible: 83

Daily life: 86

Early request for respect denied: 85

How his fellow-prisoners regarded him: 89

Initial government miscalculation: 84

Irony: How the government sowed the seeds of its own destruction: 84

Lessons: Challenging authority: 87

New generation of prisoners: Black consciousness: 94

New generation of prisoners: He ahd to earn their respect: 96

Returning to Robben Island 1964: 84

The government's dilemma in 1981: 98

Transfer to Pollsmoor 1982: 99

Visit from the minister of justice in 1976: 92

Roskens, Ronald: then president of the University of Nebraska: 183

Rubicon speech: Expectations and disappointment: 102

S

Sabotage Law

Burden to prove innocense: 77

Scams generally

Calls-to-action: 2

Changing scam: 2

Danger scammers face

A skilled negotiator: 4

The second danger: time: 5

The third danger: our sense of ethics: 6

Link to negotiating skills: 3

Obstacles we face in dealing with scammers: 4

Our cheating culture: 11

Scamming the Enron board: 7

Surrogates: 3, 4, 13

Sebokeng Township Deaths: 129, 132, 133

Segnar, Sam: CEO of InterNorth: 171

Sisulu, Walter: Nelson Mandela's closest friend

Recognized the value of interaction with warders: 88

Released on October 10, 1989: 123

Transferred to Pollsmoor Prison with Mr. Mandela: 99

Skilling, Jeff

A gambler at heart: 189

Broadband business: 200

Demand for accepting job: 189

Gas Bank: New business: 189

Skilling, Jeff: Enron CEO: 8

Slovo, Joe: head of South African Communist Party

Proposed an approach for dealing with President de Klerk's role: 159

Spielberg, Steven: Motion picture producer/director: 233

Squatter camp killings: 133

Steyn, General J. C.: commissioner of prisons: 85

Subway Test

Chalabi: 210

Emperor's Clothes: 252

Madoff: 239

The test: 9

T

Tambo, Oliver: ANC president: 104–126, 110–126, 118–126

Thatcher, Prime Minister Margaret

Forced to agree to Eminent Persons' Meeting: 106

Rejected ANC: 40

Resisted economic sanctions against apartheid government: 104

Welcomed Chief Buthelezi: 118

Whole-hearted support for apartheid government: 98

Third Force

An ultimatum: 134

Buthelezi involvement: 119

Used to undermine negotiations and Nelson's Mandela's ability to lead: 132

Transco Energy: 170

Truth and Reconciliation Commission: 38, 119, 128, 136, 137

V

Verwoerd, Dr. Hendrik: intellectual architect of apartheid and prime minister

Approach to education of non-whites: 63

Insisted Sharpeville massacre was a communist conspiracy: 74

W

Wiesel, Elie: Nobel Laureate: 233

Wilde, Oscar: Author: iii

Willemse, Colonel: Robben Island commanding officer

Opinion of Nelson Mandela: 91

Willemse, Lieutenant General W. H.: the commissioner of prisons: 107

Wing, John: Enron executive: 172

Z

Zuckerman, Mortimer: New York publisher: 233

SELECTED BIBLIOGRAPHY

ON NELSON MANDELA...

Long Walk to Freedom: The Autobiography of Nelson Mandela
Nelson Mandela, 1995

Mandela: The Authorized Biography
Anthony Sampson, 1999

The Struggle is my Life
Nelson Mandela, 1978

Selected Speeches and Writings of Nelson Mandela:
The End of Apartheid in South Africa
Nelson Mandela

Speeches and interviews 1990-99
ANC, Johannesburg and Office of the President, Pretoria

Mandela: A Biography
Martin Meredith, 1998

Nelson Mandela: The Early Life of Rolihlahla Mandiba
Jean Guiloineau and Joseph Rowe

Anatomy of a Miracle: The End of Apartheid and the Birth of the New
South Africa,
Patti Waldmeir, 1997

Fighter and reformer: Extracts from the Speeches of P.W. Botha
Bureau of Information, Pretoria, 1989

The Last Trek: A New Beginning—The Autobiography
F.W de Klerk, 1998

The Time Has Come
Thabo Mbeki, 1989

Tomorrow is Another Country: The Inside Story of South Africa's Negotiated Revolution
Allister Sparks, 1995

Truth and Reconciliation Commission on South Africa Report
Truth and Reconciliation Commission 1998

Reinventing a Continent
Andre Brink, 1996

Strange Bedfellows: Mandela, de Klerk, and the New South Africa
Mark Gevisser, 2000

ON AHMED CHALABI

How Ahmed Chalabi conned the neocons
John Dizard, Salon May 4, 2004

The Truth About Ahmed Chalabi
Andrew Cockburn,CounterPunch Exclusive, May 20, 2004

The Fall of Chalabi and the Conservative Brain Trust
Center for American Progress, May 21, 2004

Our Con Man in Iraq
Newsweek, May 23, 2004

From Friend to Foe,
Romesh Ratnesar, Time, May 22, 2004,

Ahmed Chalabi's House of Cards
Fred Kaplan, Slate, May 24, 2004,

The Rise and Fall of Chalabi: Bush's Mr. Wrong; Ahmed Chalabi may go down as one of the great con men of history.
Newsweek , May 31, 2004

The Manipulator (a critical look at the history and investigation of Ahmed Chalabi's role in the decision by the U.S. to invade Iraq),
Jane Mayer, The New Yorker, June 7, 2004,

Tinker, Banker, Neocon, Spy
Robert Dreyfuss, The American Prospect, November 18, 2002,

Bank fraud, botched rebellions, intrigues
Stephen Fidler and Roula Khalaf, Financial Times, December 12, 2002

Scandals dog the man who would be next leader of Iraq,
Anton La Guardia, Telegraph UK, April 11, 2003,

Ahmed Chalabi – Worldbeaters
New Internationalist, June 2003,

Blueprint for a Mess
David Rieff, ,New York Times, November 2, 2003,

Ahmed Chalabi's Bay of Goats
Michele Steinberg, Executive Intelligence Review, April 9, 2004

Chalabi's Fall From Grace
By Johanna McGeary et al, April 26, 2004

The implosion of Chalabi's Petra Bank
John Dizard, Salon, May 4, 2004

The Man Who Pushed America to War: The Extraordinary Life, Adventures and Obsessions of Ahmed Chalabi
Aram Roston, 2008

A Pretext for War
James Bamford, 2004

Plan of Attack
Bob Woodward, 2004

The Price of Loyalty
Ron Suskind, 2004

Intelligence Matters
Sen Bob Graham, 2004

Fiasco
Thomas E. Ricks, 2006

Against All Enemies
Richard A. Clarke, 2004

State of Denial
Bob Woodward, 2006

Cobra II
Michael R. Gordon and General Bernard E. Trainor, 2006

The Greatest Story Ever Sold
Frank Rich, 2006

Rise of the Vulcans
James Mann, 2004

Financial scandal claims hang over leader in waiting
David Leigh and Brian Whitaker, The Guardian, April 14, 2003

Odierno: Chalabi has clear ties to Iran
Politoco.com, February 17, 2010

ON ENRON

The Smartest Guys In The Room
Bethany McLean and Peter Elkin, 2003

Enron Bankruptcy Examiner's Reports
James Batson

The Role of Enron's Board of Directors in Enron's Collapse
United States Senate Report, July 8, 2002

Conspiracy of Fools
Kurt Eichenwald, 2005

The Enron Wars
Marie Brenner, Vanity Fair, April 2002

Power Failure: The Inside Story of the Collapse of Enron
Mimi Swartz and Sherron Watkins, 2004

Anatomy of Greed: Telling the Unshredded Truth from Inside Enron
Malcolm S. Salter, 2008

Enron: A Pattern of Abuses?
Newsmax.com, March 21, 2002

Original Sins
Loren Steffy and Adam Levy, Bloomberg, April 2002

Enron The Incredible
Dan Ackman, Forbes, January 15, 2002

Empire of the Sun: An Economic Interpretation of Enron's Energy Business
Christopher L. Culp and Steve H. Hanke, Policy Analysis, February 20, 2003

No Hope for Enron's Ken Lay
Dan Ackman, Forbes, July 8, 2004

Testimony of William C Powers, Jr,, Chairman of Special Investigative Committee of the Board of Directors of Enron
February 4, 2002

Enron Lawyers: If Only We Knew
Dan Ackman, Forbes, March 14, 2002

Enron's Man Who Didn't Know Too Much
Dan Ackman, Forbes, February 8, 2002

Enron: Who's Accountable?
Daniel Kadlec, Time, January 13, 2002

Enron's Board Should Have known Better
W. Michael Hoffman, Dawn-Marie Driscoll, Christian Science Monitor, January 24, 2002

ON BERNARD MADOFF

No One Would Listen: A True Financial Thriller
Harry Markopolos, 2010

Too Good To Be True: The Rise and Fall of Bernie Madoff
Erin Arvedlund, 2009

The Believers: How America Fell for Bernard Madoff's $65 Billion Investment Scam
Adam LeBor

ON NEGOTIATION AND SCAMS

The Cheating Culture
David Callahan, 2004

House of Cards
William D. Cohan, 2009

Negotiation
Harvard Business Essentials, 2003

The Art and Science of Negotiation
Howard Raiffa, 2003

Negotiating Rationally
Max H. Bazerman and Margaret A. Neale, 1992

Negotiate This!
Herb Cohen, 2003

Negotiation Genius
Deepak Malhotra and max H. Bazerman, 2007

Getting to Yes
Roger Fisher and William Ury, 1981

The Power of Nice
Ronald M. Shapiro and Mark A. Jankowski, 1998

The Culture of Collaboration
Evan Rosen, 2007

On Becoming a Leader
Warren Bennis, 1989

Positioning: The Battle for your Mind
Al Ries and Jack Trout, 1981

How to Make Collaboration Work
David Strauss, 2002

Ponzi's Scheme: The True Story of a Financial Legend
Mitchell Zuckoff, 2005

Separating Fools From Their Money
Scott B. MacDonald and Jane E. Hughes, 2009

Stolen Without a Gun: Confessions from inside history's biggest accounting fraud—the collapse of MCI Worldcom
Walter Pavlo Jr. and Neil Weinberg, 2007

Great Negotiations: Agreements that Changed the Modern World
Fredrik Stanton, 2010

Made in the USA
Charleston, SC
12 November 2010